SO-CEW-164

Babel:

The Breaking of the Banks

Now the whole earth had one language. And men said to one another, 'Come let us make bricks and burn them thoroughly.' And they had brick for stone, and bitumen for mortar. Then they said 'Come let us build ourselves a city, and a tower with its top in the heavens, and let us make a name for ourselves, lest we be scattered abroad upon the face of the whole earth.' And the Lord came down to see the city and the tower, which the sons of men had built. And the Lord said 'Behold they are one people, and they have all one language. Come let us go down, and there confuse their language.' So the Lord scattered them abroad from there, and they left off building the city. Therefore its name was Babel.

Genesis ch 11 vv 1-9

Babel:

The Breaking of the Banks

A Chronicle of the Markets 1998–2009

Jonathan Ruffer

Dedication

To Micky Ingall, strong friend and mentor

1941 – 2009

Publishers Note

There is an important section entitled *Cracking the Credit Code* written by Henry Maxey of Ruffer LLP which begins on p184.

Each year consists of an overall commentary which is printed over tints of various shades of red followed by the subtitled subject reviews and Henry Maxey's text in normal mono print.

First published 2009

by JJG Publishing
Sparrow Hall
Hindringham
Fakenham
Norfolk
NR21 ODP

Copyright (c) 2009   Jonathan Ruffer, Ruffer LLP
Text pages 184–248 Copyright (c) 2009 Henry Maxey, Ruffer LLP

ISBN 978-1-899163-93-9

Designed by Graham Hiles.

Printed by Biddles of King's Lynn

Contents

	Page
Author's Preface	*vii*
Foreword by John Plender	*ix*
Introduction	*xi*
Commentary 1998	1
One Man's View of a Mania	3
Trouble in the East	5
Has the Penny Dropped?	8
War Loan for Ever?	11
Commentary 1999	14
The Frejus Conundrum	16
An Interruption in a Deflationary World	19
Inflation or Deflation?	22
The Court Card of Stockmarket Mania	25
Commentary 2000	29
A Stock Exchange Bubble	31
Tigers are Quicker than Donkeys	35
It's Nearly Over When the Fat Lady Sings	38
A Stream of Income	41
Commentary 2001	45
Humpty Dumpty Portfolios	47
Taking the Plunge	50
The Five Horsemen of the Apocalypse	53
Making a Boob of it	56
Commentary 2002	60
Listen to the Music	62
Mr Dampier-Wetton	66
The Yield Gap : Equities and Bonds	69
Nerdy Article on Dr Bernanke's Speech	72

	Page
Commentary 2003	**78**
The Footsie Index	80
Buy Japan, Japan, Japan!	83
The Cuckoo Clock	86
The Crème Brulée Conundrum	89
Commentary 2004	**93**
The Fruit Lorry	95
T-Bones for Tea	98
Under the Rose Bush	101
Sound Money	104
Commentary 2005/6	**108**
Crossing the Rubicon	110
Contradictiousness	113
My Catechism	117
What are We Aiming to Do?	121
Alas, Poor Eeyorick?	125
Confidence and Credit : The Naughty Sisters	129
'Small Earthquake in Chile, Nobody Dead'	132
Plonk, Plonk, Plonk	136
Commentary 2007	**140**
Cracking the Credit Code	142
Ruffer: the Bear with a Sore Head?	147
A Storm or a Teacup?	150
Beware the Rock	153
Pig-Sticking a Panzer	157
Commentary 2008/9	**160**
Index Linked: The Pathway to Safety	163
Monetary Stability	167
The Crisis	171
The Crows are Counting	175
A Team and a Service	181
Henry Maxey's Foreword	**184**
Cracking the Credit Code	**188**
Appendixes	*233*

Author's Preface

Breughel's striking image (jacket and frontispiece) captures the might and absurdity of the tower of Babel. Its massive structure, based on the Roman Colisseum, dwarfs the puny settlement which sits alongside it: its builders look like ants scurrying backwards and forwards. Yet, for all its magnificence, its wayward engineering makes manifest its vulnerability. With Breughel, it is man who is the author of its downfall, not God. It is a picture of *hubris* – the idea that anything is possible if humans endeavour 'to make a name for themselves'.

We have come full circle. Once again the world – the business world, anyway – has one language. And this international construct created a way of doing business, international in scope and relying on a financial super-structure. Its engineering was not the outwork of a masterplan, but a series of interlocking priorities which reflected the partial (but only partial) coop-eration between competing interests. It became a construct of great com-plexity, but it had within it the same inconsistencies, the same contradic-tions. Onlookers would marvel at its majesty: some would wonder at the change it would bring to society, both financially and morally. But its most obvious feature was that it was doomed. When it came to grief, nobody was quite sure why. Her Majesty Queen Elizabeth spoke for all when she asked the economists, 'Why did nobody see it coming?'

September 22nd 2009

Foreword

by John Plender

Financial bubbles constitute an awesome challenge for the professional fund manager. Not because they are necessarily difficult to identify. Robert Walpole, after all, saw the South Sea Bubble for what it was. Even the scribes at *The Economist* and *The Financial Times* managed to identify the late 20th century dot.com craze as an example of what the 19th century historian Charles Mackay called "the madness of crowds". The difficulty lies rather in timing the exit from the bubble. Premature retreat can lead to prolonged underperformance, resulting in the loss of fickle clients. Hanging on too long may lead to wealth destruction (and the loss of clients anyway) on a more grandiose scale.

The credit bubble of the past decade posed a challenge that was out of the ordinary even by the extraordinary standards of previous bubbles. Never in history, I suspect, has a bubble been so well disguised. First came a long period of economic stability dubbed "The Great Moderation" by those dismal scientists who failed to heed the wisdom of the - now newly fashionable - economist Hyman Minsky. His great insight was to see that protracted stability breeds excessive risk taking and too much debt. This in turn leads to financial dislocation followed by deflationary pressure, recession or worse, and the risk that inflation will later provide the means of shrinking the debt overhang.

Most bubbles are associated with heavy borrowing – leverage, in the jargon. Yet additional leverage was provided in the latest bubble not only by borrowing but through the structure of derivative instruments such as swaps, futures and options, which expose investors to big swings in market prices in exchange for small outlays. An eternal verity of the financial markets is that estimates of the scale of leverage in a boom always turn out to be underestimates, come the bust. This time the leverage was even harder to quantify and even more sorely underestimated than in the past.

Worse, much of it was taking place off-balance sheet in so-called conduits and structured investment vehicles specifically set up to wrong-foot the regulators. Many of the securities that were shuffled off into this shadow banking system were horribly complex. Yet they were given a veneer of simplistic respectability by credit rating agencies that were paid by the authors of the complexity, the investment banks.

All this emerges fresh from the pages that follow. They constitute a remarkable and mainly contemporary stream of consciousness, both about the hazards of confronting the fund manager's ultimate stress test and the nature of the bubble itself. To convey the flavour, let me cite just one characteristic example, which concerns the unprecedented vulnerability of the financial edifice at the time of the Lehman Brothers collapse. The system, we are told, is a spaghetti junction of cross-claims. It takes only one missed catch for it to break down. The Montgolfier balloon continues to jettison inessentials, including Latvia, HBOS, Citigroup, sterling and the reputation of Gordon Brown. Rarely have metaphors been mixed with so much panache and to such vivid effect.

It would be churlish not to observe that the House of Ruffer emerged from all this with flying colours. An acute sense of the importance of history in financial markets has something to do with it. So, too, does the recognition that the problem of investment timing in a bubble can be cracked by establishing an appropriate balance between greed and fear in the composition of the portfolio. But this, of course, is an unending battle which is only provisionally won. I look forward enthusiastically to the next Ruffer book – if not to the next bubble.

Introduction

This book is a record of our quarterly reviews to clients of Ruffer Investment Management Limited (from April 2004, Ruffer LLP) to explain what we – I – had thought was going on. It was always intended to be a personal view; I was resistant to tempering observations whose shrill tone sometimes suggested desperation and arrogance, rather than passionate conviction. It is a frank account of my inner fears, hopes and frustrations in the inky night of future events.

It therefore has the quality of a diary. It is often repetitive, littered with false judgements and ideas which, with hindsight, led nowhere. The striking thing, on re-reading them, is how constant the theme of deflation – and inflation – has been over the period. There are two explanations for this – the first is that the theme is something of a hobbyhorse, and the events of 2008 were merely its Grand National. Was, then, the timing merely the accuracy of the stopped clock? I don't think so. Common sense suggests that natural phenomena like earthquakes have causes which antedate the cataclysm itself. So it is with financial crises. The seeds of this one go back half a century – mistakes are replaced with opposite mistakes, so that generally it is the last crisis-but-one which provides a parallel. The attitudes and assumptions of the governing classes were so appalled by the Great Depression that they allowed a tinderbox of inflation to burst onto a windswept world a generation ago. Our politicians and economic gurus have grown up to fear this inflation and therefore regarded the deflationary forces of (largely Chinese) global overproduction in the 1990s as a free lunch. They didn't see what even an archdeacon understood in the 1930s – deflation in the real economy coupled with big increases in borrowings leads first to rising asset prices, and then, after the inflection point, outright deflation. The outcome of this was completely foreseeable – almost inevitable – at least since the turn of the century.

The authorities' response, too, was perfectly predictable. The 1930s revealed a rock and a hard place: if governments do nothing, there is a depression; if they overspend, they compromise their currencies, the partial destruction of which is manifested as inflation. Given that the Depression was about the rock of laissez-faire governments, no surprises that all the Fund's responses since the dotcom crisis of 1999 have been biased towards the hard-place of money-creation. Bernanke spelled it out, and even went to the trouble of announcing that the printing-press was the answer. As I write this (autumn 2009), the denouement of currency compromise and inflation is not yet played out – yet it is the inevitable consequence of government choices.

Could anybody have stopped it happening? Three groups of players were in a position to understand the dynamics, and were powerful enough to have changed, at the very least, the severity of the dislocation – the regulators, the market participants (particularly in the banks, the facilitators and hedge funds), and lastly, the economists.

The regulators are perhaps the least impressive of the three. The dislocations of the 1930s brought about a battery of protective rules to ensure that the problems never appeared again. The horse had bolted, but the locks became chubbier, the ringfences more ubiquitous. Better safe than sorry was the motto – but over the decades, there were no more frights – rather, a complete absence of bolting horses. The safety nets were withdrawn. One of these nets was the Glass-Steagall Act, which had been passed to stop a manifest conflict of interest between banking operations and investment activities – but even in attenuated form by April 1998 it was blocking the takeover of Travellers by Citicorp. Accordingly, it was repealed, opening the way for bulge bracket banks to take advantage of opportunities arising from this conflict. A few weeks later, NationsBank and BankAmerica announced a merger to form the biggest bank in the United States. In the UK the problem was exacerbated by a political decision made by Gordon Brown in the late 1990s to take away the regulation of the banking industry from the Bank of England, and to create a new Financial Services Authority. The FSA took a suite of offices in Canary Wharf – too expensive, it was pointed out, for commerce, but the fines from the sharp teeth of their vigilance would pay the rent, and support its burgeoning workforce. Their teeth, however, although sharp, were tiny. Woe betide the shady stockbroking house, the junior corporate finance executive who tipped off his father-in-law about a coming announcement. But as the financial system grew in contradictions and conflicts, so did one-sided risk/reward opportunities on a gigantic scale. The FSA seemed not to notice, not to care.

Why didn't the market operators do something about it? After all, they had something perhaps less valuable than their reputation to lose, but more important: their money. One reason was the asymmetric opportunities given to hedge funds, credit rating agencies and traders (not least the proprietary desks of the big banks). It meant that they could become very rich on the upswing, and not give it all back on a downswing – that opportunity was left to the investors, the real victims, with nothing to gain and everything to lose. Some investors were ignorant of the dynamics, but soothed into somnolence by the beneficent consequences: others smelled a rat, but had not taken full cognisance of Mark Twain's famous dictum: a thing long expected takes the form of the unexpected when at last it comes.

The most interesting failure was that of the economists. It might be thought that they were in the strongest position – above the hurly-burly of the chaise-longue, so to speak, they were armed with a depth of statistics that Keynes and his forebears could only dream about. They had the time to assess, and the status to call and interrogate whomsoever they liked. Unlike the stockbroking class, they won Nobel prizes. Yet they completely missed the catastrophe – as one eminent professor said unblushingly to me this summer (2009), it was unforeseeable.

There's an obvious reason for their failure: they are too clever. It requires extreme cleverness today to be an economist and as a result they have become an elite. All elites have pronounced strengths and shortcomings, but events can occur which mercilessly expose these weaknesses – it happened to the British Navy during the First World War. The British gunnery at the Battle of Jutland in 1916 was truly dire. The reason was that to be an officer in the Royal Navy in the nineteenth century, you had to be a gentleman. This cut down the field, to say the least, and it particularly mattered in the technical world of calibration, recoil, stabilisers, pattern of shot. Gentlemen tended to lose interest in targets bigger than a cock pheasant (or possibly an elephant), and the art of sinking battleships by gunfire fell into dissuetude. Those who were in the gun turrets couldn't do it – and those who could do it weren't in the gun turrets. That's the trouble with economists. A group which is gifted at higher mathematics is not collectively gifted, too, in the dynamics of human behaviour. One got close: Hyman Minsky. He developed a model which better fitted reality. But his thinking was always considered fringe. As Edward Chancellor observed, 'Orthodoxy decreed that economies are in equilibrium and the crisis is exogenous. Minsky said the opposite.' In addition, he was supposedly difficult to model. Models need formulae – but formulae are, alas, formulaic – they require assumptions which cannot easily be nuanced. The great banking treatises of the nineteenth century – by James Gilbart, for instance in the 1850s, and the works of Walter Bagehot a short generation later (he died in 1877) are behavioural in tone. There isn't an epsilon or a theta to be seen – and yet these guys were classicists. The change came, probably with the Cambridge professor, Alfred Marshall (cheer people up at your next dinner party by explaining Marshallian-K!); a superimposition of complex and hard-to-understand mathematical formulae became *de rigueur*. Only if you could do the maths were you allowed to give rein to the social aspects of the dismal science. It was fine for J K Galbraith – he really could do both – but the one discipline which should have been able to give the intellectual and moral framework to the dangers and opportunities of the economic cycle was too narrow of outlook and understanding to do this.

One of the fascinating things about time is that its fluidity is the opposite of what one naturally expects – that the past is done and dusted and it's the future which holds out endless possibilities. The reality is arguably the other way round. We are endlessly re-writing history. Perhaps it is really the future which is shackled by backward-looking perceptions, and the past is the home of endless change, as events are reappraised in the light of today's torment. It might be that the Bourbons were wise when they forgot nothing, learnt nothing; the rest of us are inclined to forget much, and to learn the wrong things from that which we half-remember.

In January 2005, I quoted Maynard Keynes, who said that monetary disorder was 'the way in which people may postpone and cover up what may be almost unendurable facts – people struggle to maintain their previous standards by living off their capital, and the whole apparatus of monetary unsoundness allows the country to put off the worst day without recognising what it is doing'. Nearly a century later, it is hard to imagine surer words to describe the situation. With the crash, the economic prosperity of the world flickered and died away. The central authorities have come to its rescue with quantitative easing and the rest of their monetary weapons. But the prosperity is the cornucopia of the cheque book. As I write, the cheques are being honoured, and we are maintaining, by and large, our previous standard of living. It feels like the midpoint of the collapse of our prosperity: the acute phase, when the financial system was compromised, is now behind us. Ahead is the chronic phase, when the world comes to understand that wealth cannot be created artificially – central banks, with their initiatives will be seen to be as impotent as commercial banks with their leverage.

Caveat investor!

Commentary

1998 opened in a climate of nervous apprehension not of swine, but of avian, flu with 1.25 million chickens killed in Hong Kong over the course of the New Year. The avian flu did not spread, but it proved to be a harbinger of bad things to come in the Far East. Close on the heels of the chickens came the demise of Peregrine Investment Holdings, the high-flying Hong Kong deal maker, a late victim of the Far Eastern currency crisis of the previous year.

The United States had gained something of the prestige and political power that it had enjoyed in its heady heyday between the winning of the Second World War and the losing of the Vietnamese conflict 25 years later – in many ways more so, with the collapse a decade earlier of Russia's communism. Bill Clinton was ready with the helping hand of condescension, 'The US endorses additional conditional financial support from the international institutions as necessary to promote stability, structural reform and growth in Russia.' Sergei Kiriyenko, Prime Minister of Russia, begged Parliament to vote through the necessary austerity measures. Japan, too, was in trouble. Unemployment there rose nearly to nearly 3 million, its highest level ever, while the yen fell to its lowest against the US dollar for a decade. The Prime Minister Ryutaro Hashimoto was likened by the chairman of Sony to Herbert Hoover before the 1929 Wall Street crash; the Japanese premier resigned three months later. Fujitsu, too, was in retreat closing its microchip factory in London, and in America, just as Bill Clinton was giving his deposition to Kenneth Starr on his relations with the White House intern, Monica Lewinsky, similar events were unfolding at Mitsubishi, which was ordered to pay $34 million to 350 women who claimed sexual harassment in its American division.

There was a sense of the passing of the old order. July saw the last tea auction in London – after 319 years. The same month Geri Halliwell left the Spice Girls after a shorter interval. The RAC Club was bid for by a company called Cendant, a US marketing brand group, and the mighty partnership Goldman Sachs announced that it was to become a corporation, and to float its shares on the stock market. The store chain Gap began to sell its clothes through the internet. In August, into this sense of *fin de siécle* there exploded three bombs: the Omagh bomb in Northern Ireland, the US Embassies of Nairobi and Dar es Salaam (which turned out to be committed by a little-known terrorist called Osama Bin Laden), and what proved to be the biggest bomb of the lot, a financial crisis in Russia. The stock market there, as ever a leading indicator, had dropped precipitously in June, causing the sale of the nationally owned Rosneft to be delayed. After spending $9 billion of reserves trying to support the rouble in September, Russia finally defaulted on $40 billion of debt interest. The effect on the stock market was galvanic. Bank shares halved, notwithstanding the Pope's canonisation of Giuseppe Tovini, founder of the Banco Ambrosiano. It was not long before it became horribly apparent that the biggest hedge fund in the world, run by the cleverest people in the world, had gone bust for the biggest shortfall of assets over liabilities in the world. It was not long, too, before executives at UBS, slightly less clever than the boys at LTCM, admitted to a £400 million loss, closely followed by Dresdner with an £80 million provision. Barclays managed a right and left with losses on both Russian debt and then LTCM. Not even the news that a product from Thirsk had won a gold medal at the British Cheese Awards could deflect the crisis. There was talk of widespread job losses, with Kate Dereham of head-hunters Sheffield Haworth stating sombrely, 'We're winning no recruitment mandates as a lot of banks are taking the opportunity to upgrade their staff."

By the end of the year, things were stabilising. LTCM's leveraged balance sheet was strengthened within an injection of $3.8 billion by the banks. The IMF received $18 billion – again, a unilateral move by Clinton who pushed it through Congress. Japan earmarked a substantial finance package to fight its domestic recession. The start of the great reflation had begun.

One Man's View Of A Mania

April 1998

This bull market has some of the characteristics of Rasputin – shoot him, poison him, stab him, but he just rolls his eyes and keeps on going. In the last quarter of 1997, there was a devastating collapse of confidence in the economies of the Far East. Marc Faber said of it, 'Never has there been such a total economic breakdown and massive destruction of wealth as occurred against all expectations in Asia in the last six months.' World stock markets responded by dropping by about 2%. This quarter, just ended, has seen no such shocks, and the world index, expressed in sterling, has risen by nearly 13%.

At times like this, a roadmap is helpful. The first point to make is that against a background of reducing inflation, buoyant consumer demand is fuelling both stock and bond prices. Against classic yardsticks (dividend yield, earnings multiple and premium to net asset value and replacement costs) equity valuations are unsustainable, unless earnings and assets grow at ten times the current rate of inflation for the foreseeable future.

This overvaluation, while extreme even by previous excesses, is a usual characteristic in the early stages of a deflationary cycle. These deflationary forces have been a constant theme of our investment reviews over the quarters: the Asian collapse testifies that the pressures are increasing. Governments are responding by adopting as accommodative a stance as they dare. Interest rates and taxes are down, and easy money has been allowed into the system. In inflationary times, central action such as this would be disastrous: a Lawson boom writ large. This time, it provides an effective counterweight to deflation: hence the Goldilocks' economy – not too hot and not too cold, and near-universal plaudits for the policymakers. Unfortunately, a by-product of this policy leads to distortions in other parts of the system. Corporations have embraced with admirable alacrity the advantages of replacing equity with debt when the latter appears cheap.

While the consumer spends and the economy remains buoyant, this enhances equity returns. This adds to the fuel of rising asset values, which are as popular as mother and apple pie while it lasts. The problem comes when the values move in the opposite direction. Then the unforgiving nature of debt becomes apparent, and small changes in growth make big changes to market valuations. Matheson Investments have estimated that a drop in corporate profitability from 8.5% to 8% should knock one third off the value of Wall Street! (Presumably if corporate profitability is assumed to edge up to 9%, then Wall Street can go up by a similar amount.) The point is that a rise in the value of bonds and equities is mutually inconsistent in the long term – both can rise on the increase in liquidity, but ultimately the economic consequences of the underlying economic conditions and the governments' response to them, will determine their relative attractiveness. What we do believe is that any significant setback on Wall Street is likely itself to be a fundamental factor in reducing consumer demand, so that the one factor which can unequivocally offset the lack of confidence engendered by the deflationary forces will go into reverse.

What is to be done about it? To the extent that one rides the tiger, one must be aware of the risks one is taking. For a majority of one's money, therefore, it is important to have as loose a correlation with market levels as possible. In our view, the fixed interest market is indubitably the best way of doing this, because any increase in deflationary forces, *ipso facto*, will benefit this asset class. The second is to concentrate on growth stocks. In a deteriorating economy, there is a real question of 'first catch your growth', but however hard it may be to find in quantity, it will always be there, and it justifies a high rating. Meanwhile, eccentric as it may seem to be picnicking among the mountain rocks when the beach looks so inviting, if the tide turns, a number of beachcombers will have more than wet feet.

Trouble in the East

July 1998

The last quarter has been more interesting for the development of the world economy itself, than for the stock market response to it. This bear market – if bear market it eventually be – is taking effect like hemlock: the extremities lose vitality before the poison works its way towards the central nervous system. Peripheral markets have collapsed: in the last three months Hong Kong is down 25%, Chile down 19%, India down 24%, Thailand down 40%, etc. At the centre, by which we mean the major stocks of the major markets, the overall mood is no worse than cautious: some selling down of stocks with perceived risk, but the money reinvested in other sectors where the outlook looks more attractive. Overall, these markets have drifted slightly lower over the quarter.

Events in the field have been moving more quickly than the market response would suggest. Japan's persistent refusal to tackle the bad debts in the banking sector is generating real fear in the investment community, although most commentators are still of the view that if the authorities there took the appropriate action (each commentator has, of course, a different theory as to what is appropriate), with one bound the solution would be in place.

A correct assessment of Japan's problems and their resolution is, in our view, probably the key to the correct disposition of assets over the next year. The problems are more easily stated than resolved. Ten years after the end of the stock market boom, there is widespread despondency in Japan. Property prices and stock market prices have collapsed, and if the banks were to acknowledge the full extent of the fall, they would be bankrupt. The people of Japan have responded to these deflationary forces in the classic way: they have stopped borrowing, they have stopped spending, and they save. Interest rates in Japan are nearly zero. The bond yields, universally acknowledged to be safe, yield 1.3%. Nobody wants to be the first to leave the slit trench and start spending. Meanwhile the savings pile up, some of it in banks, but more of it under mattresses and in government bonds. None of it provides a decent return, and the only place that provides such a return is abroad. Sod's Law (as far as the authorities are concerned) has determined that just as it is becoming apparent that exporting assets from Japan is the sensible thing to do, the Japanese deregulation rules are kicking in, making it more possible for Mr Watanabe and his friends to do so. As the Yen has weakened, so the exporting of capital looks even more appropriate. Intervention by the US authorities three weeks ago has halted the tide for the moment, but it is only a case of buying time, and the world waits to see what the longer term solution will be. The roots of the problem in part date back to the administrative system imposed on Japan by America in 1945. Japan's elite was encouraged to pursue a career in the big trade ministries, and away from the military and political arenas which were perceived to have been the driving forces of Japanese imperialism before the Second World War. These ministries have proved to be riddled with corruption and the dynamic for a solution has passed to the politicians. But the politicians are neither by tradition nor calibre up to such decisive action. It is like asking the mayors of England's provincial towns to sort out a banking crisis.

Nor is it clear that a solution to Japan's travails will suit the western economies. The West's sense of *schadenfreude* is coupled with clear evidence that their asset values have been supported by a massive amount of money leaving Japan. Compared with the grim reality within Japan, the greener fields of America seem attractive on any valuation. A solution to Japan's problems would result in Japanese money being repatriated, with a correspondingly depressing effect on the level of Wall Street's bathwater. If, on the other hand there is no solution, the Yen will begin to slide again, setting off a series of competitive devaluations, which would be extremely detrimental to world trade in particular and economic prosperity in general. All eyes are on China in this regard. Meanwhile, after the financial crises in the Pacific Rim comes the economic fallout. Not only is Japan itself now officially in recession, but other Far Eastern economies are plunging. Industrial production in South Korea is running 36% lower (annualised) than a year ago. Car sales in the Pacific are down some 70%. Thai cement production is down 61% (this last fact is a surefire winner at country house dinner parties).

At the moment, this is having only a limited impact on the USA. Statistics from South Korea suggest that there is still no flood of goods from Asia, but one can be assured that it will eventually come, and it will be bad news for US profits when it does. The good news is that it has lowered inflationary expectations in America where there are classic signs of overheating. The result is that the American economy is developing some unusual characteristics. Economic growth generally ends when the consumer runs out of steam, and his lack of buying power extends out to basic industry, whose volumes ultimately depend on the customer not only being able but ready to spend.

This time basic industry in the US is slowing, but the consumer is still spending and borrowing. The reason is clear: strong stock markets are keeping Mr Average confident, while Asia is hurting investment. It is worth sparing a thought as to how the situation might develop from here. Brian Reading's latest review puts his finger on it:

'Is deflation a risk?' he asks. *'Recent developments in the US, Japan and Asia suggest that the nature of the business cycle may have changed. The normal cycle is consumer-led. Investment takes up the running later. It results in excess demand and ends as a result of over-heating when the rise in inflation must be checked. But this is not the only way a business cycle can develop and end. A cycle which is investment-led increases supply side capacity as well as adding to demand. This is particularly likely where financial markets drive real economies. A stock market boom can underpin consumer demand growth even when incomes are rising less rapidly than GDP. Nevertheless, profit margins may be squeezed because of an over-valued exchange rate. The overvalued exchange-rate may extend periods of rapid but non-inflationary growth. The danger is then that the boom then blows itself out, as foreign competition hits profits and the stock market collapses. Prices may fall in the subsequent recession.'*

Lombard Street Research Ltd,
Monthly International Review 76, 25 June 1998

This is the lesson from Japan in the years since 1990, and exactly describes the US situation today. It is why we remain so nervous of the equity markets, and have our faith in bonds denominated in high quality currencies.

Has The Penny Dropped?

October 1998

T he onset of a bear market is always a frightening time. The mood of the financial community has darkened, and the carefree days of July seem as distant as the summer picnics of 1914 did three months later to an earlier generation.

So far, the developments have run true to course. The ability of capital to move across national boundaries has always been a destabilising force for the world. While confidence was high, this was not apparent, but since the Asian crisis broke, capital flows have been seeking safer havens. For a while, the retreat looked benign: currency collapses and imploding domestic demand in the East took some of the pressure off America's fast running economy. The unravelling, unpleasant for those on the periphery, did not seem to have touched Western reality. Russia (neck and neck with Denmark as an economic world force) put paid to this complacency. When the IMF did not bail them out they changed the rules and repudiated their contracts. The hedge funds who thought they had covered their risks (by currency hedging out of the rouble) found that they were hit on the back of the head by a revolving door: the hedge proved to be unenforceable. An unseemly scramble followed. The fattest animal in the farmyard was John Meriwether's Long Term Capital Management, with borrowings 2% of America's GDP on an asset base 1/50th of the size. When the burst bubble stopped this particular pig in mid-flight, it transpired that a number of unexpected trotters were in its trough: not least Italy's Central Bank. When LTCM was bailed out by the Western financial system at the American Federal Reserve's behest, it was not unnoticed that the Italian currency was one of the biggest beneficiaries of the LTCM's strategy within its fund.

Damaging as has been the arithmetic, perhaps of greater significance has been the blow to the moral authority of those in charge in the West. When Asia collapsed last year, the IMF imposed a regime of austerity which many thought was unkind, but appropriate. Most commentators now question even that appropriateness, and the exercise has put into question whether the West were acting in good faith. The LTCM bail out seems like the worst kind of hypocrisy; why was Asia not offered a similar deal? Against this background of mutual distrust, the contagion of lost confidence rolls on. Alan Greenspan, the Chairman of the Fed, remains a giant, although wounded by the LTCM decision. Beyond him, it is hard to see beyond the pygmies. A stricken US President, a novice at the helm in Germany inspire no confidence: the twin bulwarks against depression, the IMF and the World Bank, are regarded as complacent and incompetent respectively. It feels like Paris in 1940: who will hold the line if the enemy advances?

After the collapse of Russia, eyes have turned to Latin America. Brazil is largely regarded as the key: it is the eleventh biggest economy in the world, American trade and investment in the region is extremely significant, and a collapse of the Brazilian currency would undoubtedly infect the whole of the sub-continent. It is clearly a moment for injecting enough money to give an unequivocal message that Brazil has the backing of the Western world. The reason that we are bearish is that we simply cannot see where the money will come from. It probably requires at least $120 billion. The IMF have virtually none, and the attempts to raise more from the West are for insufficient amounts, and are likely to fail in any case. Germany is playing a dangerous game, and has made it plain that Brazil seems as far away to them as Russia obviously did to America in its hour of need. America cannot afford to let Brazil fail, but can she support it alone? There are massive calls on America's strength. They are currently running a $250 billion trade deficit: every month $20 billion has to flow in to balance the books. As Asian companies export to survive, America is inevitably the purchaser of last resort. America is also the lender of last resort, and, as the Brazil scenario shows, these are heavy duty figures. The effect is a weakening dollar. America cannot allow Brazil to fail, but it is hard to see how she can afford to save Brazil.

The key to how things develop from here is the level of Wall Street. Buoyant markets stimulate spending at the expense of saving: poor markets reverse this trend. The Americans have responded to exuberant markets by stopping saving altogether. The Japanese have responded to poor domestic investment returns by doubling their savings rate. If the American consumer transmogrifies into the American saver, the engine of world economic growth will reverse. Commentators have, in our view correctly, made the connection between the level of Wall Street and consumer confidence in America. Given that Wall Street is still extremely expensive by historic standards, it requires an act of faith indeed to believe that Wall Street can hold its current valuation. Normally economic shocks come from unexpected quarters, but the overborrowings within the Western banking system, the deterioration of the Japanese situation (we have not even touched on this, but in normal circumstances this would be the crisis to dwell upon) and general disinclination to hazard liquidity, all point to economic difficulties. There does not appear to be a line drawn under this crisis.

Investing in this climate calls for great caution. We feel that there is within the investment community still too much of a desire to make money, when preservation should be the keystone. In a mischievous world, objects of safety become increasingly prized, so that there is, almost as a by product, a capital return in addition to underlying safety. Accordingly, what we described in our last investment review (in July) as, 'high quality bonds denominated in high quality currencies' remains the core of our investment stance.

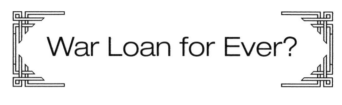

War Loan for Ever?

January 1999

The year ended on a strong note, with the fears of cataclysm which were paramount in October now almost a distant memory. The final result of the year has been, for the stock market equity indices, one of satisfactory growth – about 12% in the UK.

Yet the underlying performance of differing asset classes has varied widely. The majority of equities, worldwide, went down – the *Daily Telegraph* list of UK shares (just over 1,000 of them) showed 722 falling in 1998, as against 365 rising. This is a ratio of 2 to 1 on the downside. Commodities were in headlong retreat, with oil down 50% and copper by 35%. A clutch of 'growth' blue chips, largely in the telecommunication and drug sectors surged upwards. Fixed interest stocks performed extremely well for the second year running – the long end of the sterling fixed interest market rose by a staggering 47%.

Each of these moves is consistent with a world economy rapidly falling into a deflation – each that is, except the huge capitalisation index stocks, which moved up while the smaller brethren – those worth less than £1 billion – moved in the opposite direction.

We believe that these deflationary forces are accelerating, despite the undoubted efforts of the central authorities to counteract those forces. We therefore believe that the fixed interest markets remain excellent value in a world where inflation is disappearing, and might well be replaced by deflation – the unusual phenomenon of money rising in value, as prices drop across the board. Producer Price Indices, which reflect the costs to manufacturing industry are dropping worldwide at no less than 10% per annum. Not since the 1930s have we seen anything like it. In those days, long dated fixed interest stock yielded 3.5% or less. In Britain they currently yield 4.4%; if they fall this far in 1999 (not a prediction, but a possibility), War Loan would rise by a further 33%. It has already doubled in the last three and a half years. For UK taxpayers, the whole of the gain is tax free.

Although the UK fixed interest market remains good value against the fundamentals, it is eclipsed by the attraction of long-term German government fixed interest stocks. In the UK, the longer the duration of the bond, the less it yields. In Germany, the reverse is true. The citizens of Germany are reluctant to take a 30 year view on money – the consequences of being the silver medallist in two World Wars has made it abundantly plain to them that the long-term future is full of pitfalls. In a deflationary world, where a stream of income becomes more valuable, and less easily obtained, Britain's got it right and Germany wrong. If 30 year German yields fell to the equivalent of 10 year German bonds, long dated German bonds would give a profit of about 25%. In an increasingly hazardous and uncertain world, this is a wonderful opportunity. A chance to make money from the storm clouds.

Why are the valuations of larger companies so high? A necessary, but not sufficient, cause is the length of time that blue-chips have gone up in value – pretty much constantly for a quarter of a century. There is a deep underlying trust that they are safe, that they deliver the goods in increasing your wealth. Investors want reasons to invest. All other things equal, falling interest rates provide a platform for higher valuations. All other things are not equal, of course; the fall in interest rates is a symptom of the worsening outlook for equities. This is why it has not had a beneficial effect on the share prices of the generality of companies, but it has been sufficient to lift the best loved ones – the blue-chips.

The rise in share prices to ratings perhaps twice, maybe three times, their long term norm is therefore perfectly explainable. It is what happens next which should interest investors.

When expensive shares have this sort of momentum, there is no rule of law which says things cannot go significantly higher. But when it ends, it does so suddenly, capriciously and in spades. It looked as though it had in September: it hadn't.

If it is all likely to end in tears, it seems to us to be unnecessary to strain for the last ounce of overrated return. Events are moving in parallel to the Japanese market bubble 10 years ago, which perhaps coincidentally, ran a similar course before its final denouement in 1989. In Japan, the government allowed markets to inflate to offset the deleterious effects of an ever strengthening Yen, which was hitting the exporters. The effect was to support retail sales, but the boom came in asset prices, not RPI inflation. So, in America, it is retail demand, on the back of the wealth effect of stock market profits, which is keeping the USA afloat. The danger is that if the market drops, then the fundamentals worsen, which validates the primary fall and sparks off further stock market weakness. The fixed interest markets remain the place for regiments of cash: safe, liquid, providing a superior return. But we acknowledge this is an investment in defeat, in depression, in 'Lord, I was frightened, and I hid my talent in the ground'. Mankind is full of enterprise and the equity market provides a plethora of opportunities to make money, no matter what the overall outlook may be. 'Growth' stocks at the moment are expensively rated in the stock market. A deflationary environment is excellent for companies which can exploit an advantage, but they are highly valued. Put another way, this means that the growth must either be explosive or continue for a fair length of time, and why should the biter itself not be bitten? Much better, in our view, are safe and boring companies outside the blue-chips. Not since Nero's firework parties has boredom been so discounted. In uncertain times, such investments should trade at a premium but in fact many are on amazing discounts. They are excellent travelling companions for Captain Gilt and Fraulein Bund in a portfolio.

Commentary

1 999 saw what will probably forever be the perfect specimen of an asset price bubble. Connoisseurs may prefer the tulip bulb mania in seventeenth century Netherlands, and the 1929 Wall Street crash presupposes that Humpty Dumpty had first clambered to the top of the very high wall. But the spectacular idiocy of a wide range of the citizenry of the western world remains a marvel a decade after its event. Although the enthusiasm for the new world of TMT (Technology Media Telecommunications) seemed almost universal at the time, after its passing, its apologists were as thin on the ground as post-war Nazis.

TMT stocks had, in fact, been rising steadily, and by no means slowly, for the previous three years. The year opened with no sense that it was to be the easiest year of the entire century to make big capital gains.

It may have been easy, but clients of Ruffer comprehensively failed to benefit from it.

At the outset, the biggest event was the introduction of the Euro which promptly fell heavily against the major currencies. The *Spectator* pointed out that it was an Italian Prime Minister and Finance Minister, one of these now charged with complicity to murder, the other sent to prison for corruption, who ambushed Margaret Thatcher at the EU summit and committed Europe to a timetable for monetary union. The Europeans were triumphant. Yves Thibault de Silguy, the Commissioner for Economic Affairs in Brussels, said that for the first time since the fall of the Roman Empire Europe would have a single currency. The British government were divided. The Bank of England, under Eddie George remained inscrutable, and refrained from committing itself to any course of action. A sharp-eyed member of the public noted that the gift shop in the Bank of England had run out of fudge, but the supply was quickly restored. Tony Blair meanwhile announced a new initiative in the National Changeover Plan to prepare Britain to brace economic and monetary union; 'It's not a change of policy' he said, 'but it is a change of gear.'

It was not just the currency which put the UK government on the back foot. The EU attempted to consolidate its monetary unity with a blanket 20% withholding tax throughout the EU. It was to be another two years before Gordon Brown saw off this threat, too. The millennium bug also caused alarm since it was not clear how worrisome this might turn out to be. In July, the Orkney Islands council was proclaimed to be unprepared for the problems associated with such a crisis. The natural order, too, seemed to keep animal spirits at bay. Dou Dou, the world's oldest panda, died aged 37 in Wuhan Zoo. A peace-loving moorhen was eaten by a pelican in St James's Park, London. Meanwhile, the Euro remained on its own path falling below the value of the dollar in December.

But the story of 1999 was the bubble. Freeserve, an internet stock, demerged from Dixons the retailer, was one of the early ones to come in July – valued at £1.5 billion. QXL and Webvan (an internet grocery service) quickly followed. Bid fever is always the first cousin of an asset price bubble, and bids duly came thick and fast. NatWest Bank tried to buy Legal & General, but the move proved Derek Wanless' undoing: two weeks later Fred Goodwin made a successful bid for NatWest itself. The Industrial Bank of Japan, Fuji Bank and Da-Ichi Kangyo Bank all merged to form the biggest bank in the world. Lloyds TSB's bid for Scottish Widows the previous June seemed a mere pelican in this food chain. The Russian invasion of Chechnya and its entry to Grozny in late October of that year seemed no less chaotic than the financial world around it. In November, Edmond Safra had agreed to sell his Republic Bank to HSBC for $10 billion – weeks later in December 1999 he was immolated in his Monaco fortress, cowering in the bathroom to escape from burglars.

The Frejus Conundrum

A p r i l   1 9 9 9

In 1959, the Malpasset Dam burst, and a cascade of water swept down from the reservoir above, inundating the town of Frejus. In the aftermath of the tragedy, attention focused on the security guard whose job it was to monitor the gauges which measured any undue build up of water pressure in the dam. It transpired that he had been tremendously aIarmed some months earlier, when the needles started to push into dangerous territory, but nobody else seemed very interested, and as the gauge went well beyond the danger zone, he assumed it was miscalibrated. He was reading a newspaper when the accident happened.

For the second quarter running, a small number of mega-large companies continued their inexorable rise in price – I shall not write 'in value'. The result is that those who bought at the market peak just ahead of the Autumn crash last year have not only recouped their losses but are in profit. The effect of this has been to allay fears which were so prevalent some six months ago that the fabric of the world financial system was in disarray. It is not just that fears have been allayed – the speedy and unequivocal recovery of the markets has reinforced the sensation that brave investors are by definition astute investors. The autumn setback, it seems, provided a rare but invaluable opportunity for the slow of faith to acquire a slice of the action.

It is hard to over-emphasise the dangers of such a view. In the last 150 years there has been no precedent for the valuation that Wall Street currently enjoys. It could fall by 60% before it would be rated on an average valuation. And, of course, if the market did fall 60%, the economy would be so buffeted that the market would probably need to fall further. Our decision to avoid (very largely) an exposure to blue-chip equities is therefore a relatively easy one. The risks comprehensively and very substantially outweigh the rewards. As one respected commentator has written, 'The job

16

that inflation used to do – to bring real income and wealth back into line with economic fundamentals – must now be done by the stock market. The mechanism is different and is abrupt rather than gradual, but ultimately, it is just as certain.'

The conundrum is where this leaves the bond market. Severe market dislocations are massively deflationary, and improve the fundamentals of government bonds of long duration enormously. There would be a real chance of deflation, just as the correcting of an absurdly high stock market in Japan 10 years ago heralded a decade of paradise for bond holders. This argues strongly for big fixed interest investments, and certainly in the September meltdown last year, long bonds surged in value. In these deflationary circumstances the safety of an assured stream of income over a very long period of time becomes immensely and reassuringly attractive.

There is, however, another possibility. In such circumstances, fear is King, and there is a very real reassurance in holding cash. Is cash, or is the fixed interest market, the more prudent policy in safeguarding one's wealth? Cash preserves the capital value, but leaves the income at the mercy of falling rates. To achieve the latter, one must own long dated bonds, but this hazards the capital value if there is a flight to cash.

The precedent by which I am being guided is Japan itself. Bond yields fell from 5.5% at the time of its stock market crash in 1989 to less than 1% last year. The moral is that the deflationary conditions in the aftermath favour fixed interest stocks. But the decisive point is that bond yields first went up – and rising bond yields mean falling bond prices. Yields in Japan touched 6% in 1990, before the fundamentals reasserted themselves, and provided one of the most interesting bull markets of all time. I therefore think that it is right to raise liquidity, but not to dispose wholesale of the fixed interest holdings which remain decisively the right asset class for these deflationary times. In my view, the German government bond market remains extraordinarily attractive, being on a 5% yield base for 30 year bonds, in an inflation free society. The economy is slowing and I see little to suggest that there are any inflationary pressures in that society. By contrast, long dated sterling bonds yield less in a nation where there still are vestiges of inflation, and a history of succumbing to inflation itself as a safety valve from structural problems in the economy. Accordingly, it is the latter category that will provide the better opportunities for raising cash, although on an 18 month view, I think the enemy of the bond markets around the world will be those of default, and not those of inflation.

Accordingly, I would not want to own government bonds of those countries which have not addressed their structural problems, and this includes the United States.

Stock market indices are decisively overvalued at the moment. There are still many opportunities for value investors outside the indices in companies of more modest size. The big ones on their high ratings will find no escape, but it will be the cheap ratings of smaller companies which could provide some comfort in such an eventuality.

The extent of the prevailing onwards and upwards has swept all in its path leaving both discredited bears and hesitant participants feeling extremely giddy. It is tempting, when faced with such forces, to sit back and enjoy the ride but these rises have a finite source of power – the credit-hungry policies of the Federal Reserve. When the decisions are reversed, and it is certain that they will be, the market forces will be unleashed in the opposite direction. One cannot afford to be reading the paper when the time comes.

An Interruption in a Deflationary World

July 1999

There is a palpable sense of relief in the air. Nine months after last autumn's financial crisis, the 'business as usual' signs are hanging like bunting from the street lamps of the world's financial centres. As to where the crisis came from, the unspoken view is that it was as unpredictable as unpredicted – a financial dose of 'flu striking in random fashion. Its short duration, and seeming lack of damage to the world's financial fabric has been attributed variously to good fortune, to the pixie dust of the genial Alan Greenspan, presiding over the Federal Bank of America, and to the innate strength of an American economy taking full advantage of the flowering of the new computer age.

The origin of the crisis lay in the tension between Far Eastern inspired deflationary market forces which have dominated the world in the 1990s, and government central bank responses to those forces – of allowing the nation's banking system ready access to credit. The credit was intended to stimulate the real economy – manufacturers, retailers, traders and the like – but business conditions meant that they were reluctant borrowers. Instead it was the financial industry which had the confidence to borrow the extra money created, and most of it went into financial assets – takeovers, venture capital projects, and share buy backs. The effect of this was to trigger in the Western world an asset price boom – a sort of inflation, where it is the IBM stock price rather than IBM products which go up in price. Lending a great deal of money to the financial sector for a long period of time nearly always ends in excess. Like small boys left alone in sweet shops, it is often not the noisy ones dancing in the aisles which cause the problems; it is the Billy Bunters in the corner scoffing the cream buns. The obvious sign of the excess was the extraordinary high valuations afforded to Wall Street's blue chip shares. But the trouble came in the corporate bond market which had not been seen as vulnerable when the grandest hedge fund of all defaulted: LTCM, who numbered among its clientele the Central Bank of Italy and a number of less eminent imitators. Alan Greenspan's prompt and appropriate action in providing liquidity and lowering interest rates was an impressive feat, and effective in dealing with the primary crisis.

A side effect has been to kickstart the American economy itself. America has been for a considerable time the locomotive of world growth, and this engine has increased its powerful drive in the last six months. It has coincided with signs that economic revival might spread out to other countries. There is a consensus that the short term outlook for Japan is considerably brighter, although it has to be said there is a hung jury as to its medium and long term outlook. The United Kingdom appears to have avoided a 1999 recession which many regarded as likely last year, and even continental Europe is not the accident blackspot that it had seemed to be. This resumption of economic growth has relaxed the investment community. Everybody is agreed that Wall Street is trading at enormously expensive valuations, but now that earnings seem likely to be advancing again, there is some confidence that the economy can grow into the shoes which are currently too big for it. This is the sentiment which is currently giving investors confidence in valuations.

However, the acceleration of growth in America, and its synchronised resumption elsewhere is setting off a train of events which could just as effectively torpedo the American investor's dream. The profitless prosperity of the last few years allowed interest rates, and in particular long duration interest rates, to fall to levels not seen since the 1950s. The latest development is unequivocally bad news for sentiment in the fixed interest market. It is therefore no surprise to find that yields on long bonds have been rising (and thus prices falling). The worst affected have been US bonds, where growth expectations are highest. Rising interest rates are a sure and effective way to choke off both stock market excesses and ultimately the economy itself. With the extreme enthusiasm for stock market assets in America, it could well be that bond yields have to rise a fair bit further before they do their work.

How will things develop from here? Our view is that rising interest rates will be the mechanism by which first Wall Street, and then the economy itself in America comes back to earth. The timing of this remains the wild card: while the economy is perceived to be improving, it will take some exogenous factor to take the wind out of the sails. The poison inflicted by rising fixed interest rates may be sure in its effect, but this alone will take time. This is partly because the 'growth' phenomenon of 1999 is still more promise than reality: profit warnings still abound, and the word from corporate advisers is still of difficult markets and adverse trading conditions. It is partly that a few quarters of accelerated economic growth, bought at a price of higher indebtedness, will not be sufficient to extinguish the deflationary forces.

Translating these observations into a coherent investment strategy is far from easy. We sensed the sea change in fixed interest stocks at the beginning of the year, which is why we have cut back on an asset class which had served us well. So long as the perception of growth is prevalent, fixed interest stocks will continue to suffer. Nevertheless, they remain at the core of our investment philosophy. I believe that we will look back on 1999 as an interruption in a deflationary process which has been gathering pace all decade. In many ways the disillusionment which will follow the disappointed expectations of a return to the inflationary norm will have the same effect as the aborted 1995 economic recovery in Japan: the demons came back sevenfold. Meanwhile, it is not much fun holding fixed interest assets that go down in value, no matter how spectacular the long term outlook. We are therefore actively seeking investments which will prosper during this transitional phase. Many equities of more modest size have performed very well over the last few months. Often quite breathtaking rises have merely emphasised how cheap they had become, and how much good value there still is in this sector of the marketplace.

Some time ago we coined the phrase, 'platoons of excitement, regiments of safety'; we are endeavouring to remind ourselves that a portfolio that is correctly positioned for events in a year's time is probably a portfolio that is correctly positioned for today's markets.

Inflation or Deflation?

October 1999

S tock markets around the world remain trendless, with Wall Street, the UK and Continental Europe dropping by a few percentage points. Markets have made no progress for the last 18 months, and nervous investors are trying to assess whether, as previously, the pause is a prelude to a fresh surge upwards, or whether the mother of all bull markets is about to be given a decent burial.

Observers are in a dither as to whether the basic flavour of the world at the moment is inflationary or deflationary. This is not a metaphysical conundrum – investment strategy is radically different depending on the answer to the question. In the stock market crash of last year, the consensus view was that deflationary forces were irresistible: fixed interest stocks and defensive shares were best, and to quote Flanders and Swann, 'I wouldn't give tuppence for all of the rest'. Since then, there has been a complete change in perception, and now markets think the world will be lucky to avoid at least moderate inflation. In this environment, fixed interest stocks have done badly, with equities dragged sideways, encouraged by the possibility of higher profits, but on cheaper ratings.

The inflationists see overheating in America expanding into the rest of the world. The US economy continues to grow at a cracking pace, entirely as a consequence of a consumer boom. Moreover, other economies are looking healthier too. The UK is likely to show 2% growth in 1999 – not huge, but very different from the recession forecast a year ago. Japan has shown some spectacular growth figures for 1999 – admittedly from a low base; there is still a question mark over its sustainability. The rest of the Far East has picked up, and only in Europe is the economic news patchy – France better than expected, Italy not, with Germany still disappointing. In this view, the 'deflation' of last year was not a true phenomenon, but in large part, a reflection of unsustainably low commodity prices in 1998.

Since then, their prices have surged across the board led by oil, which has doubled. Nearly all of them have followed – sugar, paper, copper, steel and now gold. Put all this together and you have the dynamics of a boom – a widespread global warming emanating from the tropical heat of the US economy. On this basis, inflation may be deferred, but the whole basis of sound money has been undermined: like the bad penny, inflation is sure to turn up some time.

The deflationists concede that there are significant inflationary pressures in the US, which could well lead to higher prices there. A massive trade deficit, funded by capital flows from abroad has averted it so far. But the presence or absence of inflation there is not the issue. The US boom is like a bonfire burning in the Arctic Circle – eventually the bonfire burns itself out, and all that is left is the cold, polar climate. Yet there is some 'global warming' since the rest of the world is looking healthier, but even if it continues, prices are unlikely to go up much. Unprecedented competition and widespread overcapacity are likely to remain decisive in keeping inflation under control. We are deflationists. The American boom is not only unsustainable in our view, but it will lead to a deep – and deeply deflationary – slowdown there. Wall Street's strength has created more wealth for the American citizen than ever before, and that by a mile: in the last two years, stock market wealth has increased by five trillion dollars. In context, this is more than all the money in the US banking system. It is 70% of America's annual GDP output. No wonder that share ownership is wider in America than ever before. No wonder the consumer is out of control. Who needs to save when your existing savings are increasing in value like that? Sure enough, the savings ratio is negative for the first time ever; Americans are spending more than they earn. It is reminiscent of the Lawson boom in Britain in 1988, (which was based on house prices, not the stock market). When the bubble burst then, the savings ratio went from +2% to +12% in short order. The equivalent American figure is – 1% against a long term average of about +10%. However hot the present US bonfire, we believe that it will freeze over when consumer spending converts to consumer saving. The catalyst could well be a setback in Wall Street, where valuations are still running at nearly twice their long term average.

Rising commodity prices are, in our view, significant, but not *vis a vis* inflation. It will be the suppliers who take the strain of rising input prices, not the end user. Why do we think this? One only has to look at the effect of adverse currency movements on manufacturers. Fifteen years ago when the DeutscheMark went up, the price of Mercedes cars abroad went up. Not so today – the profit margins go down instead. It is hard to see that there is anything intrinsically different between higher costs due to commodity prices or currency movements.

Thus we don't see a boom developing. Suppose, however, that events go the inflationists' way and the synchronised boom takes hold and America's super-normal growth continues. We believe that rising interest rates will bring about its early – or earlyish – end. Indeed that has been the lesson of 1999 already. As growth prospects grow, yields on long bonds have grown too. In the US they have risen from 4.8% to 6.2% driving fixed interest price valuations down. Mercifully, we sensed this development and have considerably reduced our large fixed interest positions. Rising interest rates, are, though, a blunt instrument. If they do not work speedily on sentiment, it takes time for the effect to come through on an economy. The longer that symptoms of a boom persist, the higher the yields will go.

The irony is that these fixed interest stocks will once again be the star investment assets to own. Every move upwards in yield (which drives their price downwards) increases the vulnerability of the US asset bubble. Thus, as they get cheaper, they help to bring about the very climate in which they will thrive. Our judgement is to hold substantial liquidity either in cash or short dated instruments in which there is no capital risk with a view to picking the safest and best point of re-entry. For those fixed interest stocks we have retained, the capital value is suffering, especially when judged against a strong currency like sterling.

Many economists see an inflation free environment as an economically healthy one. Simply because inflation was the mad cow disease of the farm-yard in the post-war years, nothing else seemed to matter. But a debauched currency is not the only threat to an economy – other viruses are just as dangerous. Capacity has risen faster than demand, and even while consumer demand is high, there is an excess of supply. The true nature of this imbalance will become apparent when the buoyancy of demand is tested. At this point, America, with its trade deficit and diminishing consumer demand, will not look like the Patron Saint of Capitalists. The push in the name of shareholder value for improved productivity, be it through the destruction of collective labour, the unshackling of state intervention or the ruthless movement of capital in pursuit of the best return, may all become as socially unacceptable as 'collectivism' in years to come.

The Court Card of Stockmarket Mania

January 2000

T he start of a New Year is a good time to step back from the melée and have a long hard assessment as to what is going on in the world. It is appropriate that 1 January ushered in not just a new year but a new century and a new millennium: the old values, old ways of doing business and old certainties all seem under threat. The stock market has sensed that the world is in the middle of an exciting, confusing, dynamic and comprehensive change: this is the opportunity to assess where the rewards are in today's world, and wherein lie the risks.

Every age feels that it is dynamically different: Wordsworth's, 'Bliss to be alive, but to be young was very heaven', strikes an eternal chord. Yet one has to arch back through the generations to find a time when the pace of change across a range of activities was so frenetic. Most of the 19th century must have felt like this: from pony to railway, from Dundreary whiskers to the bobbed and shingled haircut. The internet is rightly accorded the sobriquet of revolution: it will have implications across the widest range of industries – it will change the way we do our business.

The lessons we draw from this are twofold. The first is not to be sucked into speculating in the shares of companies whose outlook is exciting but uncertain. Manias are a well established court card in the stock market stakes: they are surprisingly hard to make long term money from. The fundamentalists either don't own them at all, or sell them much too soon. The players who are left tend to stay until the end – there is always a valid big picture explanation which provides justification of sorts for intergalactic valuations. The second lesson is not to ignore the big picture itself.

Outside the charmed circle of large-cap stocks and 'new paradigm' companies, markets have spent a second year in a bear trend. It is hard to believe that the NASDAQ, up 87% in 1999, had more fallers in its ranks than the shares which rose. Or that the S&P 500, which rose 21% in 1999, had twice as many down stocks as up (the same ratio applied to it in 1998, as well).

Traditionally a market in which a small number of stocks perform extremely well while the majority settle into a pattern of decline is a bad sign. It is a phenomenon that rarely lasts a long period of time, but when it has in the past, it has occurred at the end of two decades of seemingly effortless rising equity markets, and has signalled a major setback to come in market valuations. Some commentators, which emphatically include ourselves, have felt that the absolute level of the stockmarket, combined with the narrowness of breadth, presages difficult times ahead. But this has not been the way to prosper in 1999. A part of standing back has to be to consider whether this bearish attitude is a mere manifestation of middle age and whether we must get used to new valuation models in the brave new world in which we live.

Last year there was a major shift in investors' behaviour towards risk and away from safety. The phenomenon itself has occurred on a huge scale. It is always hard to capture a subjective trend in figures, but the capital flows chart below goes a long way to help.

All foreign countries – net purchases of all US securities less US Treasury Notes and Bonds (line) and net purchases of US Treasury Notes and Bonds only (bars)

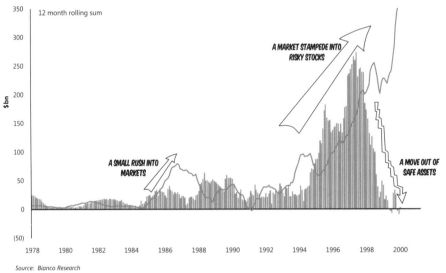

Source: Bianco Research

We cannot know what people think, but we can see what they do. The line shows how powerful these capital flows are; the bars on the chart show whether the capital flows are into 'safe' assets (the case when the bars are as high as the line) or into 'risky' assets (the case when the line is high above the bars). It gives an awesome message – two messages in fact. It shows a tidal wave of money moving into financial assets, absolutely dwarfing the 1987 buying spree, which felt exciting enough at the time. Moreover, this surge is more than wholly into risk assets. The sharp drop in the bars show that the wave of money into risk assets was exacerbated by a sell-off of safe investments.

There is, today, an overwhelming acceptance that equities give a better return than any other asset class; it is a proposition which is, however, least true when it is generally believed. We are now at a period when equities have gone up without any setback at all for 10 years. They have gone up elevenfold without a major setback over the last 20 years. The last period of sustained grief was in the 1970s. Every society depends for its coherence upon patterns of belief in practice which determine what ideas are plausible to that society and what are not. Because of its pedigree, the cult of the equity remains plausible despite its massive historic overvaluation on every conceivable yardstick.

Why has this happened?

An avalanche of money has been created by the US Federal Reserve in particular, but other Central Banks as well. In the past, money growth has led to inflation in retail prices. In present conditions, it is leading to inflation of asset values. The predisposition to equities has meant that more money has meant higher stock prices – the length of the bull market has temporarily suspended the constraint of traditional valuations. The idea that the stock markets were pushed up by the creation of money, rather than pulled up by the attractiveness of the asset class, is reinforced by the observation that momentum investing has been the best (and indeed only successful) investment strategy: what went up last month should go up further this month, to the exclusion of all else.

Our strategy remains low risk. But this is not to say there is no excitement to be had. Outside the narrow mania, it is still possible to buy growth with low risk. The arrival of Ruth Keattch as head of our Investment Research broadens our perception of growth and value in a time of dynamic change. This is a two-tier market with dull companies trading extremely cheaply, and world beating companies trading extremely expensively. In the real world, most companies fall somewhere in between, and either a comparatively small change of direction by a company, or even the perception of this, is enough to show that the lady in the boiler suit can yet be the belle.

Stockmarket overvaluation owes more to the technicalities of Federal Reserve action than to profits and dividends. In usual circumstances, stock market behaviour is not very important. In today's conditions, it is the pivot to a great deal of what is going on in the world. The level of economic growth is pretty much wholly explained by the exuberance of the American consumer: an exuberance based on the beneficent effect his stock market investments are having on his personal balance sheet. About 10 cents of every dollar spent is attributable to this wealth factor. Other distortions have played their part. The US balance of payments has gone from bad to terrible. Again, in normal circumstances such a bad and deteriorating balance of payments would lead to a dollar crisis; at the moment foreigners are happy to hold dollars, since the highest risk counters are largely to be found in that country. The NASDAQ index of 100 shares is now capitalised at $3.4 trillion (or approaching half America's GDP). Not only the economy in America, it seems, but also the currency is dependent on Wall Street's level. Of all fixtures and fittings, it is hard to imagine a less reliable one. In this deflationary world, it took a long time for the inflation in assets to infect the real economy, and make it grow at an above trend rate. It has taken even longer for this development to translate into inflation in retail prices. The irony is that it is probably just this development which will bring about the ultimate downfall of this seemingly virtuous circle.

Commentary

2000

The year 2000 brought the relief that the millennium bug was a mirage. The Chairman of National Westminster allowed himself a joke about the £50 million spent on its computer protection: 'our computers only count to one, but they do it very quickly'. The boom continued, and the Millennium Dome – a kind of reverse Eiffel Tower, in that it was intended to be permanent, but actually quickly closed down – announced that a money zone was to be incorporated. Not just the Millennium Dome: the Millennium footbridge across the Thames opened and then closed on its first day because of an alarming swaying motion.

In March the tide of the equity boom turned. To begin with, it was felt that the speculation was only in minnows, and the blue chip growth companies involved in technology, such as GEC (by now, Marconi) were still riding high. Yet the leaves were brown on the trees. In June the FTSE 100 players were re-organised and Psion, Baltimore, Thus and Kingston, TMT darlings each of them, left the index. Getting rich may have become more difficult in the markets, but the desire was still there: India launched its wannabe game show, *Who Wants to be a Crorepati* (a person worth 10 million rupees or about £148,000). As far as could be seen, the world was cloudless, but as is often the case when the weather is good, insignificant events turned out to be larger than they seemed at the time. A global-warming cartoon appeared in the *Spectator* in August, the same month as America bombed Iraq. Sadam Hussain's son Uday won his seat in the Iraqi elections with a 99.99% majority. On the last day of 1999 President Yeltsin of Russia resigned to be replaced by a small chap with funny eyes: Vladimir Putin. Tony Blair, recently heckled by the Women's Institute, went and visited him, and was quickly on 'Tony and Volodya' terms. There was an international get together at the Hague to discuss climate change, but the main message that came out of it was John Prescott's un-gentlemanly way with the French delegate Madame Dominique Voynet, and the English language: 'She got cold feet, felt she could not explain it, said she was exhausted and tired, and could not understand the detail and then refused to accept it.'

The year drew to its close with George Bush winning a controversial election in the United States, with the results dependant on the votes in Florida, which were too close to call. The world learnt to thrill to the dimpled chad, noted the relationship between the President nearly elect, and Jeb Bush the Governor of Florida. In December came the news that the official rescue by the French Government of Credit Lyonnais had cost more than £10 billion, a world record for a bank bailout. It remained a formidable figure for a number of years.

A Stock Exchange Bubble

April 2000

One day last week, the Dow Jones Index rose 2% at the opening bell, dropped 7% by lunchtime and then rose by a similar amount in the afternoon. Its sister index, the NASDAQ, was twice as volatile, dropping by 14% before recovering. Two hours trading took away, and then gave back, more than two years return of money on deposit. It is, perhaps, time to consider the nature of investment. What should an investor expect from his investment? What should a fund manager promise? From time immemorial, managers of money have tried to make money for their clients. In the last decade, there has been a fundamental change in the industry approach; the overwhelming majority of money is now invested by managers whose stated aim is to outperform their relevant indices. For much of the time, the behaviour of professionals trying to make money and those trying to outperform the indices is achieved by a similar investment strategy. This is not, however, always the case and we argue that now is just such a time.

How should one invest? Because no one can predict the future, it is an inherently risky exercise, and anything one buys could turn sour. Future developments may be uncertain, however, but the price one pays for an investment is fixed at the moment of purchase. At the risk of irreverence, one can compare stock market investment with a game of roulette. On a roulette table there is a 50% chance (nearly) of red coming up rather than black, and a successful 'investor' will receive £2 for every £1 risked. If the croupier mistakenly offered to pay out £5 for every £1 risk, an investment on red would represent a terrific opportunity, although the chances of one losing one's money would remain as high as ever – at just over 50%. Likewise, if the croupier was looking the other way, and you managed to have two attempts on the spinning wheel to see if red came up, your chances of winning would be higher, although the payout on the actual win at 2:1 would remain the same. The market can be likened to such a game of chance, where the wheel is malfunctioning, and the croupier is drunk. Some investments are safer than they seem, and others give better odds than they should. The fund manager's job is to beat the odds, and the successful ones will make money, and, as a by-product, outperform the indices.

But suppose an external factor comes in: the players themselves can place their bets in such a way that the outcome is self-fulfilling – hence we have to leave the analogy of the roulette table for the simple world of supply and demand. If demand for one type of investment becomes overwhelming, then its price rises regardless of the fundamentals. Ultimately, the fundamentals always win, but the future being forever inscrutable, it is always impossible at the time to know whether a decisive shift in valuation is based on fundamentals or fantasy.

At this point, the two investment styles will differ enormously. The investor who wants to make money will be as nervous as a cat in Battersea: if the boom is based on fantasy, there is a lot of money to lose, but if based in reality, then he misses out on a big opportunity. The 'index' investor has no such concern, for if it is fantasy, the fall in the index is of no concern to him provided he outperforms. While markets rise, the distinction is blurred; it is a distinction which is likely to become apparent in retrospect.

In today's language, is the information technology (IT) revolution, and are the dot com valuations soundly based or not? Over the last six months there has been a struggle between two polarised views, centring around IT, and it is the resolution of these views which is presently causing the volatility in stock markets. We touched on the internet revolution in our last investment review, and we return to it now.

Our analyst, Henry Maxey, went to the Berlin IT Conference last month. His conclusion is arresting. The investment significance of this revolution is to be found much more in the outlook for its victims than its champions. 'It is', he writes, 'a powerful tool to help companies to cut their costs, but an even better tool for customers to force those companies to do precisely that.' He concludes, 'It is a bleak landscape. However, while growth in a deflationary world is difficult this does not mean that anything outside of TMT (technology, media and telecommunications) should be consigned to the scrapheap. The key is to distinguish between companies where excess capacity for the internet holds little or no threat.' In short, an investment world which has driven the value of internets upwards and old economy stocks downwards is, in principle, a sound response. The broad indices peaked two years ago, in 1998, and, numerically, most stocks have fallen – a fall which has gathered pace since Christmas time, which has only partially been reversed in the recent rally in 'old economy' stocks.

Turning first to the 'status quo' stocks, the internet is just one more, albeit very powerful, force for the reduction of price to consumers. Across the world, any company which has been in the position of being a 'middle man' has suffered. This has obvious effects on retailers and manufacturers in the middle of the supply chain. For instance, the big three American car producers have indicated that they might standardise their components, and then, rather than give contracts to a range of manufacturers, instead invite bids for the work on the internet. It does not require the imminent collapse of Rover to see that a whole swathe of Midland industry is under a profits threat from this. The consequences extend to the far from obvious. Thus the shares in Avis, the car rental company, have suffered. Why should this happen? The answer is that as consumers have seen that the cost of car purchase could well fall significantly in the near to middle future, it has had an immediate on second hand car prices. Avis have a bathtub full of second hand cars, which are now less valuable than they were a year ago. Coupled with this ill wind from economic pressures, governments too are beginning to flex their muscles in the commercial arena, really for the first time since Mrs Thatcher came to power. Thus banks are told not to close branches, drug companies are told that the NHS cannot afford their products, utilities find that the ground rules have changed, independent of the regulator. As one looks, company by company, at future profitability one sees that there are a host of pressures which are either new or magnified in their force. No wonder there has been a bear market in this constituency.

Turning to the new economy, Marc Faber put it rather well, 'I believe that despite a difficult economic environment characterised by a secular fall in profits, 90% of the 'old economy' companies will manage to survive. At the same time, based on the history of previous 'new economic sectors' (which, after all, may be a useful guide), it is almost certain that 90% of the now perceived 'new economy' will go out of business.' It is something of a Grand National; the winners will do extremely well, but the ferocious speed of technological change, and the fact that commercial success depends on lowering prices to the consumer means that a very high discount rate for the inherent uncertainty should prevail, whereas the opposite is pointedly true.

Our conclusion is as follows. As a whole, the markets are extraordinarily high, and the outlook does not justify the levels at which they are trading. This is of paramount importance as one considers the new or the old economy within this observation. In fact, most of the overvaluation is in the new economy. This does not mean that they are totally to be avoided, but, taken as a whole, the risks outweigh the rewards by a considerable margin. It is like shopping for antiques in Bond Street – you may find a bargain, but the mark-ups argue against it. On the other hand, a scattergun approach to the bran tub marked 'cheap and cheerful' might yet lead to indigestion. We have become considerably more interested in this sector with the shake up of the stodgy blue chips; six months ago they were cheap on a comparative basis to the market, but still not obviously so in absolute terms. They are now extremely lowly rated, which, of course, makes the risk/reward much more compelling. Buy the wrong one, and you find that the bad news was already in the price – find one which had fallen in sympathy, but with no fundamental problems, and there is a real opportunity for capital growth. Moreover, industry pressures create a need for industry consolidation, and the premia at which sound companies are privatised or taken over would make even a dot.com addict envious. (Well, nearly.)

We continue to believe that we are in an stock exchange bubble, and that it is unwise to make bold dispositions until there is a clear resolution of this. Our roadmap continues to be: watch out on 'new economy', do not be afraid of 'old economy' where valuations have become one's friend, always remembering that in a deflationary age, the fixed interest markets with their relentless payment of interest, will once again shine when the transient problems of inflation, stoked up by the Federal Reserve and the Central Banks, have passed.

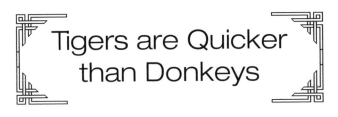

Tigers are Quicker than Donkeys

July 2000

This was the quarter when old fashioned investors found that the organ stops on the stock market Wurlitzer started working again. The companies whose names one didn't quite recognise have left the FTSE 100 Index, to be replaced by the likes of Scottish & Newcastle and Hanson. Solid old-fashioned businesses were found to have some virtue after all, and the pearls of the new economy may indeed be pearls, but not beyond price. This false world of black and white investment has past, and it is now possible once again to think in terms of overall market levels. Indeed, for all the excitement of the last year, the level of the market is exactly where it was a year ago, having dropped by some 10% from the beginning of 2000. The sense of impending doom has lessened, but a world where interest rates have risen, and could easily rise further, has left the bulls feeling equally uncertain that much progress can be made in an already expensive market.

Although 'value' has performed well against 'growth' for a few months, a sense of unreality still billows around the cathedral doors of the equity markets. The cult of the equity is still sacred. Twenty years of superior – and consistent – growth have seen to that. Telecom and bio-tech conferences still bring out the fund managers anxious to pick the next winner. Above all, equity investment is still about making money, and the lesser achievement of its preservation is universally taken for granted. The result is that most investors are treating the equity market as a fast ticket to wealth: why ride donkeys at Skegness, when sitting on the tiger gets you to the end of the beach so much quicker?

Nevertheless there is a sea change of perception to investment following the deflation of the dot.com bubble. The insurance companies have provided a most interesting straw in the wind. At the same time that stock markets have continued relentlessly providing superior returns, one by one they have been writing to policyholders alerting them to the dangers that their policies may not prove to be as valuable as predicted. These letters base their pessimism on a matrix of future returns: 4% (low case), 6% (flat) and 8% (high case), and justify these low forecasts on the fact that we now live in a low inflation environment. If 6%, or worse still, 4% was the likely return, what are the self-same insurance companies doing anywhere near the equity market? They should be in cash, which would provide their middle projection with no risk to capital values. It might seem that the investment strategists of these insurance houses are not talking to those who drafted the letters and, indeed, this assumption would be right. All the letters (amazingly similar) are the product of compliance departments, who were humiliated by the last mis-selling scandal of the 1980s. They see only too clearly the gulf between perception and the arithmetic of likely stock market returns in the future. And the arithmetic makes interesting reading. The growth in corporate profitability is limited by GDP growth and the share of GDP which makes up corporate profits. At the moment, profit margins are high, competition from new technology is fierce, and so the profits share of GDP might easily fall. It is hard to construct an argument for profit growth of more than 5% over the medium term. Investors will, of course, get a dividend of perhaps 2% on their investment, which, added to the capital growth in the shares resulting from the profit increase, gives a return not unadjacent to that on cash. Unless stock markets are re-rated yet higher, the game is over.

A bearish view of the stock market does not mean there are no opportunities for making money. Emphatically the reverse! There are some exceptional opportunities among shares with high yields which are beginning to benefit from the fall in Sterling from its high levels. Commodity shares do not reflect the likely possibility that the rise in raw material prices will stick, even if the economy slows down. Most excitingly, this has become a stockpicker's market, and the more true this is, the better we estimate our chances of doing well.

The real conundrum remains the fixed interest market. Our view remains that, when the next economic downturn comes, it will be accompanied by severe deflationary conditions. In this environment, long dated government bonds could be a truly wonderful investment, providing a regular and certain income at a time when cashflow will be increasingly difficult to rely on. However, between now and then, there is a distinct possibility that there will be some frighteningly awful inflation figures out of America. Interest rates will rise there, and the dollar will fall, adding to the bad news on the inflation front. Our view is that the economic slowdown that would be precipitated by this development will make this period of inflation short lived – those with longish memories will recall the period of 1920/21 in the UK – in this regard. But the fixed interest market could well not take the same view, and yields could go up sharply in such an environment. Thus the dilemma: do we lock in what we believe to be the right assets for the future and risk being hurt in the short term, or do we hold off for a fall – a fall which perhaps never happens, and we find that we were indeed on the right railway platform, and we watched the train draw away without ever getting aboard? This dilemma was first highlighted in 1999; the economic boom in the US has raised the stakes as to the answer, but the passing of time has given us no clearer answer as to the likely outcome. The question remains: is the next move a spontaneous slowdown towards deflation, or must we first suffer an inflationary crisis before the slowdown comes about? Our own conclusion is to hold a fair bit of fixed interest, but with firepower in reserve in case there is a buying opportunity later in the year.

It's Nearly Over When The Fat Lady Sings

October 2000

The mood among economic commentators is one of petulance. Optimists and pessimists alike attribute to the other the foolishness of perversity. As they assault one another with slogans, the investor has to draw his own conclusions as to where lies the safety, and where the opportunity.

The American economy continues to grow at a blistering pace, having risen uninterruptedly for 10 years. Traditionally, economic booms end in production shortages, wage pressures, inflation and high interest rates, but it has not happened this time. Wages have stayed down and it has not been the wage earner who has benefited from the boom, but the stock market investor – and the house owner. There is, of course, a big overlap between the two categories. With lowish interest rates in America and few amber lights ahead, Paul Krugman, a respected commentator, has 'seldom felt more positive about the global economy'. The pessimists take their cue from Eliza Doolittle – 'Just you wait, 'Enry 'Iggins', without being very sure as to what it is we are to wait for – perhaps that the oil price increase will be very bad news for the economy.

Indeed it might. But the worries are more closely at hand than oil. The world's economy reminds us of nothing so much as an elderly prima donna who is having difficulty reaching her high notes, and who achieves them by forcing them out at full volume. The sound is, of course, magnificent, but the volume is also a sign of weakness – it's the only way that it can be achieved. And so with the economy. Consumer demand is very strong (the high notes), but it is coming increasingly from borrowed money, and not from savings. This is not healthy: the level of the stock market becomes a crucial factor for continuing demand. The stock market is both the source and the destination of the mania. Looking backwards, it has created the wealth which has given such confidence: looking to the future, it is attracting both domestic and foreign money through its doors in the hope of future reward.

If it is possible for lust to form a virtuous circle, it has done so in the US stock market. America is the central player in this, and the rest of the world must convert its money into this casino currency if it is to play the American game. Thus the virtue includes a rising dollar, which has ramifications back in the real world. The strength of the dollar is crucial to America's favourable economic statistics. It keeps commodity prices low, and it stops domestic demand from overheating, as cheap imports pour into the United States. All this (seemingly) validates the idea of American capitalism winning the gold medal for lifestyle values. The fat lady hits the high notes, the chandeliers rattle and everybody is impressed.

But suppose for a moment that the stock market stops going up; indeed, it hasn't gone up for over a year. Suppose – wild thought – it went down, and stayed down. The answer is that all the currently favourable factors would become unfavourable factors. We will consider them in turn.

A weak stock market is very likely to shut off consumer demand very rapidly. Traditionally, the Americans and the British have saved rather more than 10% of their annual incomes. When people become afraid, this figure goes up: Japan has been in economic distress for 10 years or more, and the savings ratio there is more than 30%. In America the ratio is minus 1% and the UK is at its lowest level for decades at 3%. If Wall Street fell, whether for good reasons or bad, it could easily lead to a very sharp contraction of consumer demand. Manufacturers and service providers could not possibly avoid a very sharp profit downturn if this happened. This would, of course, weaken the stock market further. Once asset values deflate, the attraction of holding one's assets in the casino currency becomes less compelling. Hot money will leave the US and return to its various homelands. The hot money has masked America's requirement for some $400 billion of money each year – going up by about $60 billion annually – from its trade deficit. When a country is seen to need foreign capital, there is an inevitable loss of confidence in its currency. The trade deficit, in the past two years a stabilising influence in the virtuous circle, suddenly becomes the mad cousin from Milwaukee.

A few commentators have latched on to this, and generally take the line that there is nothing to fear except fear itself: provided that we all keep our nerves there is no need for the cycle to turn vicious. While one can sympathise with this pious hope, the reality is that the virtue lasts only as long as markets continue to be attractive. This is as realistic as marrying a Rottweiler and hoping for a serene and happy life. Stock markets are unpredictable beasts, and it might be that they continue in a good mood for a few more weeks or a few more months, but when the music stops, the lady's top C may sound more like a seizure.

A Stream of Income

January 2001

Scholarship candidates for Imperial China's civil service had to respond to a single command: 'Tell all you know.' The difficulty, of course, is in marshalling an assorted jumble of material into a structure which passes information across to the reader. An understanding of the investment outlook is every bit as inscrutable as the Chinese students' agenda: the enigma is how to distil that jumble into something simple enough to comprehend and act by: Here goes ....

The entry point to understanding the Western world's economies is the amount of money that has been created over the last 5 or 6 years. Since 1995, money supply has been growing 5 times faster than inflation. Although 'money supply' sounds a technicality, it is simple: when a man borrows £100,000 from a bank, the bank literally creates that £100,000. The banker does not reach for a stock of money in the way that a car dealer might supply a new vehicle from the forecourt. This money never existed before the bank had granted the loan.

This creative act comes at a cost: the bank does not give the money, it lends it. Another way of saying that money supply has grown very quickly is to say that debt has grown very quickly. In America, for example, private sector debt has grown from 50% of the US economy in the 1950s to 200% now. In 1950 the total outstanding amount of private debt was the equivalent of six months of total American production: it's today 24 months.

Much money, much borrowing: what has it been spent on? The answer is not at all as one might expect. Normally a borrowing spree finds its way into the economy – whether you hire a cook, buy a car or improve your house, it will all show up in the economy. The rule of thumb is that for every dollar borrowed, 70% of it gets into the economy. But the relevant percentage for 1999 was only 27%, and the provisional figures for 2000 suggest that for every $1,000 borrowed, less than $200 was spent. Why would people borrow money if they didn't mean to spend it? The answer is that people have been borrowing to invest, and it is striking that the growth of money supply took off exactly at the time when the stock markets re-rating began. The chart below shows the extent of this re-rating. It shows the value of the stock market as a percentage of the whole US economy. It therefore makes irrelevant whether or not the economy has grown quickly or slowly, thus highlighting the uncomfortable fact that the rise in Wall Street has been a phenomenon of increasingly expensive valuation, not a reflection of a booming economy.

Stock market capitalization as a percentage of nominal GDP

Source: Bianco Research

It takes only one variable – that of confidence – to turn a virtuous circle into a vicious one. Over the last five years economic confidence has been based on asset prices being high, which has been brought about with borrowed money, which itself requires confidence on the part of borrowers and lenders alike. The breaking of confidence is like breaking wind – it sours the atmosphere remarkably quickly. And this appears to be what is happening at present. Two months ago there was talk of a slowdown in the American economy, and the big issue was whether or not there would be a hard landing or a soft landing. Then there was an optimistic consensus that the slowdown would be gradual. The tone today is decidedly more pessimistic. The Fed's abrupt lowering of interest rates on 3 January 2001 has persuaded even the optimists that we are in the midst of a sharp, not to say precipitous, slowdown. There is talk that Greenspan's actions will revive confidence, and the investment community seems very relaxed that by the Autumn of this year, lower interest rates will mean that there could be a synchronised worldwide economic recovery.

We think it unlikely, and this does not bode well for the equity markets which, in the round, are a play on world prosperity. Current valuations have more to say about the increasing level of confidence built up by decades of relentless growth. We believe that the days of making broad swathes of capital appreciation from growth equities are over for the foreseeable future. Now is the time to benefit from its successor sport: compounding the cashflow. If our timing is right, this is not a time for long faces. The credit based asset bubble that the Western economies – but notably the Americas – have seen in the last five years occur regularly, but rarely, throughout economic history. The last one occurred in Japan in the decade to 1990. It is worth recalling the events. The Japanese stock market went up sixfold in 10 years. It is instructive to see what happened subsequently, because the unfolding facts took exactly the form that the imbalances created by the bubble might have suggested they would.

The first thing that happened was that the market dropped precipitously, with the Nikkei falling from 38,000 to 22,000 in 6 months. There have been some very unpleasant stock price falls in the world technology sector in the latter half of 2000, so perhaps we have had all the pain of this first phase, perhaps not. The interesting part of the Japanese roadmap is what happened thereafter. Between 1990 and 2000, the Nikkei dropped from 22,000 to 13,800. There have been some very tradeable rallies during this 10 year period, and there were plenty of opportunities to make big sums of money in individual stocks, but the key was to change one's mindset in 1990 from trying to make capital appreciation, to locking in a steady stream of income from one's capital. By 1995, it was too late for the Japanese to make this mental switch: cash on deposit yielded 0.3%, bonds yielded 3% (they went on to yield as little as 0.7%!) and equities yielded only a headache. In 1990 it was still possible to buy bonds with a yield of more than 5%, and fixed assets whose financial characteristics meant that the longer they were held, the more value was accreted to the owners through the relentless accumulation of its cashflow. Those who eschewed capital growth for such an income stream in 1990 found that, almost as a by-product, they not only received their income, but they received, too, significant capital growth as well because the assets were re-rated to reflect the growing value of their income stream.

For many months, we have been waiting to make this call. Act too soon, and the result is missed opportunity in the capital appreciation game and worse: the very safety of the cashflow counters looked suspect in an exuberantly dynamic world. Act too late and, like the Japanese in 1995, the window of opportunity closes. Our judgment: now is the moment, and I'm jolly excited!

Commentary

2 0 0 1

The new year got off to a mysterious start – who gave £2 million to the Labour Party? When it turned out to be a British citizen, and part of the establishment (Lord Hamlyn), interest quickly fell away – but it was a straw in the wind that the relationship between business and politics was a matter of increasing public interest.

Particularly so, as a general election was not far away. A ruling party, riding high in the polls, is always inclined to go to the country four years after its last mandate – and that suggested a summer polling date. Gordon Brown produced a 10p tax-rate lollipop for the poor as a sweetener – it would be a number of years before it would come back to choke him. Tony Blair fired the starting gun, somewhat bizarrely in a girl's school. The result was both predictable and, for the Government, satisfactory. The Conservatives won, on balance, a solitary seat.

The victory was an acknowledgement that the country was in pretty good shape, but the low turnout, perhaps, was a sense that all was not well. In the countryside, this was testified to by the pyre of smoke which accompanied the slaughter of cattle to control the worst outbreak of foot and mouth for a third of a century. It first appeared in an abattoir in Brentwood, Essex in February – the authorities missed a vital opportunity to stop the movement of livestock in the early days. By election day, 3.2 million head of livestock had been destroyed.

It was not the beasts alone who were the victims. The effect among rural farming communities, falling on a community already under pressure, was scarcely bearable. But, as with the destruction of coal mining communities a decade earlier, the trauma fell in a narrow and concentrated way on those outside the mainstream of Cool Britannia.

For the rest social mobility meant winners – and losers. Lord Archer started his prison sentence in July; Conrad Black was ennobled. It was a bad year for Peter Mandelson (a second resignation owing to a little overseas difficulty), the Millennium Dome (all its assets sold at auction ready for the knackers' yard), and the Royal Mail (which suffered the indignity of a dog-Latin rebranding: its name changed to Consignia). All three made a subsequent comeback.

In September came the generational event which passes the 'what was I doing when it happened?' test. The British came back from lunch in the early afternoon of 11 September to hear of the atrocity of the attack on the World Trade Centre. Those who responded quickly were in time to see the shocking sight of the second plane flying into the South Tower – as it happened. As news came in of further attacks – the Pentagon, possibly the White House, it became apparent that a world event might be just that: global. Lloyd's of London was evacuated from its trophy building. The markets plunged, and everybody waited, waited to see what had changed. A hundred years earlier, the century had ended not with the arithmetic of 1 January 1900, but with the death of Queen Victoria almost exactly a year later. So it was to be with the coming of the 21st century. Today's generation had to wait a further few months for the true start of the new century.

Humpty Dumpty Portfolios

April 2001

A year ago, stock market barometers started to send a warning of bad weather to come; now the first hailstorms are upon us. The barometer continues to signal a further deterioration, and investors are faced with a dilemma; is the stock market double counting: falling last year for fear of the squalls, and falling again this year because they have duly arrived?

The facts themselves are opaque. Authoritative evidence of a recession is always too late to be of any use – by the time you know it's a brick wall, the ambulances are racing back to the infirmary. But the early evidence is sobering. In February the World Leading Indicator (OECD) went into recessionary territory for the first time since 1990. Many businesses in the US are showing turnover declines of 10% or more since Christmas: across a wide range of businesses there is significant slowdown, and surveys in technology-related sectors are showing some precipitous falls in both volumes and confidence. But the figures do not point universally towards a slowdown. Interest rates are falling everywhere, and money growth – the oxygen of economic activity – continues to grow at a cracking pace. Consumer spending is holding up remarkably well, encouraged by the prospect of tax cuts.

These powerful cross-currents are the result of irresistible market forces meeting an unmoveable central bank in the United States. Most of us grew up in an inflationary world, where prices tended to go up. Sellers had the upper hand, and any increase in demand fed through to higher prices. But the last few years have seen the balance of power shift from sellers to buyers, who shop around, and won't tolerate higher prices. The economic consequences of this change are remarkable. In times of prosperity you get the best of both worlds: no inflationary bottlenecks because of the surplus of supply, and plenty of demand to meet that supply. But the darker side comes when the good times give way to bad, at which point you get the worst of both worlds. Supply continues to grow, but buyers go on strike. In these circumstances, deflation can take hold remarkably quickly, and lead to a deep and lasting recession *à la Japonnaise*. The central authorities have sought, if not to remove absolutely, at least to delay an inevitable downturn. Low interest rates and easy money have ensured that the prosperity has lasted far longer than in a usual economic cycle. This elongation of the business cycle has come at a grave cost. A by-product of central bank action is that a great deal of borrowed money has found its way into assets, driving both the stock markets and property values into unprecedentedly high territory. This asset price inflation seems a good thing on the way up, but is a manifestly bad thing on the way down. When a heavily borrowed consumer finds that he is suffering big capital losses, the desire to save and to repay debts reinforces the slowdown in consumer demand; profits decline, putting further pressure on asset values, thereby delaying the recovery in a malign circle of events.

This bad weather therefore should be taken very seriously, and could easily build itself up into a hurricane. The central authorities are doing all they can to stop it. The chances of them overcoming the problem are, frankly, small, but there is always the possibility – perhaps even a probability – that they will be able to delay this end game. The weapons at the Federal Reserve's command remain the lowering of short term interest rates, and a policy which allows for money supply to grow quickly. It can influence consumer demand only indirectly (the stock market is probably the key here, hence the debate as to whether the Fed is targeting Wall Street), and wages not at all. The extended economic boom has at last – late in the day – caused upward pressure on wages in America. They are rising at 6% – 6.5% per annum, and commodities, too, are showing signs of life. All this means is that buoyant economic activity is more likely to manifest itself in the form of rising prices than rising profitability. This makes the equity market a dangerous place to be on either eventuality. It does, however, keep us from wholeheartedly embracing the fixed interest market, which is the natural asset class to own in this macro-environment. It also means that there is sense in owning commodity shares – oil, metals and softs – which would be the beneficiary of an inflationary scare at which point both the equity indices and the fixed interest markets could be expected to weaken.

The following principles seem to us to be appropriate at the present time:

1 In a world of uncertainty, cheaply rated stocks are a better bet than expensive ones. Why pay a premium price for the favourite when the riderless horse can unseat everyone?

2 The worrisome levels of debt, both corporate and personal, have a threefold message. Heavily indebted companies are most at risk, but general liquidity concerns can impact asset values more powerfully than economic activity itself. Financial companies (still trading near their high points) are early victims from a proliferation of bad debts.

3 Income is more certain than capital gain in a naughty world, and will be correspondingly prized. This argues for a portfolio with a highish yield. (Zero coupon stocks are attractive, the dividend being rolled up within the capital value.)

In these circumstances, it is hard to know what strategy is appropriate. The last year has shown that Humpty Dumpty portfolios built on naïve optimism are liable to fall apart when gravity takes over. They will not be easily mended. We are entering a period when the increasingly difficult economic conditions will change the whole pattern of economic life, and in a way not seen for several decades. It will not be enough to be cautious, although that makes an excellent starting place: it will be necessary also to sense the nature of the dangers ahead and we believe that we are in a strong position to do so.

Taking the Plunge

J u l y   2 0 0 1

In our spring report, we described the battle raging between market forces, which have been slowing down the economy, and the response of the central authorities (interest rate cuts and high money growth) which are designed to counteract this deterioration. As with all battles, the advantage can move in an instant from one side to the other; the last three months have shown neither the victory. The pendulum has perhaps swung somewhat in favour of pessimism, with Japan doing what it does best – matching England's cricket team in disappointing its wellwishers. Germany's economy is in trouble, and France, until recently the brightest spot of the Continental majors, is running out of steam. But these are sideshows: it is America which matters, and it is simply too early to say that the good times there are over. The one-off effect of corporate destocking, whilst startling in its intensity is largely over, and retail demand is holding up well in its aftermath. In the short term, the question is whether the knock-on effects of the slowdown will lead to redundancies, further loss of confidence and recession, or whether the bad news has been absorbed, and the Federal Reserve's lower interest rates and the Bush tax cuts – $40 billion of them – will carry the day.

From this analysis, one might conclude that the stock markets are over-valued if the slowdown continues, whereas investors should be increasing their stock market exposure if consumer confidence remains high. The reason that we remain on the side of the pessimists is because we believe that, even if the consumer remains confident, the outlook for corporate profits and the stock market generally is far from attractive. In either eventuality, the world that we see in America (for the American outlook is the absolute key to understanding the outlook for the rest of the world) is one of increasing fragility. The sharp increase in the amount of money in circulation has allowed the consumer to continue writing the checks, but at the price of an increasingly problematic legacy behind it. At the moment broad money is growing at the rate of 15.4% per annum; an increase in money supply is precisely the same as an increase in borrowing, since each new dollar has been lent to a borrower, and at such a growth rate, every seventh dollar circulating in America has been created in the last 12 months. One only has to look at the American housing sector to see the nature of the risk. The fuel of lower interest rates has caused property prices to go up, and the availability of easy money has allowed house owners to borrow more. Seen from a short term perspective, the house owner pays a similar monthly mortgage (thanks to lower interest rates) while the increased mortgage has not reduced the proportion of equity he has in his property (thanks to its rise in value).

Either way, we see problems ahead for the stock market. A further slow-down is self-evidently bad news, while the lifeline of lower interest rates can so easily result in misallocation, further destroying the fundamental outlook for corporate profitability over the medium term. Indeed, it is unlikely that short term profitability would be much helped by a last hur-rah of the consumer, so the purchase of equities on the basis that there is a greater fool out there to whom one can sell them, might mean that the fool is the one in the mirror. There is an old saying at the blackjack table: 'If you haven't worked out who the patsy is after five minutes, it's you.'

Nevertheless, to those who know the sensibilities of the investment industry, it will come as little surprise that fund managers remain steadfast-ly confident. Despite the increasing uncertainties, the percentage of stock market bulls is unprecedentedly high. Fund managers are more fearful of failing to make money in a bull phase than losing money along with every-body else. The reason for this is partly the overwhelming prevalence of fund managers whose role is to outperform the indices, rather than to make money in absolute terms. Buying the dips, however dangerous it has appeared to be, has always paid off. The last 20 years has seen the bears routinely discomfited. They missed the start of the big bull market in 1982 for fear of Mexico's default; they thought that 1987 was the grand climax before a depression set in; in 1997 they thought that America's economy was overheating, but the Asian crisis proved to be the cool breeze which assuaged the problem. The 1998 crisis appeared to vindicate those who thought the world would be overwhelmed with systemic financial risk, but instead asset values ballooned to new highs. Although the last 18 months have not been easy for the bulls, the white-bearded loons predicting the end of the financial world seem as fantastical as ever.

The irony is that the outlook for the fixed interest market is increasing in attractiveness as the sun sets on the cult of the growth equity. Almost all commentators are agreed that growth has slowed down from the fast rate of the 1990s, and a low growth environment makes the comparative attraction of a 5% – 6% return in a fixed interest stock considerably more attractive than an equity yielding less than half that. The wildcard of a financial crisis would make bonds – at least of government quality – extremely attractive, and a rumbling indigestion of low growth and earnings disappointment is a good breeding ground for capital gain in the bond market. The dangers of a short period of inflation cannot be completely discounted, but the appropriate way to manage the inherent risk of this is by careful juxtaposition of those assets which would rise in value on such an eventuality. Although we are nervous of committing more money to fixed interest stock, we have taken the plunge in the closing weeks of the last quarter.

The Five Horsemen
of the Apocalypse

2 0 0 1

Has the world as we know it changed forever? It is unsettling to try to translate human tragedy into investment opportunity, just as it is invidious to assess what military outcome should form the basis for our economic future.

In every aspect, the world has become more uncertain – militarily, socially and politically. Ironically, if there is one constituency in which the future is reasonably clear, it is economic. While it is true that the outlook has deteriorated sharply, it has done no more than accelerate what was coming upon us, anyway. The economy was already falling down the stairs: the terrorist attacks produced an unwelcome push from behind.

In previous reviews we have painted a picture of expansionary central bank initiatives being pitted against deflationary market forces. These two warring pressures have given ambivalent signals, and will continue to do so as the battle rages. The battle has, however, escalated following the atrocity: market forces are more deflationary, governments are responding with more 'inflation' being pumped into the system in the form of lower interest rates, emergency money supply and the likelihood of increased government spending.

We remain, unhappily, confident that market forces will prevail over the government initiatives. Here's why. The role of government is not unlike a farmer in a field of bullocks. There is more bullock than farmer, but farmers have more brains than bullocks do. The latter can usually cajole, confuse and direct the bullocks in the desired direction. The farmer here, is the Federal Reserve who is fearful of a systemic lack of confidence, and has responded with almost unlimited liquidity to markets, a cut in interest rates, a Federal spending package and tax cuts. This array of roars and armwaves would in normal times be sufficient to impress the livestock, but occasionally, bullocks get a warble fly in the brain and run amok; a collective failure of confidence causes the equivalent chaos in financial markets and can override the usual responses to central authorities' blandishments. Liquidity and low interest rates are no good in themselves – they require the money to be borrowed – and borrowed by sound companies anxious to expand. Today's would-be borrowers are the airlines and the telecom industries: there's no recovery to be had from throwing good money at bad situations. Low interest rates certainly help weak companies, who need less cashflow to service their debts, but it also encourages a lack of robustness in addressing bad loans – pretty much the reason that Japan's bad debts have rumbled on unresolved for a decade or more. Tax cuts only work if they are spent, not if they are simply saved. The final arrow in the financial farmer's quiver is government expenditure. Again, Japan is an interesting precedent – there the government has spent the last 10 years spending, thereby destroying its finances, but with no obvious benefit to economic growth. The moral is clear: bet with the bullocks, not with the bulls.

We have remained confident of the fixed interest markets, because the certainty of a given income flow is increasingly valuable in deflationary times. Nevertheless, the first reaction to the events of 11 September, deflationary as they are, was for long dated bonds to lose value, albeit slightly. It is instructive to consider why this happened. The markets are afraid that the escalation by the American government of monetary liquidity and government expenditure could destroy the fabric of sound money. Seen through the eyes of the American authorities, anything is better than the certainty of its debt-laden citizens drowning under the weight of their borrowings in a 1930s spiral of an ever-slowing economy. Left to its devices, this is a distinct possibility; why not risk perhaps reckless inflationary actions in an attempt to neutralise these forces? It may buy time; it might, *mirabile dictu*, solve the deflation. The drowning man is happy to take the lifesaver down with him if the alternative is certain destruction.

It is hard to say that Mr Greenspan will not take such actions, but to take the Japanese experience, such policies have merely kept the corporate world on life support, thereby not allowing bankruptcies to reassert some price stability, nor creating enough confidence for the consumer to take up the running. We also believe that, even if an inflationary problem is squeezed into the system, it is an American problem, and that it would be the value of the dollar which would suffer, rather than the world's financial system generally. We see no such recklessness elsewhere.

It seems utterly extraordinary that one should be writing an Investment Review chronicling the total destruction of the twin totems of capitalism, and seriously considering whether the central authorities are responding with policy errors so egregious that the very bastions of sound economics are threatened. But that's the way it is: certainly, this is a time to be thinking thoughts which embrace the world in its entirety, rather than wondering whether Marconi is worth buying as a punt.

Making a Boob of it

January 2002

There was a time when evening dresses were an exercise in virtual engineering. They stayed up most of the time, but nobody could work out why. For the deb's delight the art was to assess which ball-gowns were improperly designed – sooner or later the impropriety would be revealed to all.

Much of the world's economy today seems to operate on a similar principle. Its precarious nature is there for all to see; the difficulty is essentially one of timing. Throughout 2001 the Argentinian economy looked completely unsustainable. In December, it duly collapsed; what had looked to be true proved, in the event, to be the reality. Problems in Japan look equally intractable – but is the chemistry of events there subtly but crucially different, and the parallel a false one? Time will tell, but while we wait, it is worth remembering that inexorable events do inexorably happen – but events move more slowly than the inexorability would suggest.

We have just completed a second year of double digit declines in world stock markets, as the expected world growth disappeared, and we now know that America has been in recession since the first quarter of 2001. Profits have declined by 19% this year after a poor 2000: stock markets, which entered the millennium at mountain top prices were unable to withstand this breeze. In fact, profits have fallen faster than prices, so that on today's earnings, markets are more expensive than they were at market peaks two years ago.

In the light of the facts and stock market valuations, it is extraordinary to find that there is a strong bullishness among the investing classes. It is perhaps no surprise to find that the investment house strategists are going, on average, for an increase of between 10% and 15% for the stock market in 2002. This is a similar prediction to the ones they made in 1998, 1999 and 2000 (when they were wrong) and also in 1997 (when they were right).

It should be obvious to all that this is the optimism of the used car sales-man, for whom it is never quicker by rail. Nevertheless, the disconcerting feature of the bullish case is the somewhat tabloid feel of the arguments themselves. 'We are already two years into a bear market, longer than they usually last.' Maybe, but will it be so this time? Japan's bear market is just entering its twelfth year. 'The stock market rally since late September has all the hallmarks of a leading indicator of economic recovery. It is always darkest before the dawn.' The bold illogicality of this is a reminder of General Joffre in World War I: 'My left flank is collapsing, my right is in retreat: I advance.' In the words of another French general two generations earlier, '*C'est magnifique, mais ce n'est pas la guerre.*' The one ace which the optimists claim is the actions of a powerful and radical central banker in America who is willing and able to manipulate markets. There have been no less than eleven interest rate cuts this year, and money creation continues to grow at around six times the rate of inflation. Such stimulus is unprece-dented. For several quarters, however, our argument has been that these tools of his trade postpone the darkness, without extinguishing it. We repeat the mantra of previous reviews: this is a battle between the deflation of mar-ket forces and the expansionary responses of the central authorities. We con-tinue to think that market forces will win – only the timing is uncertain.

A long overview of history makes the point clearly. By the end of World War II, the US private sector was unborrowed and there was no unemploy-ment. Europe and the Far East were war-shattered: the Marshall Plan in 1948 whereby the US funded overseas recovery ensured that there would be global demand for US goods. The economy grew on a worldwide basis – and it grew fast, based both on the fundamentals, and the constant rise in the level of indebtedness. By the 1970s this debt was unsustainable. It was extinguished through systemic inflation whereby a combination of high taxation and negative real interest rates ensured that the borrowers triumphed at the expense of the lender. By 1980, thanks to that inflation, the West was again unborrowed, and we have seen another generation of fast growth, and, once again, this growth has been magnified by an increase in debt ratios. Like all things too good to be true, it suffers from the law of diminishing returns. In 1980 the American economy grew by $189 billion on total money creation of $267 billion (70% economic growth/money growth). In 1988 the figure was $398 billion of economic growth on total money creation of $956 billion (41% economic growth/money growth). In 2001 the figures were $312 billion and $1,783 billion (17%). The latest quarterly figure showed economic growth of $7 billion, against money creation of $597 billion. As Dr Warburton has acidly pointed out, taking on debt the size of Brazil's economy has led to growth the size of Paraguay's economy. The spring in the coil has unwound.

This phenomenon seems to us to be the conundrum which is the key to economic developments going forward. One of the features of the slowdown has been the profit collapse of 2001 throughout the whole world. This has occurred without any abatement in consumer spending; with appetite for credit so freely and cheaply available; this engine has been on full throttle. On the contrary, it has been a sharp downturn in investment which has caused the damage, and it has been made worse by the fact that the previous investment pattern had been concentrated in software and computer services, which are depreciated over a short period of time, unlike factories and heavy machinery, which have a life of many years. At the point of investment, it looks the same, but a higher depreciation charge comes straight off profits. In the old days, investors were encouraged by high depreciation charges because they judged a company by its profit line: since a depreciation charge does not affect a company's cash, a high depreciation charge means more cashflow £ for £ of profit. Not so today. Now analysts concentrate more on EBITDA (earnings before interest, tax, depreciation amortisation) so that the depreciation charge is bad news: when two companies have the same EBITDA, the one with higher depreciation has lower profits. This might appear somewhat technical, but it is not. A nation's wealth comes from productive investment of its savings into profitable enterprise. Borrowings play the same role, but need servicing. Expenditure on non-productive goods consumes wealth, and if done with borrowed money, strikes a double blow at the ultimate health of a nation's economy: the debt-shackle remains, and there is no legacy of profit-generating assets. That is becoming apparent in today's US corporate profit pattern.

If this analysis is correct, then the stampede of the consumer into the shopping malls makes as much sense as the Charge of the Light Brigade. The sooner it stops the better, despite the fact that a widespread lack of confidence could well bring about the deflation and 'liquidity trap' which the central authorities fear.

In investment terms, to be forewarned is to be forearmed. We remain confident that government fixed interest stocks of long duration (emphatically outside the United States) remain the preferred asset class. At the close of 2001, the yields have increased, as it became clear that low long term yields were allowing an unprecedented surge in monetary growth to occur through the 'refi' markets in America. The fall in such fixed interest stocks makes them doubly attractive – first, because they now offer a rather higher yield, and secondly, because they act as a custodian on sound money: it is impossible to renegotiate lower mortgages in the light of high government yields. When the mania for borrowing has passed, there will be time enough to reap the rewards of a capital gain in these instruments.

Commentary

2 0 0 2

The year of Queen Elizabeth's Golden Jubilee did not open in the sunny uplands. The monarchy was in good shape, notwithstanding the death of HM's corgi, Kelpie – the agonies of the past seemed to be just that – in the past. The previous year, the mutual love which Charles and Camilla showed for each other had been acknowledged by her future mother-in-law.

So much for the real world. Elsewhere, things were unravelling. The stockmarket was lower than it had been five years earlier. Tony Blair seemed not to notice, and announced in July that it had risen £250 billion under the Labour Government. The economy had formally entered recession in the middle of the previous year, and a wave of corporate defaults shocked the world – the early victims, Enron and WorldCom, through dishonesty, and in August, through incompetence, down went GEC, renamed Marconi after an Italian émigré who settled in London, and helped catch Dr Crippen. It happened barely three weeks after the death of its founder, and all-round good-egg Lord Weinstock. Equitable Life sank further into the mire, and increased penalties (again) on those who tried to withdraw their money early. Things became blacker still in the autumn. One of the 'safest' investments, much beloved of school-fee payers was a recherché instrument known as zero coupon preference shares – 'the one year old which lets you sleep at night' – purred one of the purveyors of these things. Unfortunately, when the dust settled, it transpired that there was rather less of the preference, and rather more of the zero.

These were conditions which made for grumpiness. The Rural Development Minister in the Scottish Parliament, Ross Finnie, had to apologise to Digby Jones, Director General of the CBI, for calling him 'an English prat'. Capitalism seemed under pressure. In July came the twin blows that the next Archbishop of Canterbury would have a Che Guevara beard, and that the statue of Maggie Thatcher had been decapitated. Railtrack shareholders who had been told by Stephen Byers the previous October, 'I can say for certain that there will be no taxpayers' money made available to support shareholders', received £4 per share from the taxpayer. Indeed it was not Railtrack's stock which fell, but Mr Byers's: he resigned a couple of months later.

There were other resignations: in February Lord Wakeham resigned as chairman of the Press Complaints Commission, but retained his £156,000 salary. Many felt that this was the wrong way round, since it was his role on the remuneration committee of Enron which had been the trouble, not his relationship with either the press or its complainants. Sir Roger Hurn left his chairmanship of the Pru prematurely, presumably to keep his time free for his other chairmanship, GEC/Marconi, whose existence had some two months to go. The last to go, unmourned, in mid-December, was Paul O'Neill, the Treasury Secretary of the US. He remarked: 'I like to see a strong Dollar.' Christopher Fildes pointed out that the last Treasury Secretary who had said that, under Jimmy Carter, had the nickname 'Typhoid Mary'.

The darkening outlook caused a swing in financial opinion that the world might be facing a depression. The Fed responded with alacrity. It published in the autumn a weighty retrospective on the lessons to be learnt from the Japanese deflation of the 1990s (subliminal message: it won't happen again) and was followed in late November by one of the most startling statements ever to come from the Federal Reserve.

A Governor of the Fed, Dr Benjamin Bernanke, already talked about as Alan Greenspan's successor, made a momentous speech. It was quite unlike anything which the delphic Alan Greenspan might have said: Bob Woodward in his biography of Greenspan records that his wife failed to decode his first two offers of marriage. Indeed, Greenspan famously said of himself, 'If you think I understood what I said, I need to repeat myself.' On the contrary, Bernanke's speech was unequivocal and of great clarity, and earned him the nickname 'helicopter Ben'. It highlighted that the Fed had grasped the truth that, in an over-indebted economy, the greatest threat to prosperity was deflation – but a vigilant central bank has the power to counteract it.

Listen to the Music

April 2002

The All American family potters through the glade, Dad in his Bermudas, Mom in her slacks and dark glasses. Junior is winding up his sister, whose high pitched whine sounds rather like a telephone left off its cradle. The whole cinema wants to shout out, 'Listen to the music, you oafs! This is no time to toy with a bagel! Watch out for the Tyrannosaurus with sharp teeth and luncheon voucher eyes!' When they meet, what is seen and what is heard tell the same story.

The investment world is rather like Jurassic Park. Focus on the viewing, and all seems pretty well in cosyland, but the orchestra's tune tells of danger. The purpose of this review is to assess whether sight or sound is the better reflection of reality. First, the scene from the viewfinder.

1 Events are unfolding along classic recovery lines. America emerged from recession before the commentators had even realised that the second quarter of 2001 marked its existence. Inflation is low and not an immediate threat. Interest rates are low and consumers are confident. Corporation de-stocking was radical, but by definition is something that can't go on happening: when a company has run down its stocks, it has nothing left to de-stock. Easy money has ensured that investor confidence has not been damaged. This has been exactly the pattern from which earlier recoveries have been born; why, ask the optimists, should it be different this time?

2 There is a high degree of confidence in central banks in general, and Alan Greenspan in particular. Over the last 10 years there have been several financial crises, and on each occasion, the response from central banks has been radical, with lowered interest rates and money being made freely available both within the banking system and outside it. The Russian currency crisis of 1998 was over before the widespread loss of confidence could do damage. The Japanese alternative (hope for the

best and experience the worst) looks to be proof positive that such bold moves are both effective and soundly based.

The US financial dream still sparkles. Following the fall of communism, the political supremacy of the United States has been integrally bound up with the onward march of the globalisation of markets along the American model. Its cheerleaders have become positively Papal in their *ex cathedra* pronouncements. Jack Welch (lately retired Chief Executive of General Electric, the largest corporation in the world) attributes his management success to 'six sigma' principles. Amazingly, people take him seriously. His disciples await his cure for scrofula.

3   Investors have been encouraged at how well-publicised problems have been shrugged off. Investors like to feel brave and they know that they must think contrarily to the crowd. 11 September and the collapse of Enron provide the frisson of nervousness which can persuade them that they are buying to the sound of gunfire, and will in the future be able to sell to the sound of the violins. Market volatility is low, suggesting that investors are reassured; surveys show a high degree of optimism.

What music do we hear coming from the film?

1   *Complacency, not bravery*. The response to the Enron crisis is perhaps the most salutary. Enron's equity and debt has dropped in value from $120 billion 18 months ago to nothing. There is widespread evidence that profits were overstated and debts kept out of sight in off balance sheet entities. The radical innovations which Enron brought to the worldwide trading of energy would not have been possible without a great deal of corporate and legal work provided by a wide range of bankers, lawyers and accountants. The company was at the very heart of the economic system, and the widespread grant of financial and corporate favours ensured that it was at the heart, too, of the political system. Yet when Enron collapsed there was an assumption that it was an isolated incident, and that the true villain of the piece was its auditors, Andersens. This head in the sand approach is very serious. The idea that a cockroach was found in the kitchen but got trodden on, belies the real issue: can the kitchen really be clean at all? This is not the only case of the wakeup call which the financial establishment has determined to sleep through. Another example from the insurance world: the claims on the destruction of the World Trade Centre run at $40 billion but only

$28 billion are admitted to – the rest is sloshing round in the system, laid off, reinsured against, contracted away to some shadowy entity: a real liability which is someone else's responsibility. There are plenty more: Fannie Mae growing its balance sheet by 25% per annum by lending to absolutely anyone who can sign their mortgage form, and then securitising it with a gold-plated 'AAA' rating. The list is as long as you like.

2 *The Tyrannosaurus of the marketplace: the credit cycle.* The seemingly smooth outlook for the economy is a central bank artefact. The dangers throughout the 1990s were that a collapse of confidence would threaten the economic prosperity which has been in place since the recession which ended in 1992. Alan Greenspan therefore subordinated every other consideration to ensuring that consumer demand remained strong, and this he has done essentially by guaranteeing cheap and plentiful credit. He overcame the 1998 crisis by making aggressive moves in this direction, and is doing the same thing again today. It is the Danegeld approach: an effective escape from an immediate problem, but with the creating of another one, which in the long term proves to be considerably more worrisome. He has marvellously kept demand expenditure growing, at a time when such demand was vital to keep the economy intact. But the cost of doing so threatens the very fabric of America's financial system. Money growth has resulted in leveraged corporations, and private individuals with more borrowings than ever before. Debt inevitably means distress when times get hard. Optimists point to the sustainability high debt levels when interest rates are low – but this is bad analysis. Low debt service charges leads to the Japanese problem of economic stasis: if you can pay the interest, but not repay the principal debt, the poison is never cleared from the system. The magic of the 1970s crisis was that interest rates were high in nominal terms, but negative in real terms: it was sink or swim: debt laden companies either collapsed, or came through with a debt burden which had been largely removed through inflation.

So, is it a horror movie or not? Only if there is something horrid in it. Frolicsome children from a Julie Andrews film have nothing to fear – the sound of music tells you that. The answer will therefore not be found in the bull story, the picture of a world of low interest rates, brave consumers and the broad path back to the prosperity of the 1990s. The key is whether or not there is something worrisome and largely unperceived threatening the economic fabric. We believe there is. Its footprints are already clearly in evidence for those with eyes to see, both in the credit statistics, which speak of unsustainable and unresolved pressures, and also in a number of recent failures, which are systemic in nature, but which the financial world chooses to regard as isolated incidents. As an investment house we've locked up our children.

Mr Dampier-Wetton

July 2002

My father once met a water engineer called Mr Dampier-Wetton. An unlikely story, you may think, but no more so than the man who has driven a stake through the heart of the US and world stock markets. He is a cowboy from a place called Clinton. Bernie Ebbers' company, WorldCom, was capitalised at $160 billion at its peak. His presentation to investors consisted of just one slide – a chart of the company's stock price soaring upwards. He once famously told the Financial Times reporter that he didn't care whether the return on capital was 6% or 60%, provided the share price went up. It is the contempt of the prostitute for the client.

Make no mistake, once investors lose confidence in the wholesomeness of the product, the basis of valuation changes completely. The art world well knows the ravaging murmur that an artefact is not 'right'. Nowadays the Mona Lisa is regarded as Leonardo da Vinci's masterpiece, but it was not always so. Lord Bessborough sold it in 1801 for 50 guineas, reflecting its doubtful provenance. In the 19th century it was the Spanish artist Murillo who fetched the big money, until his peasant scenes proved easy to fake. Everything now depends on confidence in the stock market product; it is hard to see how this will be maintained. To those within the village of the stock market, the scandals have occurred among the likeliest suspects. No doubt investigative journalists are combing through the whole of corporate America for further evidences of misbehaviour and will be concentrating on those companies which seem most likely to have overstepped the mark. Each revelation will seem as though the whole system is rotten, whereas it is only the petals nearest the radiator which have wilted. The prize victim would be General Electric, the biggest, most prestigious company in the world, and it is hard to believe that it will escape unscathed. The problem for GE, and indeed for corporate America as a whole, is that accounting practice is an art, not a science – an artistry which might well look decidedly black to a kangaroo court of disaffected investors.

The result is a mood which has darkened perceptibly over the last three months, tellingly at a time when the economic news has been perfectly satisfactory, with the post 11 September recovery still more or less on course. But the confidence thing cannot be calculated arithmetically: it's more a mood than a measurement. One example will do for a multitude. The markets have hammered the share price of Glaxo which is believed to be considering a bid for its rival, Bristol Myers. Their purchase of SmithKline three years ago on exactly similar reasoning was feted. With Bristol Myers the markets see only that Glaxo will be hard pressed to grow its sales, whereas with SmithKline it saw the cost savings of a merger. Both true then, both true now. It is not just the share price of Glaxo which has been under attack – so has its management. And, as confidence wanes, the damage to reputations will grow apace. J K Galbraith in his Great Crash 1929 wrote: 'The prestige of the bankers had in truth been falling even more rapidly than the market.' This was in the context of the discovery that those who were in control were powerless to do anything about the erosion of confidence in the markets. Today an entire industry of stockbrokers, analysts, salesmen and intermediaries have been selling a dream about the future. They are always bullish, and have now been wrong for over two years. It should go without saying that they have no more idea of what the future will hold than Mystic Meg. The mischief is that, when discredited, they will not be able to offer cheer, no matter how bullish and how right they subsequently prove to be. Discredited too, will be the central bankers whose laying on of hands has kept the blessing alive. Over all stands the Colossus of Greenspan whose only perceived weakness is that his age might necessitate his retirement in the next couple of years. Greenspan's adulation has lasted longer than Sven Goran Eriksson's, but it, too, will not survive a series of poor results from his team, the US economy. This is a distinct worry for the future. A mightily fallen Greenspan will be completely impotent – much more so than a mediocrity who has stumbled platitudinously through a crisis. Once confidence in him has gone, the US economy will be rudderless. While economists are looking at whether there will be a hard landing in the financial figures, they should be looking at the dangers of a hard landing among the financial figureheads.

With popular dismay moving inexorably towards disgust, it now becomes more certain that stock markets around the world will retreat in deflationary disorder. Stock markets are still trading expensively, even assuming a profit recovery, which is, in our view, far from certain. We are therefore retreating somewhat from our already underweight position in equities, particularly those which still enjoy high ratings. Our policy remains to achieve for clients double the return available on cash, come rain, come shine. The barometer reads 'rain' and we are confident that our galoshes of Swiss Bonds, a Euro umbrella and a mackintosh of the US Bear Fund combined with a covered currency will see us through the wet weather. The rain will end one day, the mushrooms will grow, and we hope that our stock picking will then be evident.

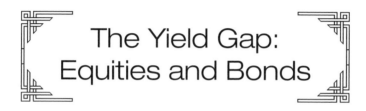

The Yield Gap:
Equities and Bonds

October 2002

Three months ago we wrote, 'popular dismay is moving inexorably towards disgust, and it now becomes more certain that stockmarkets around the world will retreat in deflationary disorder'. Equity markets are down a further 20% this quarter alone. The wet weather galoshes which we referred to have continued to make progress, so that we are in the happy position of being able to reverse a strategy which has worked well; but should we be selling our fixed interest stocks at high prices, and buying back equities which daily are hitting levels not seen for some 6 years? One of the famous failures to capitalise on a successful strategy was that of N M Rothschild in the 1974 bear market. Directly anticipating trouble, it had big positions in gold shares. In the words of Barry Riley, 'As a result it handsomely outperformed its peer group of pension fund managers in 1974. In early 1975 however when the UK equity market rocketed by 130% Rothschild was stranded. It never recovered its reputation – (and, now, the fund management business is up for sale).'

The purpose of this report is to consider whether we are right to hold to our strategy, or whether we are guilty of a complacent stubbornness, making us hold firm to a strategy which is now fully reflected in stockmarket and fixed interest prices.

It is the spectre of deflation which has caused the divergence of assets, gilts going up and equities going down. The hallmark of a deflation is not just a fall in the prices in the shops, but a fall, too, in the returns that investors receive on their capital. At corporate level, this means falling profits – hence the fall in the stockmarket. It means falling dividends, and it also means falling interest rates. A retreat by investors into cash on deposit safeguards their capital – a virtue not to be underestimated in a bear market – but it locks into the likelihood of a falling income stream as rates go lower. The hard thing in a deflation is to keep up one's spending power. That is the pleasure of the fixed interest market – a relentless stream of regular income, which becomes more highly priced as other income sources falter and dry up. Hence the rise in top quality bond prices.

The question is whether these factors are now reflected in prices. We have been worried about deflation for many years, and what seemed a cloud no bigger than a man's hand some 10 years ago seems now to be an approaching storm. One can chart the market's response to this growing threat through the price of War Loan, the government stock issued during the First World War to pay for the Sopwith Camel and the Big Push. Issued at 100, trading at 102 only 50 years ago, inflation drove its price ever lower, and in the 1970s its yield rose higher than its price (16 to yield 17%). A slow recovery saw it above 30 in 1991, and, as the Western world pulled out of recession, it became apparent for the first time that inflation was no longer the dominant force that it had been. Pricing power was on the wane, and by the time of the 1992 general election, War Loan had risen to 37. Sterling's devaluation in September 1992 was the first practical test for the deflation theory: would wages go up, and the competitive advantages of the lower pound be passed away on a Friday night, or would wages hold and the UK obtain a jump start because of the improved terms of trade – exactly what happened when Britain devalued in the depressionary circumstances of September 1931? It proved to be the latter, and War Loan continued to improve, breaking the 8% barrier (July 1993), then 7% (August 1997) and 6% (February 1998). At the end of 2001, it had a yield of 5.0%; now it is standing at 77, a 50 year high, giving a yield of 4.5%.

Today's investor is faced with this practical issue. If long-term government bonds yield, as they do, between 4.5% (UK) and 5.3% (Australia), is an All Share yield of 3.7% compelling? By the standards of the last 40 years, the relationship between these two yields suggests that equities are very cheap against bonds, but the last 40 years has been an era of inflation. Go back to the pre-1959 period (the last year of nil-inflation in the UK) and equities had a higher yield than gilts, on the perfectly respectable premise that a government guarantee of an income payment to gilt holders was more certain than the discretionary dividend payment by corporations to a shareholder: it was therefore more highly valued. When the first gilt to yield 5% was issued in 1961, the old wisebeards whispered that such an offer was too good to be true. 'Look through the current uncertainties,' they opined, 'and apart from one issue in the heat of battle of 1916, no such coupon has been seen since the Peninsula War.' The argument was compelling, and quite wrong. Those who fell for it discovered that peacetime inflation wiped them out. Today the boot is on the other foot. Conventional wisdom says that gilts below 5% are unsustainable. Even vicars know that you have to take inflation into account. The market, ever wiser than most of its participants, is beginning to sense that it is the last 40 inflationary years that have been the anomaly – not the 150 years which preceded it. The dark horse of deflation has come from being a rank outsider to the favourite. Favourite odds, of course, demand that the favourite win the race, but that is looking increasingly a probability, not a possibility. We are happy with our fixed interest stocks!

Nevertheless, we remain bigamists at heart. Having defended our exposure to the fixed interest markets, we feel an equal loyalty to a representation – albeit a diminished one – in the equity market. We are ever mindful that it is picking the winning companies of tomorrow which makes clients serious money. Never mind whether you bought Marks & Spencer in 1929 at the top of the market, or 1933 at the bottom – provided you bought it, your grandchildren are certain to be fat and complacent. Already the falls in the market have thrown up compelling valuations in a number of areas of the stockmarket. This is not the same thing as saying that their shares are compellingly attractive, because valuations deteriorate when the fundamentals deteriorate: cut dividends and cut profits make a stock look expensive at the lower levels, as many investors have found to their cost over the last 3 years. At the risk of sounding like an old gramophone record, we reiterate our commitment to trying to produce a balance of investments which will ensure that, whatever the economic and financial position, clients will be fully protected, and enjoy a return substantially in excess of cash.

Nerdy Article on Dr Bernanke's Speech

December 2002

There is consternation amongst the self-appointed vigilantes of sound money. For years the archbishops and doctors of economic theology have been hoping for a chance remark from the US central authorities which reveals a monetary heresy: Dr Bernanke, a federal reserve governor, has obliged with a speech which has spelled out in compelling simplicity the steps which it would take to avoid the mischief of falling prices. Simply print more money! While there are trees, a paper currency can always outrun a deflation. Ten out of ten for honesty, but perhaps Dr Bernanke should have lunch with Gerald Ratner to be appraised of the dangers of such homespun honesty.

Why did he do it? A likely first reason is that he thinks that the spectre of deflation is pretty much a false one. Encourage the front line troops with talk of the reserve army if the enemy breaks through, and the likelihood of having to use those reserves is correspondingly reduced. There is also some complacency in his remarks. Dr Bernanke represents the nerve centre of the greatest brand name in the world – the US dollar. He sees only its rock-like immovability, not the threat represented by the irresistible force of endless paper money in undermining its value.

It was not always so. A look at the history books is instructive. There have been a number of ozymandian currencies over previous centuries. The pathology of their destruction varies enormously – military defeat is not helpful, as the Germans discovered twice in the last century. But the last 40 years have been unusual. Fiscal and economic irresponsibility has tended to lead (in the First World at least) to a higher level of inflation, rather than the complete destruction of a currency. Thus a feckless Italy has had inflation at over twice the rate of its German neighbours, and this was reflected in the falling value of the Lira – again, no crisis in an age of flexible exchange rates. The result was that even in the extreme conditions of the 1970s, currencies did not fracture, they merely bent. It was the era of the rubber currency. But in a steady-state or deflationary period, the pressures are more akin to those on metal: the pressures build up, nothing appears to happen until there is a sudden break. The period between the wars is a good example. Britain was then the economy whose glory was in the past, but whose reputation – and currency – stood higher in the lists than an objective assessment would suggest. In September 1931 after agonising indecision, the Labour government devalued: the pound went from $4.87 to $3.90. Almost immediately, things looked up for Britain, but the very idea of devaluation was regarded universally with horror – including by Keynes.

How so? Skidelsky wrote (*Politicians and the Slump*, Macmillan 1967, page 349) 'Every official and unofficial memorandum the government received from its advisors stressed the immense dangers – the dislocation of the world's trading and financial system, uncontrollable inflation at home which would result.' To understand the advice the government received, one only has to look at the experience of the previous 10 years, to put their advice into context. Failure to balance the books, and political haphazardry had resulted in the total destruction of the Germanic and Russian satellite currencies. France was down 86% against the dollar, Portugal 93%, Spain 50%, Italy 70%, and with only the Nordics, Switzerland, Japan and, to our eyes, amazingly, Argentina escaping the downdraft. The message was clear: bad behaviour brought you up before hanging Judge Jeffries. Yet every player could see that a strong currency meant poor terms of trade, and the cut-throat competitive pressures meant that those with a strong currency suffocated from its strength. It was the economics of the Siberian labour camp: those nearest the brazier died of the fumes, those furthest away died of hypothermia. To move away from the brazier was wise, although dangerous. Skidelsky again (*op cit*, page 343) 'Up to 1 August 1931 the financial crisis was not regarded as England's fault. The nature of the crisis changed with the publication of the May report, and the conclusions drawn from it. It was now suggested that London might not be such a safe place to keep money as had been thought, because the Labour government was bent on inflation leading to a devaluation of the currency. Once doubts of this kind had been suggested, it was also noted that Britain was running, in 1931, a balance of payments deficit which was interpreted as part of the same inflationary tendency. Hence a real crisis of confidence in Sterling arose. In order to counteract these fears the Labour government was urged to take immediate steps to balance the budget.'

It should be clear from these extracts how similar were the proximate events to those in present-day America and yet how different were the attitudes then of the international financial community, the government's advisers and the government (for government then read Dr Bernanke today). The attitudes in 1931 had been forged in the crucible of the regular economic collapse of world powers. Today the past strength of the dollar, and universal survival of all currencies in the First World leaves its spokesmen unalarmed at extolling of the pleasures of the printing press.

It is clear today that the balanced-budget Micawberism of the government's response to the events of the 1930s was a policy mistake, but they were in reaction to market sentiment which was far from irrational in its assessment of the dangers. It is easy for us to overlook the absolutist power that financial confidence plays in the outworking of policy. Thus far, America in general, and Greenspan in particular, have been given indulgent treatment by the markets. One only has to look at the fall in corporate heroes to see that the first victim of a loss of confidence is flexibility. Many is the CEO of a stock market darling who has made reckless statements, believing wrongly that the markets will understand. It could be that Dr Bernanke's words will come back to haunt him – Gerald Ratner often made his joke about the quality of his product – but suddenly one day it mattered, and then it looked less like his funny side than his suicide.

Déja-vu all over again!

The Great Depression of 1873-98 followed a period of high-jinks in the financial markets. This was the contemporary (1873) observation:

True, some great event may prick the commercial bubble, and create convulsions; but while the Secretary of the Treasury plays the role of the banker for the entire United States, it is difficult to conceive of any condition or circumstances which he cannot control. Power has been centralized in him to an extent not enjoyed by the Governor of the Bank of England. He can issue the paper representative of gold to the amount of scores of millions.

After the World Trade Centre

January 2003

It has become our custom at the year end to step back from the minutiae of the perspectives and concerns which are manifest quarter by quarter – and look at the world as it appears across a broader front.

There are many grim things to consider, so let us start with one which seems to us to be less malignant than the consensus view. There is widespread concern in the investment world that things will go sufficiently badly in Iraq to reinforce the downward spiral in equity markets. This is not our view. Bullies rarely stand up to concerted aggression, so we are considerably more hopeful that there will be a 'regime change' speedily in the medium term. Such a conflict could, of course, engulf Saudi Arabia, the Kuwaiti oil wells or exacerbate the Israel/Palestine inferno, but, if it happens, it will owe more to the instabilities themselves, than the catalyst of the US/Iraq war itself. We think, when looking back on 2003, that an Iraq conflict will be an uncertainty resolved.

The distress and uncertainties created by the World Trade Center atrocity still remain and ensure that the world remains a frightening place. Uncertainty is never a helpful ingredient in the world economy, but today in particular we are living at a time when world economic growth is being held together by the confidence of the consumer in spending his own – and increasingly his borrowed – money. In the last 5 years consumer expenditure in America has grown at 3.9% per annum, as against 2.9% for the economy as a whole. It has become the only engine for growth in a world beset with oversupply, lack of pricing power, and a tendency towards falling prices: the hallmarks of a deflation, a quicksand from which it is hard indeed to escape. There is a major battle going on between these deflationary forces raging in the marketplace, and the inflationary responses of the central authorities anxious to avoid the quicksand. Their policy of low interest rates and easy money in America has kept the consumer consuming. We have been constant in our belief that the battle will be won by the marketplace, on the simple premise that a good big'un beats a good little'un. For the first time there is some clue as to how this battle will play out. We think the arena will be the currency markets, and we think that the US dollar will be the casualty. This is why:

On 21 November 2002, one of the Federal Reserve governors, Dr Bernanke, gave a very significant speech to the National Economists Club, Washington DC. While discounting the probability of deflation becoming a practical issue, he argued that a US central bank which was determined to ensure that deflation would not occur could issue as many dollars as necessary to ensure that there was a sufficient supply of them to keep prices from going down. His argument was that, in the old days, when currencies were based on gold, this freedom was not open to governments, because there was not an unlimited supply of gold. With paper currencies, there is no such issue. This speech fluttered the dovecotes of the professional economists, but has been given little publicity beyond that constituency. It is, nevertheless, an extraordinary thing for the Federal Reserve to have announced – and there can be no doubt that Dr Bernanke was speaking on behalf of the Fed. If any government except the American had said that they planned to print their way out of economic difficulty, the result would be a drop in their currency. The prestige, the wealth and the history of the United States monetary system (combined with Dr Bernanke's complacency that it will ever be so) has meant that the threat to the US dollar has not been widely perceived. But in our view this is nemesis deferred, not avoided.

Our prediction is, therefore, that when the irresistible force of deflation hits the immoveable object of US central banking, it will be the dollar which is the victim. This is a new development, not because the dollar has only recently become vulnerable, but that there are signs that its vulnerability will be tested in the near future. Let us assume for a moment that we are right, and the dollar does fall significantly. All US assets will be depreciated by that amount, but what are the consequences for the rest of the investment world? The currency winners are likely to be the Euro (by default rather than on merit), and even more likely, the Swiss Franc: the latter has been the best performing currency for a while. Looking at the broader picture, a weak dollar is likely to benefit the United States (terms of trade improve, and an inflationary influence offsets the deflation) but at the expense of Europe and the Far East, whose exports suffer along with their savings in the depreciated dollar. Not good news, therefore, for equities. The effect on the fixed interest market (which is of more significance to our investors here) is less easy to divine. It introduces a layer of uncertainty, and valuation volatility, into an arena which doesn't respond well to these characteristics. An adverse currency move of, say, 15%, is a killer in a world where returns on interest rates are at 5% or below. On the other hand, when a currency rises its fixed interest stocks benefit from all the concomitant economic effects, as well as the currency movement itself.

Our conclusion is that fixed interest stocks in the right currency will be excellent in 2003, and poor in weak currencies. It is another example of trying to find investments in riskless asset classes. The exposure we put into place in the Swiss Franc last year is paying dividends, and we are minded to look to increase that exposure. We are beginning also to dip our toe into the gold share market, for similar reasons.

Commentary

2 0 0 3

On the last day of 2002 a further ten countries joined the European Union, each of them adopting the Euro currency; Sterling remained the hound of the Baskervilles – a country whose geography and shared traditions should be at the heart of a pan-European initiative, was not a part of it.

But Britain had ever been the bridesmaid, not the bride, of Europe. The early steps towards integration under the initiative of Jean Monnet had not been attractive to successive UK governments, not least because they had centred on the steel industry, whose long term viability did not seem to be in doubt. When it became clear that Britain should join, de Gaulle blocked it. Andrew Marr cites Edward Heath at a meeting at Chequers. Pompidou had told him in French, 'If you ever want to know what my policy is, don't bother to call me on the telephone – I do not speak English, and your French is awful. Just remember that I am a peasant, and my policy will always be to support the peasants.' So it was that the Common Agricultural Policy became the hurdle to British entry. Britain, led by Edward Heath, held its collective and not inconsiderable nose, and joined. A decade later when Maggie was on the warpath, she won two decisive victories: one in the Falklands, the other in Brussels. The Tory leader may have won the battle for a budget rebate in the EU but the whole issue of Europe destroyed the party's unity and, by extension, its credibility.

This was the legacy which Tony Blair inherited. He made it plain to his European colleagues that he wished to join the Euro. The Governor of the Bank of England, Eddie George, was against it ('There were those who argued that the City would suffer if the UK failed to join from the outset. That clearly has not so far happened – quite the reverse.' he stated in June 2000). But the Bank of England didn't count. The Chancellor of the Exchequer, however, did. The division of Labour: Tony for Prime Minister, Gordon a free hand at the Treasury, turned out in reality to provide Gordon Brown not with a free hand, but a mailed fist. He unilaterally hijacked the decision by declaring that five tests had to be satisfied before

Sterling could enter the joint currency – and like a Mormon preacher of yore, declared, too, that he was its interpreter. The 2001 election had been presumed to be the decisive event – the *Spectator*'s banner headline on Labour's victory was, 'Now the Battle begins' – a reference to the debate over the Pound. The virtual Euro had existed since 1999 – the rates of each participating currency were fixed: the €500 note was to become the bank-note of choice for those whose acquaintance with their taxing authorities was distant.

The markets had dropped throughout 2001 and 2002, continuing to fall in early 2003. (The US had bottomed six months earlier, but the weakness of the Dollar meant that foreign holders of Wall Street stocks were no bet-ter off than elsewhere.) By the April, the FTSE had halved, which included a period of eleven straight 'down' days in January when the market fell by nearly 500 points. Equities had a yield greater than gilts, a point which many bullish commentators saw as a sure sign that equities were going to recover. (There was less self-congratulation in early 2009, when, on an his-torical basis, the FTSE had a yield of 5.8%, and five year gilts less than half that.) Once again, it was the invasion of Iraq which saw the turn – as it had in 1990. The bull run was to last a full four years, and saw the market near-ly to its 2000 high.

The Footsie Index

April 2003

A t the start of the year the markets had fallen for three years in a row. The turmoil in the stock market has not been matched by events in the real world – the shortest and shallowest recession in America over, interest rates low, consumers continuing to spend and some spectacular corporate defaults that signally failed to destabilise the banking system. Notwithstanding this calm, the stock markets have continued their downward trajectory. By mid-March, they had lost another 15%; the UK market has halved in three years. Equities yielded as much as gilts for the first time since 1957, the year Toscanini died. Since then, markets have staged something of a rally, but the pressing question is whether the chasm between sentiment in the markets and the seeming calm of the real world will be resolved positively (ie, markets recovering) or the opposite (ie, we learn what it is that the stock market is discounting). Although there is a lot of fear, it is remarkable how bullish the investment industry remains about future prospects. Everybody is on the lookout for 'capitulation' – when the last seller has panicked, markets can recover on a 'wall of worry'.

But is it true that people have capitulated? A selling climax is much more typical of an intermediate low – true market bottoms are accompanied by disgusted indifference. The real buying opportunities of 1932, 1940, 1949 and 1975 were all markets where low volumes were the order of the day – no fish were being caught, and the fishermen had moved on. Today, too many people are bottom-fishing. A couple of years ago we printed a US chart (see p82) we entitled 'Patsy Country' showing that 63% of professional investment managers were bullish. Since then the fall in the market has highlighted that they were indeed patsies. The bullish percentage is now even further up to 65%: one can perhaps draw one's own conclusions from this.

The consensus view in London is that the problem for equities is essentially a technical one: forced selling by the insurance industry has been met by a temporary absence of buyers, thus driving the stock market to abnormally low valuations. This has made the market 'cheap', and three factors are usually cited: a price/earnings multiple no higher than average, a dividend yield as high as that available in the gilt market, and the fact that the stock market has halved. The FT columnist, Philip Coggan, asks, 'If a store reduces its price by 50%, shouldn't this bring out the buyers, rather than turning them away?' Our answer is, no! – if the store is a greengrocer trying to palm off brown bananas, and, no! – if the pre-sale price reflected the optimism of Voltaire's Dr Pangloss. Alas, the brown banana syndrome and Panglostershire are very much in evidence.

We do not see a cheap market. Looked at through the prism of earnings, ratings in the UK are about at their historic average. The trouble with the earnings yardstick is that there are two fast-moving plates: markets become expensive either if prices go up, or earnings go down. Prospective earnings therefore need to be earned – and, while analysts in aggregate are predicting higher earnings, the economic outlook points to a different picture. Earnings, in our view, do not support market levels. How about yield considerations? The current yield on the FTSE Index (3.67%) is, by historic standards, a warning bell. In the 70 years until 1995, arguably when the stock market 'bubble' began, there were only 8 periods in which the market had a lower yield. In every case except one, the market dropped by over 30% – in the one exception (1959) the fall was 18%. It is striking that in half this period gilts yielded less than equities, and in half they yielded more. The significance of this is that equities historically have required a yield well in excess of 4% to be worth buying, regardless of the inflation rate, the main motor of gilt prices. The message seems unequivocal: whether times are inflationary, deflationary, or all square, 3.7% is too little.

Other measurements – price to book, price to sales, Tobin's Q (this is, of course, showing off), price to free cashflow and comparisons with average wages all paint the same picture. But in a world where investors are no longer so interested in making money as they are in outperforming indices, the absoluteness of market levels is less important. The industry is more terrified of missing the big bounce than of losing money in a market setback: there has probably been no other factor so powerful in keeping investors locked into this relentlessly falling market than the fear of selling at the bottom.

One of the great conundrums of investment is why fundamentals play such a small part in investors' considerations. This long-term perspective is probably less in fashion than it has ever been. Markets have been volatile, and have taken on the frenetic aspect of a football match for 11 year olds, where 22 excited youngsters chase the ball wherever it happens to go, without any strategy or cohesion. Active managers redouble their efforts to master the skill of market timing – but the gyrations are wholly haphazard. We prefer to adopt an approach where time becomes our ally, not our enemy – understand the fundamentals, and sooner or later they will assert themselves. The great economist, Lord Keynes, thought this a rotten way of investing. 'Investment based on genuine long-term expectation is so difficult today [1936] as to be scarcely practicable. He who attempts it must surely lead much more laborious days and run greater risks than he who tries to guess better than the crowd how the crowd will behave; and given equal intelligence, he may make more disastrous mistakes.' We sincerely hope he's wrong – it's the only way we know. Our roadmap tells us that markets are far from cheap, and we remain concerned that the imbalances consequent on the financial bubble which burst some three years ago are still unresolved.

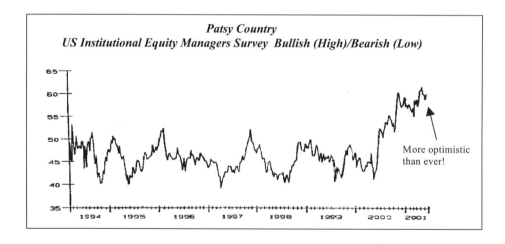

Buy Japan, Japan, Japan!

July 2003

The moment has come to invest in the Japanese stockmarket! I write these words with enthusiasm, alarm and not a little surprise: the emotions, perhaps, of a 45 year old bachelor who takes his dog for a walk in the park, and comes back with a wife. It is 18 years since my clients last had any meaningful investments there, and the place has changed a bit since then. At the top of the market, Japan represented about 42% of the world index by market value; it is now 8.7% (MSCI World Index). The pendulum is set to swing back again – a sentiment repeated many times by commentators but never – until now – by us. This investment review is about the thoughts which have led to this conclusion.

The world's economy is not doing well, we think. The problem is that timely statistics which prove or disprove this are not available: by the time they are in, the worries are about 2004, not 2003. The snippets of information, the straws in the wind, are insubstantial – a survey here, an order there, advertising revenues up, and a stock market recovery: but they don't add up to the real thing. It's like judging Gordon Brown's five economic assessments of Euro entry by his body language the weekend before. Our pessimism is based on a single premise: the economy was fragile in 2002, and will not have been helped by commercial hesitation before the Gulf war, and the SARS alarm, although mercifully of short duration, was extremely dislocative to world trade. The best news will be out of the United States, but the growth will have been 'stolen' from the rest of the world on the back of a weaker dollar.

What is the significance of this? The backcloth which we have articulated quarter by quarter is of a battle between the deflationary forces of the marketplace, and the reactive forces of central banks and governments which are of themselves unequivocally inflationary. The general assumption has been that the central banks would prevail, but it should not have been very much of a surprise that the armoury of weapons at their disposal has been unable to overwhelm the marching army of a thousand million commercial decisions made by individuals around the world. Against this slowdown, the Federal Reserve has used the elephant gun of interest rates (effective if your timing is accurate, otherwise not, as the last 14 have shown in America), and the mustard gas of easy money. Easy money is, of course, borrowed money, and low interest rates mean that the cheese of low servicing costs is more apparent than the mousetrap of how the capital will be repaid. Properly used, easy money provides a device for creating the opportunity to eat tomorrow's lunch today, and sometimes this extra demand is just enough to fill the gap – but the Fed's problem is that this gap is too big – a yawning shortfall of demand growth, met with the relentless response to debt creation, more debt and yet more debt.

Mr Greenspan has made no secret of his fear that if existing channels of demand falter before the economy picks itself up, the result could be a deflation from which a cure is notoriously difficult. That is why we continue to allocate assets into long government bonds which don't default, and give a regular and safe source of income in a world increasingly barren of yield. But Mr Greenspan has made it clear that he will try 'unconventional methods' to stave off this deflation, and he is a powerful figure with the will and the means to compromise the value of the currency, which (as he has pointed out) is only made of paper. This could 'spook' the bond market and provoke a nasty fall. The analogy is Iraq's: the very success of the coalition army in getting quickly to the gates of Baghdad made it likely that Saddam's Republican Guard would bring about a last stand. The conundrum is this: should we abandon ship at what feels like the moment of victory? Ultimately, we believe that our long bonds are safe, since market forces will play themselves out, however desperately the Federal Reserve twists and turns to keep the show on the road. But there is no doubt that sentiment could turn against this asset class if this Zeus, with his inflationary thunderbolts, were thought to compromise the soundness of money. And that is where Japan comes in.

Japanese businesses have been coping with deflationary conditions for more than a decade, and they have become adept at restructuring their activities to accommodate a lower revenue stream. As a result of this, they produce prodigious amounts of free cashflow, and the Japanese stock market judged on this basis is very cheap indeed. The market does not appear cheap because profits do not look as bright as the cashflow, partly because of asset writedowns which come about because the blue chips in Japan tend to have cross holdings with one another, and as the market falls, each has to reflect the decrease in value through the P&L account. And there is a technical reason for this fall (at least among the blue chips): the *Deiko Henjo* effect where companies have been forced sellers of cross-holdings in the companies to the detriment of both parties. The key to the Japanese stock market is therefore not so much the level of general retail prices, but rather the level of asset prices. As the market has gone down, it has made Japanese stocks look more and more expensive. If they recover, then the write offs become write-backs, and one could find the anomalous situation of the true cheapness of Japan only being apparent when the market has gone up. And US-inspired inflation might well be the catalyst for this. In other words, inflation is a risk in the rest of the world (as bondholders we cower) but in Japan it would be thoroughly good news for equities.

Our philosophy has always been that safety is achieved through juxtaposition of different types of asset. The Japanese equity market thus provides a series of insurances which protect our core positions. If Diana smiles, and all the world is gay, then we believe that the Japanese equity market will outperform the other major markets. It therefore protects us from being over-bearish in outlook. If the thunderbolts hit our long bonds, it could well help turn asset price deflation in Japan into asset price inflation. Moreover, the fizz and spittle of that market means that a comparatively small exposure protects a far bigger block of money in the bond market, whose price movements – both upward and downward – tend to have the stolidity of the policeman's ball.

The Cuckoo Clock

October 2003

T he markets have enjoyed a second quarter of recovery and the flowers have re-appeared: not the rhododendrons and begonias of extravagant exuberance, rather the buttercups and snowdrops of a cautious optimism. The cuckoos in the clock have reversed, the wet weather bird behind shutters, and the other, marked 'dry' is enjoying a modest cock-a-doodle-doo of self-congratulation.

Over the last three years we have been cautious, and any change of direction towards bullishness was always likely to put our defensive stocks under pressure. Sure enough, it has. The bond markets generally have been weak with the ultra-defensive Swiss 'gilts' particularly so – not so much watching the paint dry, as watching it peel. We have, however, been rescued by a bold move into Japan in the late Spring, which has performed spectacularly well. Somewhat to our astonishment, it has played out exactly as we predicted in our Summer newsletter: the waterspout of Greenspan's inflationary rhetoric may have flooded the fixed interest markets around the world, but it has irrigated Japan. The juxtaposition of these two asset classes has had the effect of giving a safe and positive return.

The situation today is finely poised. Events could unfold over the next six months in a number of different directions, some of which could drive the markets a fair bit higher, and some of which could result in the sort of financial mayhem which has been a sub-theme of these Investment Reviews for some little time. Although the battle could rage across a wide front, there are three separate armies – elements of the portfolio – which, properly balanced, should see the valuations safe through this coming period of intense uncertainty.

The central army remains the holdings of long duration government bonds (gilts in the UK, but primarily in Germany and Australia). We believe that the deflationary forces of the market place will prevail over the central banks' attempts to resist them. In such times, returns on assets become unsatisfactorily low. The obvious example is UK bank interest rates – 10% in the early 1990s, 6% four years ago and now not much more than half that. In Japan, the *reductio ad absurdum* deposit interest is £30 per million (before tax, of course). But it can be seen, too, in cut dividends, and missed profit targets – all these are threats to an investor. But the threat becomes an opportunity if one can find a guaranteed stream of income which will not default (hence government bonds) and which goes on for a while: preferably 20 years or more. Fears of too much supply as governments increase borrowing to match their deficits are misplaced. One can never have too much of a good thing, as the thunderous issuance of equities in most bull markets testifies. There is a danger, of course, that even the governments themselves default. (They do this via a collapsed currency, such as in the Weimar Republic in 1922/3 and in South America every five years or so since 1825). So this central army is a good one, but it needs protection from both an investment boom (which has inflationary implications) on the one hand, and a deep deflation and concomitant default on the other. Let us look at the other two armies to protect this core central army.

The second army is the Japanese equity market. The long hard slog of thirteen years of unwinding the bubble markets in the late 1980s has taken Japan to the opposite pole of the economic conditions seen in Anglo Saxon markets. In America and the UK, there is far too much borrowing, and long term borrowing commitments at 5% look to be a bargain. In Japan, businesses and consumers have been grappling with deflation for the last 10 years and have learnt the hard lesson that debt without inflation appears cheap to service but the principal loan gets bigger as the asset falls in value. The resultant behavioural pattern is to accommodate a lower revenue stream and both Japan corporate and consumer have done this – both are cash generative and this is what gives Japan its stability and growth prospects in any possible recovery in the world's economic situation. We do not believe that the recovery engendered by an unprecedented range of stimulants in America will prove to be anything other than a flash in the pan, but we accept that we may be wrong either as to the length of time it is before any disappointment in growth becomes apparent or because the growth does indeed come through. In this circumstance, Japan should serve us well.

The last army is to protect against financial dislocation in America and, by extension, the rest of the world. This arsenal is the 'store of value' into which fearful investors can retreat: our own preferred vehicles remain the Swiss franc, and gold (that's why we have launched the CF Ruffer Baker Steel Gold Fund). The main danger confronting the financial industry in America is the level of debt. Perversely the West appears to be approaching the long and hard lessons that Japan has had to face over the last decade. The apparent ease and cheapness of borrowing and rising asset prices has created a complacency with debt that could shatter as and when asset prices fall. In America last year, 8% of the value of residential equity was removed by way of remortgaging, and the worrying thing is that the money was not spent on yachts and high living, but the humdrum business of making ends meet. A downturn in property values in America could have serious and pretty immediate effects on economic growth there. What is true for the American citizen is also true for its government. They are running a large deficit, and the balance of imports to exports is huge: nearly half the containers leave America empty (nobody wants American products) whereas every container into America brings goods, thus widening the trade deficit. Our bet is that it will be the dollar which breaks the complacency which currently snozzles the world. A weak dollar would quickly cause problems within the financial system, not least because the world's savings are largely denominated in that currency, and a sharp fall would, *ipso facto*, destroy those savings. America has overspent well beyond the bounds which any ordinary entity could have got away with, but, like the profligate Victorian duke, it can be a long time before economic fundamentals stare such an eminent personage in the pocket. A sharply weaker dollar could well throw into question the very survival of fiat currencies over and above the plight of the dollar itself. Not good for our core army of Euro denominated fixed interest stocks, but good for gold.

The Crème Brulée Conundrum

January 2004

The economist Paul Krugman tells an economic parable which goes like this: There was once a babysitting community which swapped babysitting duties – you do it for me, and I'll do it for you later. Vouchers were issued as a future 'claim' on a babysitting, but it turned out that the vouchers were hoarded: too many babysitters, and not enough revellers. The organisers issued out more vouchers; the result was that they were no longer hoarded and a healthy equilibrium was established. So it is, he argued, with economies. Central banks print more vouchers (this time as money) and no longer do we have the deflations and the slumps which punctuated the years before World War II. 'Policy was ineffective because policy makers didn't know what they were doing.' (Krugman, again.) 'The 1970s,' he averred, 'added a caveat: if you printed too much money, you ended up with inflation.'

Printing money! Provided inflation is kept at bay, a sovereign remedy! Very interesting as a theory, but, on the back of such economists as Mr Krugman, Mr Greenspan has made it a real-time experiment. He is on the bridge of the battleship, and the rest of the crew must wait to see if it is a success. It will be a great source of debate for the economic academics and will give the journalists much upon which to comment, but we investment managers have no such luxury. Our effectiveness is judged not by the elegance of the argument, but in arithmetic. We remain deeply sceptical that the American initiative will prove a success over the long term. However, we believe that the effect of this initiative in the short term will be to push asset prices higher until such time as there is a decisive dislocation, with the potential for a significant fall in prices. In practical terms, this means that we have a preference for assets, such as gold, the Swiss Franc and euro, that are furthest removed from the dollar experiment, whilst at the same time investing in those fundamentally attractive equities, principally in Japan, Europe and the UK, that will gain some benefit from a liquidity driven rise in the markets. Our investment stance is therefore to have prepared for a sharp break in the markets, but to continue to lick the crème until the onslaught of the brulée.

What makes us sceptical? Five things

1 The first is a widespread refusal to face facts. The US official figures, for instance, are full of sand. Take employment. Every month, 40,000 individuals are arbitrarily added to the employment figures on the basis that this is the assumed number who start their own businesses during a recovery phase of the economy. The annual figure (to May 2003) was revised down by 400,000. Why the charade? Because the monthly figures are market sensitive, whereas the historic revision is not. Fannie Mae, the government sponsored mortgage agency wrote off $10 billion from its balance sheet earlier this year – but took a similar profit through its P&L. Why so? Because the profits are market sensitive, the balance sheet less so. The US economy was heralded as growing at a real rate of 8.2% annualised in the third quarter of 2003 – a sensational figure if true in a meaningful sense – but it is not. The US economy grew by 2% between the second and third quarters: annualised, this gives the published 8%. But growth in the third quarter of 2003 was only 3.5% higher than in the third quarter of 2002, and that growth was only achieved through tax cuts and yet more borrowing, plus a Dali-like treatment of the growth of computer-related sales.

2 The second is the increased size and sophistication of the markets. Sometime ago I compared Greenspan's relationship with market forces as being like a farmer with a field full of bullocks. Most of the time the farmer can control the bullocks, but sometimes he can't. Since I wrote that, the bullocks have been joined by a whole lot more. The derivative market is now four times the size of the world's annual economy. It is easy to imagine this as a zero sum game, for every winner there is an equal and opposite loser, but it is not. Dynamic hedging (you have to be clever to understand it) means that you don't take out the full insurance, but play 'chicken' with it – taking out just enough to cover today's risk position, with tomorrow being another day, another risk. But markets are not always continuous and liquid, ie, they can gap up or down with-

out allowing the hedgers to enact the trades necessary to hedge their positions. That is how Fannie Mae lost the $10 billion which it put through its balance sheet. It also makes it easier for fraud to fester and grow as derivatives allow risk to move more easily from the regulated and informed to the unregulated and ill-informed. The unedifying story of Parmalat, the yogurt company bust to the tune of £7 billion, shows how the financial community allowed Parmalat to take a bet on its own demise to sustain a lower rate of interest on its debt instruments (to help profits . . . see (1) above).

3   The third is that the real-time experiment is throwing up some old-time rhythms – and blues. The growth of credit, together with asset-price inflation is a well recognised phenomenon, and is the hallmark of a deflation with interest rates declining, but no corresponding investment opportunities in the real economy. The effect of this is for the borrowed money to flow into investments in financial and property assets, rather than commercial ones. The nature of financial institutions round the world means that different asset classes are more attractive: in the Anglo Saxon world, it tends towards a bubble in property prices. It is significant where this is not the case, such as Continental Europe, there is no such overheating. The striking feature of the stock market rally in 2003 was how similar it was to the last year of the stock market boom in 1999 – momentum driven – and the greater the risk, the more substantial the rise. Investors display the characteristics of the Bourbon regime, learning nothing and forgetting nothing from the last experience. It highlights that the dynamic of markets in 2003 has a common cause to 1999 – the response of liquidity targeted at the markets by the US central authorities.

4   The fourth reason for scepticism is that the behaviour of the US economy is not consistent with strong fundamentals. Savings at a post-war low (we are talking Berlin here, not Baghdad) and borrowings at a high. Borrowed money represents tomorrow's lunch today; savings the opposite. The figures are the wrong way round for a healthy economy. Low interest rates and high asset prices protect the investor for the moment, but both are vulnerable. There is some fear that interest rates will be driven up if the economy gets too strong, but that is to underestimate Mr Greenspan's real-time experimenting. Since high interest rates will certainly finish the good times, it is equally certain that they will not go up. The vulnerability is to asset prices. They have to go on rising to sus-

tain economic recovery, but how precarious a platform this is! It highlights the asymmetry of risk implicit in all those portfolios which are judged against stock market indices: until the bubble bursts, markets will continue to rise, but when they burst, they could fall far. Surely the wise thing is to leave the party a little early?

5 Market valuations are very extended. US profits can be calculated in several ways, but they throw up PE multiples of between 22 and 34 times (the long-run average is under 15). Dividend yields, price to book and replacement cost valuations all suggest an extremity of valuations, certainly in the American market. These high valuations first became apparent in the late 1990s, and even at the bottom of the stock market setback in 2003, they hardly dropped lower than fair value.

Marc Faber quoted Mark Twain (see also page xii) in saying, 'A thing long expected takes the form of the unexpected when at last it comes.' The tendency in the West for borrowed money to keep the economy growing adequately, and asset prices growing strongly, has looked unsustainable, arguably for more than a decade. It means that those who identified it in its early stages and acted upon it have been humiliated – houses sold at 1992 prices, and the stock market abandoned at barely half the levels ruling today. The rest of the world has gone on with the business of making money, and either ignored the doomsters, or laughed at these phantom fears. It is yet possible that this is the crackling of thorns under a pot (*Ecclesiastes* ch7, v6). The brulée may come in 2004, or it may not. We repeat that we have endeavoured to create investment portfolios which will make steady progress whether the outcome over the coming months is benign or malignant – ever mindful that cash, which produces a steady upward return, is the true rival to what we do.

Commentary

2 0 0 4

The Federal Reserve's policy of easy money continued unabated. Interest rates were down to 1% in America by June 2004. They had been 6.5% only three years earlier. One or two odd phenomena were beginning to appear in the system. In the UK first-time buyers were up 36% in March on the figure a year earlier. Money – and debts – were appearing in previously unlikely places. Arnold Schwarzenegger, the new caliph of California, unveiled plans to issue a $100 billion bond. Police in Madhya Pradesh were paid a bonus of 35 pence a month to grow moustaches in a drive to increase their authority. Hedge funds had grown in number and size – up from $300 billion in 1999 to $1.5 trillion. But the statistic which summed up the febrile financial world was the conviction of Miss Joyti De-Laurey who had stolen £4,303,259 from the accounts of her bosses, who hadn't noticed the resulting shortfall. Almost the same week, a blushingly modest Chancellor of the Exchequer announced that Britain was enjoying the longest period of sustained economic growth for 200 years.

Regulation was on the back foot. After the Enron and WorldCom scandals of the previous boom, Congress passed the Sarbanes-Oxley Act, which among other things required the chief executive and chief financial officer of public companies to appraise the internal controls over financial transactions within 75 days of the end of the company's fiscal year. It was an act with sharp teeth – and a prodigious digestive system. It cost General Electric about $30 million in extra payments to its auditors in 2003. (After Sarbanes was abolished, GE was to write off $5.8 billion from its dodgy finances and reserve a further $7.5 billion for future losses in 2008.) The London market crowed over this red-tape. Britain had unwittingly become the poster-child for *laissez-faire* regulation. No longer could it be said that London was the Wimbledon of Finance. ('We provide the tournament, but it is dominated by foreigners'.)

Back in 1999 Don Cruickshank, in a report on the banking sector for the Chancellor of the Exchequer and Tony Blair, had stated that 'regulations and competition are each other's enemies'. This was helpful advice, as it ensured that regulation could not compromise the economics of the banking system, and to the extent that competition stifled exceptional return and capital, the bank mergers accelerated. The regulators themselves hissed and spat: Sir Howard Davies, the first Chairman of the FSA, was said to have powers which transcend the Bill of Rights. Powerful he might have been, but it was the power of the Maginot Line – the regulators at the FSA and the regulators at the Bank of England didn't cover the waterfront – what Paul Tucker of the Bank of England described quaintly as an underlap. The devolving of power into two disunited bodies was to prove a significant factor in the difficulties which became apparent in later years.

Meanwhile at the G8 meeting world leaders called for oil providers to produce adequate supplies of oil to keep 'lasting global economic prosperity and stability'. At much the same time Beagle 2, which had landed on Mars, sent back to an enquiring globe a message of similar weight and authority.

The end of 2004 brought about a financial crisis in America, which once again clearly demonstrated the bankruptcy of the American financial model, and gave an insight into the extreme steps which were being taken by the Fed to keep the economy growing through the acquisition of debt. It concerned the government-sponsored entities, Fannie Mae and Freddie Mac. These two siblings, with their 'come up and see me sometime' names, were a colloquialism for the instruments of government creted to provide mortgages for American citizens (Fannie Mae was born the Federal National Mortgage Association, founded in 1938 during the Great Depression and Freddie Mac, the Federal Home Loan Mortgage Corporation, founded 1970). By the 1990s they were sizeable entities; through the decade, they became outsize – growing at 20% a year, chosen by Greenspan as the instrument to bring an effective response within the US economy to Federal Reserve policy. All central bankers know that there are just two levers at their command – interest rates, and various indirect methods of controlling the money supply. That's where those twins came in. Under US law, mortgagors can take the benefit of lower interest rates by refinancing – but are not exposed to suffering a higher rate of interest if rates go up. Re-fi became the catalyst for interest rate cuts – within ten weeks of the interest rate cut, ordinary Americans had money in their pockets to spend on consumer goods. It worked a treat at the macro level, but the twins weren't up to it, in terms of management, structure or conditioning. It was a bit like entering a wood-pigeon for a cock fight – and the feathers appeared in the autumn. The stakes were rising, and so were the risks, but the year ended with a crisis of a quite different kind – the tsunami.

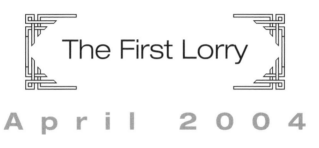

The First Lorry

April 2004

S ome time away from the markets rarely does one any harm, and for me it was a week near Amalfi, long enough to revel in a world of Italian friendliness and piracy, in evidence when the local bus broke down: we were shepherded on to the verge, and the driver flagged down passing vehicles, cajoling, threatening, pleading with them to take the stranded flotsam to their various destinations. His judgement was shrewd: the old biddy in black got the Mercedes; the Ruffers, with Panama hat and pressed trousers, the fruit lorry. But nothing in Italy was quite so bizarre as the 24 hour television programme put out by CNN Business, a 24 hour stream of consciousness about the investment markets around the world. It might be thought that the complex economic thread of events which weave and unravel through the course of a single day could certainly justify such a venture, but the monochrome message and jejune informational output was astonishing: it was like playing the Siegfried Idyll on the cornet.

It is easy – and wrong – to be snooty of such things. Whatever it may lack in finesse, it is the sort of investing-by-numbers which creates the shining bright consensus, ignoring the cobwebs of maybes, ullages of uncertainty and the patina of finely balanced pressures. The investor whose intelligence is too exquisitely refined needs to learn the lesson of Palmerston: 'What the damn fool predicted,' he complained, 'and what the wise man said could never happen, has come about'. These are times for foolishness as well as wisdom, and the art – and art it is – is to know how to take acceptable risks when the fundamentals look so dangerous.

Although the last three months appear to have been dull – sideways markets with no decisive bets to be made – we have made a significant strategic move. For the first time in years, we have begun to sell down our holdings in the fixed interest markets in the UK, and, more particularly, in Germany. The latter have served us well and, given our view of the world, this is far from obviously a correct move. I am using this Investment Review to set out the reasons that we have made it.

Our basic belief is that the world is gripped by deflationary forces, and, when the asset bubble – primarily in the housing market, but also in Western equities – bursts, this will act as a further force for deflation. In that environment, fixed interest stocks which will not default – government stocks – are the obvious investment. This is why we continue to hold fixed interest stocks. However good the fundamentals are in this big-picture sense – there are a number of possible outcomes which would show them in a sorrier light. We are concerned that there is a great deal of speculative money 'playing the yield curve': borrowing short term in the US at 1% or so, and reinvesting in ten years fixed money yielding 4%. If interest rates were to rise, the speculative money, which is playing this trade on a geared basis (you have £10 of investments on the table for every 20p you invest of your own money) would be embarrassed. A rush to sell would drive prices lower, and we could be placed in the position where the very eventuality we were investing for – financial dislocation – proved to be our downfall. It's a bit like going off to enjoy the pleasures of a public hanging, and finding out that it's you that's being hung. We retain significant, although smaller, investments in Germany because it is as far as can be from the United States in philosophy and behaviour, but the two bond markets have tracked one another, and we think may continue to do so. We live in the Lewis Carroll world of mirrors where the crisis which makes our bonds better value could be the same set of events which drives the prices of those very bonds lower.

Not a time, then, for exquisitions or cleverness. There will be time enough, no doubt, for that later.

That is the bravest thing we have done during the quarter. We are conscious that, in our attempt to find safety around the world, our investments have increasingly had an international flavour to them. This has been fine while sterling has been a docile currency, but we were somewhat alarmed by the increase in value of sterling following the decision by the Bank of England to put interest rates higher. This has abated following some US-style awful trade figures, but it has led us to take measures to protect the currency. This has involved the foreign exchange market on occasion, and it is another reason why we have reduced the German bonds.

We have increased our Swiss franc positions – that currency, too, has been weak against sterling, but that is a piffle of a premium to pay for its insurance qualities. The Swiss government bonds (not really a fixed interest play at all – more a way of holding the currency) and Swiss utilities have been in the portfolios for many a long month (and pudding-dull they have been, too). We remain cautiously optimistic on gold shares – fair weather friends, alas, since they go up when the portfolios need no help from them, and go down when they do. They are the mustard, not the meat, of the meal.

In these uncertain times, the element of the portfolio which is hardest to fill is 'investment in prosperity', which would benefit from an increasingly favourable outlook. Here, we have concentrated on Japan. The domestic sector of the stock market remains achingly cheap on most investment criteria, and the fundamentals are moving decisively in their favour. There are tentative signs of domestic reflation, falling unemployment, and corporate profits are improving, along with sentiment. The behaviour of the Bank of Japan under governor Fukui has been to support recovery rather than to look for the first opportunity to make monetary conditions tighter.

Turning back to preoccupations of the market place, sentiment has been improved by some apparently excellent payroll (US employment) figures published in the first week of April. Those who have predicted a conventional economic recovery to accompany the stock market revival of 2003 have been discomfited by the failure of this recovery to produce jobs for Americans; since the 2001 recession, job numbers have actually fallen by 1%. After very weak February figures, the March figures were much more positive. We remain unconvinced by the progress of this important indicator. The volume of total private hours of work actually fell, as did average weekly earnings. More part timers joined the workforce, and the number of full time workers fell again. The net gains in payroll employment remain healthcare, construction (a direct result of the housing boom), leisure/hospitality and administration. We continue to believe this recovery is not soundly based, and if the consumer starts to retrench (as he must do at some point), the idea of a recovery in America will seem a distant memory.

T-Bones for Tea

July 2004

The senior partner of the stockbroking firm I worked for in the early 1970s was not a man to put his head on the block. I remember him once examining the price chart of some shares. He considered first whether they were going to go up ('a distinct possibility') or down ('reasonably likely'). Would they perhaps go sideways for a while ('a fair chance')? Just in case the shares did none of these things, he added a caveat – that he did not believe in charts anyway. At the time I was rather contemptuous of his equivocation, but age has persuaded me otherwise.

Six months of directionless markets have left investors frustrated. Bold bets have not paid off – Japanese smaller companies, China, Russia, gold, commodities – all have been under the cosh: currency calls, switches from equities to bonds (or vice versa) have been a zero-sum game. Only the stock pickers have flourished – mid-cap and smaller indices are nicely up on the period. It has not suited our big picture, diversified asset allocating style, and in the next 6 months we will need either greater skill, luck or a following wind to achieve our annual aspiration of a 2x cash return.

The consensus view sees a battle between high valuations and growing profits – on this view, the passing of time is the market's friend: as profits grow, ratings become less demanding. This view is, in our opinion, considerably too complacent. First, it is a strong likelihood that US profits will not continue to grow. They are already at exceptionally high levels as a percentage of GDP – significantly the last time they were this high was 1929. Over 40% of these profits come from the financial sector (again reminiscent of 1929) – it doesn't take a genius to see that they are largely the profitable exercise of borrowing money at low rates and investing them in longer-maturing assets with a higher yield. This game, known as the carry trade, is over, the window closed either by the Federal Reserve putting interest rates up, or if the window latch is sticky, by the markets' upset at this inappropriate delay. Scale back this 40% – and it requires some optimism to believe that it will not be replaced with losses – and the US market would be dramatically overvalued.

This impasse is not an unusual one when market conditions are deflationary, and the Federal Reserve fights back with low interest rates and a policy of easy money. The last time was in 1994, an almost exact rerun of Greenspan's present-day policies, put in place to overcome the US banking crises of 1990/91. But then interest rates only got down to 3%. In those far off days, recent memories of inflation meant that 3% was startlingly low, and the banking sector was unsophisticated enough to need to be shown how to play the carry trade. This time no such lessons are necessary, and the leverage achievable by a bold operator is much greater with interest rates at 1% – sorry, now 1.5 % – than at 3%. No surprise, then, to find that US bond market leverage has reached $800bn, four times the peak in late 1993. Nor should it be a surprise if the hangover is rather worse than it was in 1994.

Although it feels as though we are in a world of uncharted territory, the pattern of the path is pretty clear. The key thing to grasp is that these events have the hallmark of deflation stamped on them, although conditions currently have more of an inflationary feel to them. Here's why. The low interest rates and easy money are a reactive force to the oversupply and lack of pricing power. They are an attempt to stop those deflationary forces gaining first a foothold and then a stranglehold on society. But, as people use cheap money to buy investments on a geared basis, they create an asset-bubble, the bursting of which is itself deflationary. The US stockmarket halved following the bursting of the technology bubble of 1999; this was despite massive easing and yet further lowering of interest rates by the Fed.

The Fed's actions were not without effect: two more bubbles were created, one in housing, and one in corporate and securitised debt. The time of the asset-bubble is rather like the killing of the cattle in a Midwest drought. It appears to be a time of feasting (T-bones for breakfast, T-bones for tea!), but thoughtful observers know that the stranglehold has begun. It is fanciful to imagine that the stockmarket will come to the rescue if asset prices should deflate in these two huge markets. And the Fed has fired its only two weapons – it is without any further conventional defence. The Fed has one unconventional weapon which all central banks possess, but which they never use except *in extremis*: they can compromise the value of their currency. There are precious few examples of this card being played deliberately, simply because it is a scorched-earth policy: Germany did it in the 1920s – so did Portugal. It has never happened to a Reserve currency, although it was forced on Sterling in the 1960s, and resulted in its devaluation of 1967. The victims of the Sterling crisis were the unsophisticated – the newly powerful oil-majors, and the colonies. This time round it would be everybody – effectively a default of that proportion of savings which are held in dollars.

This takes us to the very heart of the nature of a deflation: streams of income become more and more valuable, but less and less secure. It is well-illustrated by Equitable Life in the UK. The 'guaranteed' income became more and more attractive until the day when it wasn't attractive at all because it wasn't honoured. Nobody saw it coming at the Equitable because it was a market leader and, ahem, the smart money – the judges, the politicians, the chatterboxes – were invested in it. The moral is: beware the dollar.

So what should our coracle of an investment house do in a gathering storm? The keynotes are 'streams of income' and 'stores of value'. Investments have to have both characteristics. Our ambivalence about the government fixed interest stocks, even in Germany, is the fear that it is a promise based on a piece of paper – if the Reserve currency is compromised, what price the B-list? But income can be found elsewhere, in utilities, in PFI contracts, even in cash-generative Japanese domestic corporations – although the latter don't pay much of a dividend. The stores of value remain real assets: Swiss francs, gold – we've even flirted with New Zealand timber, but clients will be relieved to know that we think we have got over that.

Under the Rose Bush

October 2004

The year 2004 continues trendless, to the great frustration of the investment industry and investors alike. It doesn't always seem that way to the professionals – barely a fortnight goes by without an alarum or an excursion, but the alarums turn out to be false, and the excursions end up being a round trip. It is fun to laugh at those who jumped out of the charabanc at Rome only to find it was Frome, but the brutal truth is that there are more bunkers than pin flags on this year's golf course. For ourselves, a positive third quarter has moved the performance indicators towards 'adequate'; nothing much going wrong, and nothing going particularly right.

Some things have been rising, even if not the market indices. Interest rates are up in America and the UK, the oil price has risen, and so has the temperature in the political arena as the American election draws closer. Of these, the most significant is the rise in the oil price. Despite an undercurrent of belief that the new highs in the price of crude oil are driven by speculation by the hedge funds, the underlying trading position suggests that the rally is driven more by the old fashioned pressures of supply and demand. China now consumes 7 million barrels of oil a day, still a small absolute percentage (world consumption is 80 million, 26 million of which is in the United States); but in the first 8 months of this year oil consumption grew at a 40% rate in China. This is quite enough to tip the fragile balance between production and usage.

One other development is worthy of note. We identified in our January 2004 review our concern that the fever of borrowing against assets was centred around two government sponsored enterprises which facilitated the provision of mortgages for house buyers in the United States: Freddie Mac and Fannie Mae. There was a scandal last year when it became apparent that Freddie Mac had tried to 'smooth' its profits by holding in reserve some undisclosed contracts. A long awaited spotlight has now turned to Fannie Mae, Freddie's older sister, and it transpires that all has not been well in her woodshed, either. The significance of this cannot be overstated. These entities have grown at 30% per annum compound for the last fifteen years, and their book of business is now one third the size of the entire American economy. Fannie Mae and Freddie Mac has allowed the lowering of interest rates in the last five years to transmit through to extra consumer spending, through the existence of the refinancing opportunity. Essentially, when interest rates come down, house owners can get a better deal from their mortgage providers, and this has by tradition, if not by prudence, been money that has been regarded as money to be spent. It has been the transmission system by which Mr Greenspan has ensured that the lowering of interest rates has given a boost to the US economy itself. The hallmark of the monetary merry-go-round has been a lack of fear of debt and the damage that it can do to families and their dependents. A lack of rigour in Fannie Mae and Freddie Mac's accounting policies are to some extent reminiscent of the enormities of Enron, and they show a generally complacent attitude to the whole issue of debt.

Our policy in the face of this uncertainty, and our fears that the amount of borrowing in the worldwide financial community will end in dislocation, is to invest heavily in those assets which will benefit from a widespread fall in equity values. The centre of this remains the Swiss currency, a jewel which we have placed in a golden setting, since precious metals tend to reveal their qualities as a store of value when 'other leading brands' prove less efficacious. We have identified a third opportunity, which is particularly appropriate for sterling investors – gilt edged stock which mature in the years 2008 and 2009. These currently yield 4.8%, and are scarcely to be treated as an investment at all. They should perhaps better be looked at as a cash instrument, because whatever interest rates do between now and maturity, the redemption value dominates the return. The deal is: 4.8% per annum until you get your money back at redemption. We think that 4.8% could be absolutely the wrong yield base. Here's why. Imagine that our fears come to pass. Those who have borrowed money find themselves having to make distress sales of investments, and the great community of the consuming public hesitate in their desire to spend money. Equity values drop, amid widespread fears that a recession could occur in short order. Central banks around the world would respond as they always have responded, by lowering interest rates and encouraging more money into the system. But the coil in the spring is broken in the United States, where money is already freely available, and interest rates are under 2%. The same is true in Japan and, to a great extent, in Continental Europe. But the one place where it is not true is in the UK. The Bank of England has put interest rates up (to precious little effect, one might add), but with interest rates approaching 5% there is plenty of ammunition for them to respond effectively to this threat. We can see UK interest rates falling sharply, and the effect of this would be to drive gilts of this maturity sharply upwards. The art is not to buy gilts so short in maturity that you receive your money back before taking advantage of falling interests, but not so far out that an extended length of time before maturity turns the instrument into a risk asset, rather than a cash instrument. The effect of this could be to give investors 5% capital gain in addition to the 4.8% yield. For UK capital gains taxpayers, a 5% gain in the gilt is the equivalent to an 8% rise in gross terms, since gains on gilt edged securities are free of capital~gains tax. A cash instrument producing a gross return of 13%! Sometimes the best opportunities are in the back garden, under the rose bushes.

Sound Money

January 2005

N ot everything has a big meaning,' wrote Andrew Marr of the tsunami which prevailed along the oriental coastlines on Boxing Day. Perhaps so, perhaps not, but one striking thing was apparent – the dislocation between its cause and effect. It is an unsettling reminder that mankind's enterprise is occasionally overwhelmed by distant and elemental forces.

In the 19th century, economic misfortune was categorised as one such elemental force. Astute bankers such as Sir James Gilbart would observe the climate like some financial countryman and take shelter when the winds blew; the age of economic macro-management awaited the arrival of Maynard Keynes, and a rigorous collection of data which made accurate observation possible. Like the grand old Mississippi, with flood defences put in here, water volumes controlled there, and flood warning systems in place, it is easy to think the beast is now tamed. There is a settled view that economic prosperity can always be achieved provided only that its river wardens, the governors of the Central Banks – in particular, Alan Greenspan, Chairman of the US Federal Reserve – do their jobs properly. Mr Greenspan is held in high esteem. The US has completed its fifty-second consecutive quarter of annualised economic growth, up 3.2% last year, and much the same expected in 2005. The stock markets have made solid progress for eighteen months, house prices are sharply up, and household wealth is at a new high. The (US) stock market, not obviously expensive is about 15½ times price to earnings, interest rates are in goldilocks territory, inflation is steady at about 2.2%. What could disturb the susurration of the breeze in the fronds of the sweet smelling frangipani?

Not all economic statistics are so benign, to be sure, but it is to exogenous factors that the bears must turn. We believe that there is just such a powerful factor abroad today – centred on the United States.

The citizens of America are spending more than they produce: the trade deficit is now 6% of the US economy. Every second container leaves the nation's shore either empty or filled with hay. The citizens of America are spending more than they earn. Indebtedness is now 300% of the economy; it has been rising inexorably for 20 years. The budget deficit indicates that the government shares this characteristic. In a well-ordered community, these things are self-regulating: mummy says no more sweets, the hole-in-the-wall cash machine becomes bolshy, the mortgage provider turns down the latest application. But it sometimes happens that circumstances conspire to allow a community to live beyond its means without having any concern that it is doing so.

Maynard Keynes, with his careful eye for these things, analysed and described exactly this phenomenon in Europe's financial dislocation in the years following the First World War (*Present Disorders of the World's Monetary System*, Oct 1920). First there was an inflationary boom in 1919/20 – the governments made it worse by keeping interest rates too low and themselves overspending. Keynes's diagnosis is chillingly close to the mark for today. He defined monetary disorder as 'the way in which people may postpone and cover up what may be almost unendurable facts – people struggle to maintain their previous standards by living off their capital, and the whole apparatus of monetary unsoundness allows the country to put off the worst day without recognising what it is doing.' He believed that deflation, 'although its immediate evils are greater, is a derived phenomenon, brought about by the inevitable collapse of the inflationary boom'.

Today that same unsoundness – government overspend and interest rates fixed too low – is manifest in asset price inflation, not conventional retail price inflation. As house prices rise, it is possible to borrow money, spend it on day-to-day living, and still feel richer, because the value of the property has exceeded the borrowing. Since the overspend – and the borrowing – is chronic, the veil is not removed until house prices stop going up – they don't need to fall. This process of overexpenditure, once underway, is difficult to stop because no one wants to precipitate the deflationary consequences spelled out by Keynes. So, of course, it can continue for a long time.

How could events unfold from here? The early 1920s, about which Keynes was writing, give a helpful insight, because there were two distinct responses. The Anglo-Saxons plumped for sound money. Interest rates doubled in the UK (to 7%) and the US tightened its fiscal and monetary stance. Tears at bedtime, unemployment, a deep recession, but the currencies held value. On the Continent, governments broke the other way, and took no such steps. For them there was initially a 'sweet spot'; their depreciated currencies meant that their industries took the lion's share of the diminished trade, and foreigners noted how cheap the cost of living had become. The currencies of Germany and France held up well – indeed, rallied (to the great discomfiture of Keynes who was speculating against them). It was not long, though, before the earlier currency weakness caused domestic inflation, and the bankruptcy of government policy quickly undermined the Franc and the Mark. Interestingly Czechoslovakia, starting from a similar position in 1920, protected its currency with deflationary measures, and prevailed:

	Germany Marks to £	Czechoslovakia Koruna to £
Jan 1920	340	250
June 1920	160	181
Oct 1920	240	261
Oct 1921	580	385
Oct 1922	14,000	135
Oct 1923	400,000,000,000	160

This was the backcloth to the US Government's policy response to the Depression ten years later. Confronted with a stark choice between unemployment or currency destruction, the authorities plumped for the former – the consequences of the latter were too awful, too close at hand. Today, all the evidence is that the decision would break the other way – currency collapse is a distant memory – whilst depression, though many years ago, has become folklore, and was replicated in pastel shades in 1990s Japan. It is uppermost in the Fed's mind. Moral: watch out for the dollar!

We believe that, sooner or later, the citizens of the Western world will have to lower their standard of living, just as they had to after the prostration of the First World War. Then it was delayed by the 'money illusion' of inflation: today a true appreciation is disguised by asset price inflation and by the ability to borrow large amounts seemingly without any problem.

Could these grim truths become apparent in the very near future? Certainly! Could the world muddle through for a long time, with no apparent crisis? Certainly! Could this analysis be quite wrong, and the imbalances prove to be as sustainable as New York's problems in 1975 and Mexico's in 1982? That's a real possibility, but the question is whether an investment policy which ignores the present nature of those imbalances is a reckless one. In our view, it is. We make no predictions as to whether 2005 will be a crisis year, a year of impending crisis, or the year when the stormclouds disperse. We have, nevertheless, tried to create a balance of assets within portfolios which will bring about a decent return whichever of these come about.

Commentary
2 0 0 5 / 6

One of the uncanny features of a bubble is that in retrospect it appears to have been a frenzy of brilliant excitement, but at the time it seemed to be a steady un-newsworthy sequence of events of little import. Each ship that comes home is of great consequence to its owner, but for the rest of the world, it's not a big deal. So it was in the second half of the equity rally from the beginning of 2005. Those who had lost their nerve at the bottom of the market in 2003 had regained it by then. Investment again became a world of performance against indices – the escalator was going upwards, no doubt about that, but was the investor standing still, or going up – or, even, walking backwards?

The equity research of Citigroup Smith Barney, selected at random, is typical of the flavour: their 2005 predictions ('Sticking with it') expected healthy returns, the market valuation cheap to boring, profit outlook up 9% in the UK. The market delivered about twice what they expected. Their verdict on themselves: 'At least we didn't fall into the trap so common amongst the top-down bears 12 months ago. They suggested that analysts earnings forecasts were too high. Analysts' forecasts for overall market earnings were wrong, but they were too low, not too high.' Their 2006 prediction ('More of the same'): healthy returns in the stockmarket, profit outlook, up 8% in the UK, equities up 10% to 15%. Their verdict on themselves for 2006: 'At least we didn't fall into the trap so common amongst the bearish strategists. Some suggested that analysts' forecasts were too high and that 2006 would be a year of profit downgrades. Quite the opposite.' Their 2007 prediction the bull market continues.

Those who stood up against the prevailing wind made little headway. Bill White of the Bank of International Settlements warned the Jackson Hole conference (the annual meeting of the world's central bankers) about the risks to the credit system – nobody, not even the clever ones, took any notice.

The facts were relentless in favour of the bulls. Milestones were passed: HSBC's £9 billion reported in early 2005. Economic growth hot, but not furious – around 3.5% per annum. The key was not to be – in Citigroup Smith Barney's words, a 'top-down' analyst. The 'bottom-uppers' (those who looked at investment opportunities company-by-company) could see that if a company substituted debt for equity by buying back its shares, and shaving its capital-at-risk, then quite modest economic growth translates into strong earnings growth. Equally, a modest slowdown would translate into a significant slowdown in earnings. Not surprisingly, the top-downers (the big picture men) saw the phenomenon as an increase both of reward and risk. Hindsight proved them wrong in 2005 and 2006. The band played on: by the end of 2005 the market had recovered by 75% from its low point – but was still 16% below its high nearly five years before.

But a cloud no bigger than a man's hand was observable in the US mortgage market. It had been clear for a longish time that mortgages had been given not only to those who had difficulty reading, but also to those who could read, and read the wrong sorts of things. By the fall of 2006, the mortgage failure rate started to rise sharply. Nobody took much notice, but everybody knew that there was a great deal of leverage based on mortgage collateral, some of it pretty dodgy. The branch on which the investment community sat felt solid, so they took no notice of the chainsaw at work cutting into the branch between themselves and the trunk.

Crossing the Rubicon

April 2005

Whimsies are often irritating, and none more so than the thought of 'what would it be like if, one day, there wasn't any news! What would the newspapers do?!' The answer to these fatuous questions is manifest each week to readers of the *Herts & Essex Observer*, but nevertheless it is something which has come to mind as I write a commentary on the events of the first three months of 2005. The stock market indices dropped a bit in Dollar terms, but rose slightly in Sterling. The oil price went down, and then up; the Japanese market went up, and then down.

Small events, however, can be telling. When Caesar crossed the Rubicon in 49BC, he passed over an insignificant stream outside Ravenna. But the significance was enormous – an ancient Roman law forbade any General from so doing and this act of treason plunged the Roman Republic into a civil war. The art of the prophet, no less than the historian, is to identify those insignificances which are in fact loaded with meaning.

We see a rubicon in the downward move in the one month US LIBOR futures price, which has moved from 96.5 at Christmas time to about 95.7 at the end of March. This rubicon is scarcely a puddle, but its significance lies in the fact that it prices in a year end expectation of US interest rates of more than 4%. At the moment, the interest rate is 2.75%, having been raised from 2.5% on 22 March.

Why the significance? Last year, I painted a picture of the Federal Reserve (the central bank of the United States) being increasingly boxed-in by events. The lowering of interest rates in America in 2002/3 to 1% brought about a mountainous increase in borrowing, the proceeds of which were largely invested in almost riskless US Treasury stock of three year duration yielding 3%. Baboons couldn't grasp it, but most other primates could see that the more you borrowed at 1%, the more you could invest at

3% and – here's the point that the baboons missed – you got to keep all those two percents. Forty two percent of all US profits came from the financial sector in the first half of 2004 (it was about 6% when I started in the City in the mid1970s): the carry trade was of Olympic dimensions.

This massive distortion of economic activity helped liquidity in the US, but it could not last for ever, and the question arose 'what would happen to this carry trade when interest rates start to go up?' However unrisky three-year Treasuries might be, if the entire population of America paid off their borrowings and tried to sell these assets, there could be dislocation. So Greenspan went gently on rate increases, and employed a symphony orchestra to sound the warning note that they were on the way. 'It is time to leave the party,' he bellowed, 'when the police arrive, they will round up all the pretty girls who are misbehaving.' But the message was undermined by the tacit understanding that the police were still someway distant and peddling towards the party on bicycles. The result was that the carry traders were not frightened, and far from the phenomenon being curtailed it has taken on an altogether more malevolent form. If interest rates are approaching 3% then there is no point in investing in 'riskless' assets yield-ing the same amount. Carry traders have been seeking investments with enough yield to justify their borrowing costs – and these are, by definition, more risky. Low volatility in the marketplace, and no dislocation … yet … has disguised the inherently riskier nature of these investments.

Nine months on, things seem to be reaching a climax. Although the appetite for risk has increased, the outlook is considerably less benign than it has been. The dilemma for Greenspan has always been that if he puts interest rates up significantly, a crisis will be created from the leverage in the carry trade. If, on the other hand, he fails to put interest rates up, then the markets will sense that Greenspan lacks credibility – unwilling or unable to do the necessary thing in the light of current circumstances. The most dangerous phenomenon in this regard would be a resurgence of infla-tion. We have long spoken of the essentially deflationary forces at work in the world, but it is perfectly possible for weakness in a currency to engen-der domestic inflation. The deflationary busts of Germany in the early 1920s or South America in the last 30 years saw prices in local currencies go up enormously, but this was a reflection of the failure of those local cur-rencies to be a store of value – a phenomenon much more common in defla-tionary conditions than inflationary times. This is what is beginning to hap-pen in America. Greenspan has been much helped by the official inflation statistics in America which have routinely shown unrealistically low inflationary figures (thereby boosting productivity, but that is a different story). The markets now sense that the cost of living in America is moving up uncontrollably. Oil at $60 a barrel is its harbourmaster, but there is a legion of other factors which point in this direction. The markets now desire what the dollar – and by extension the United States – needs: higher interest rates to combat it. The LIBOR future pricing tells us that markets not only desire it, but they are expecting it. But can the carry trade take it? The financial community goes on piling up the borrowing just at the time when such risk taking is becoming increasingly dangerous. The launch of a $600m, 7x leveraged mortgage backed securities (MBS) fund by UBS shows the former, and the potential downgrading of General Motors' debt to 'junk' status, shows the latter.

The spread of our investments has not changed much over the past few months. We have a great deal of money which stands to benefit from a financial dislocation – our Praetorian guard is held in the form of Swiss francs, and we remain keen on gilts of five year duration in the UK. Japan continues to intrigue us, and has been modestly beneficial during the quarter; our happiest allocation has been in the oil sector, which we think will continue to prosper while the markets hold firm. We should have been equally keen on commodities generally, but our nerve is not quite sufficient. The overall returns from the portfolio have been positive but unexciting – given the Chinese nature of the financial world, and its curse (may you live in interesting times), we are reasonably pleased with this outcome.

Contradictiousness

July 2005

Captain Frederick Burnaby, a 19th-century swell, heard that the Foreign Office had forbidden all journeys to Russia and thereupon decided to ride to Khiva. His nanny was not surprised, for she always dubbed him 'contradictious'. We have an unpleasant feeling that his nanny would recognise a similar characteristic in us. For ten long years – maybe more – we have advocated investment in the longest duration of quality government bonds. Every quarter the valuations have shown a solid phalanx of German bunds, and from time to time there has been a regiment – sometimes an army – of British War Loan, issued to the sound of the Somme gunfire and paying a coupon of 5% (a Conservative government reduced it to 3.5% *pour encourager les autres*). The arguments which took us into these investments are now routinely believed. The deflationary forces manifest in the world today are increasingly well understood; the difficulty of finding secure streams of income in such an environment is now a pressing problem for investors. Long government bonds are the natural place to benefit from these twin developments, and yet we have sold the whole lot of them. A clear case of 'contradictiousness', as nanny might have said.

Why then have we retreated from a long-held strategic investment, just as it appears to be so right? It is only partly a matter of price. In the ever-lasting assessment between the balance of risk and reward, higher prices always disadvantage the fixed interest sector, since the 'what you get' is a constant: a steady stream of nominal income until redemption. In a growing business, by contrast, a company's equity may actually get cheaper as the price goes up, if the fundamentals are improving at a faster rate than the shares. However, deflation can continue to make fixed interest investments attractive at levels which in past environments would have looked enormously expensive. So high prices are not the issue.

The real reason for the shift in allocation has more to do with the increase in risk than the paucity of any future reward. The mantra for deflationary times is that streams of income become more and more valuable, but what can default will default. Up until now, we have looked on the benign part of this mantra; we have treated the fixed interest market as the classic means of producing a safe stream of income. Governments rarely default, and one can therefore concentrate on the increasing value of the stream of income, and the more of that future income there is, and the longer it lasts, the more valuable today will be the value of that instrument. Hurrah for long dated bonds!

But what can default, will default. There is a circumstance where the fixed interest market is far from safe, and that circumstance is when money is no longer acting as a store of value. Those of us who lived through the 1970s need no reminding of the uncomfortable nature of that period. The world, particularly the western world, is heavily leveraged, with the consumer using the strength of the house in his balance sheet to continue to borrow, and the carry trader trying to squeeze the last ounce of effectiveness of borrowing at low interest rates, and investing for a higher running yield. In short, we are worried about default.

Why do we worry about default? Rising debt has also had a worrisome effect on asset values. It has changed the very nature of the economy – asset prices have become the driver of economic activity; consumers will only spend if personal balance sheets are strong enough for further borrowings. Every day, every month, every year, there is a wave of goods and services pouring in from the East. Every day, every month and every year, it has been met by a surge of demand from the consumer. In the 1990s the consumer spent his wages which were going up – now, there being no great increase in wages, he is spending money he has borrowed. Our concern is that the current equilibrium (loads of goods matched by lots of demand) will give way when asset prices hit the buffer. The result will be financial dislocation. That means default – too many claims on too few assets: too many bottoms for too few chairs when the music stops.

The key to the relative effectiveness of the fixed interest market as an investment allocation depends on who bears the brunt of this default. At one extreme, the borrower takes the burden of the problem. When the bubble burst in Japan in 1990, the Yen remained uncompromised, and individuals and corporations had to pay off their mountainous debts through belt-tightened savings. This led to deflationary conditions, such that the more the Japanese saved to pay down their debts, the more burdensome those remaining debts became. Fifteen years on, and Japanese society has scarcely recovered from this dislocation.

The other extreme is where no attempt whatsoever is made to preserve the currency. If the borrower had not been Japanese 1990s style, but German, 1923 style, the million Reichmarks which he borrowed would have become worthless: he would have been able to repay the debt with the cost of a decent lunch, excluding the wine. Knowing which bottom will end up on the remaining chair is essential. In one circumstance, the stream of income delivered through a fixed interest stock designated in a sound currency becomes by far the best investment: in the other circumstances, the default falls firmly on the lender – and the owner of a government stock will find that he has lent his money to a borrower with unsound currency.

We have long been conscious of this as a theoretical concern. We now regard this as a practical issue. We regard a sharp fall in asset values as a distinct possibility – after an immodest lunch, perhaps even a probability. The question is whether western society has the resilience to allow the over-borrowed to take the full consequence of their actions. Take housing in this country. Those over the age of 45 are old enough, and perhaps clever enough, to own their own house, and to take the benefit of the relentless rise in capital value. Those under the age of 25 have probably not addressed the issue of the price of buying a property yet. But between these two ages lies a generation of middle-class and middle-income family men and women, who would simply be crushed by a sharp fall in house prices. The Japanese experience shows that 15 years is scarcely enough to correct the imbalance. A generation of victims! Is it not much more likely that we will have a situation where the grief is shared by borrower and lender alike? This would occur through compromise in the underlying value of the currency. There is no need for a Weimar wipeout: a partial default of the currency, combined with a real fall in asset values would have a very 1970s feel about it. It would be bad both for equities and the fixed interest market: hence our decision.

The observant among you will have spotted that the portfolios are still laced with long bonds, denominated in Swiss Francs. We believe this to be the exception which proves the rule. There is an element of the two way bet here. If the default is Japanese in nature, then long bonds in all the major currencies will do well. There is no reason to suppose that the Swiss will be any different, although it will seem a rather eccentric place to go to obtain benefits just as easily achieved in the home market. On the other hand, if the situation involves currency compromise, then we believe that the Swiss Franc will be a major beneficiary, since it has a proven track record in thriving in difficult economic conditions. In such a circumstance we think that the major gain will be in the value of the Swiss Franc and long dated Swiss bonds there will be an effective way of holding a lifeboat currency.

My Catechism

October 2005

I am just young enough not to have had to learn the Collect of the week each Sunday when I was at prep school (hurrah for the seventeenth after Trinity – only three lines long). But I certainly had to recite my catechism (Q: What is a parable? A: An earthly story with a heavenly meaning.) This quarter's review is my economic catechism. Some of you will have heard bits of it – indeed, many may have heard most of it – at investment meetings in Wigmore Street. If the thrust of it is true, then it bears repetition. The links between today's situation and the 1970s – set out in the penultimate paragraph – are a recent refinement of thought (and a very nasty one, too, if I may say so).

The starting point is that directionally the world has moved from being inflationary to having a deflationary bias. Rather than defining inflation/deflation as prices going up/down it is better to think in terms of the relationship between a buyer and seller. Put simply, a single purchaser of tomatoes at a county fair with three tomato sellers is more likely to get a better deal than three such purchasers from a single stall.

Over the last twenty years, the number of the world's stallholders has increased. The fall of communism has released Eastern Europe, and indeed Russia itself, from the shackles of a command economy. The Pacific Rim has been growing at 10% a year since the 1950s, but that is 10% of a much larger figure today. And over it all, the productive capacity of China vomits its beneficence into all corners of the earth.

When supply is plentiful, times of prosperity are sun-kissed indeed. Prosperity brings profits, good wages, good bonuses, and where these three graces are found, animal spirits will be in attendance. A superabundance of supply satisfies a whirlwind of demand; in earlier times, the inherent shortage of supply was unable to cope with such demand – the resulting bottleneck and price rises had to be choked off with rising interest rates. The stop-go of those inflationary times has given way to a more gradual but nevertheless powerful growth which continued for many years – in the case of the US, 37 uninterrupted quarters of growth from 1991-2000.

Alas, while prosperity is golden in a deflationary period, a downturn is unusually nasty. In a world where supply exceeds demand, a recession becomes a slump very easily – such slumps punctuated the nineteenth century, and, most famously in the 1930s. In those days of innocence, central bankers and governments had no idea that these alarums and excursions had anything to do with them. They were the monetary equivalent of a bad harvest – an act of God. No longer. Today the central authorities, exemplified by Alan Greenspan, beady, imaginative, watchful and radical, understand that such a mismatch between supply and demand must be avoided – avoided at all costs. Moreover, Greenspan has been aware of this danger at least since the middle 1990s. The key to averting its onset is to concentrate on keeping demand healthy – the only way of dealing with the supply side seems to be protectionism, which most able-bodied economists agree is a wasteland policy.

How do you keep demand going when an economy is naturally rolling over towards recession? If the consumer has no extra money to spend, then he must borrow. That requires an easy accessibility to borrowings, and Greenspan observed that the government-sponsored mortgage providers, charged with giving Mr America a chance to own his own property, were well placed in this regard. They have grown tenfold in the last 20 years; it is possible to see the Fed's hand in this extraordinary increase. Lower interest rates, coupled with rising asset values, are a terrific spur to a growth in borrowing. Say you borrow $700,000 at 7% on a $1 million property ($49,000 a year interest, leaving $300,000 of equity). Two years later, you borrow another $300,000 to bring the debt to $1 million, when interest rates have reduced to 5%. The total interest burden is almost unchanged: up from $49,000 to $50,000. If the house is now worth $1.4 million, your equity has gone up from $300,000 to $400,000 – and you've got the extra $300,000 of borrowings to spend. So a policy aimed at encouraging rising asset values, and increased borrowings has been a key driver of Fed policy.

And the policy has certainly worked. Asset prices, particularly home prices throughout the US, have risen relentlessly for 15 years and, in the last 5 years, quickly. Borrowings have also done what was expected of them. In the last generation they have doubled as a percentage of GDP in America from 150% to over 300%. And the last piece of the jigsaw –

spending – has also come up trumps: the savings ratio is now negative for the first time since Gettysburg.

In our view, this is certain to end in tears. Not because it's immoral, not because there is a rule which says that the credit machine blows up at 302% of GDP. (Why not 350% or 450%?) The reason that it will end in tears is because it requires asset prices to rise, and one day they won't.

Increased borrowings raise the stakes, both for good and for bad. If you own a £1 million house and it doubles, you are £1 million richer. If you own two £1 million houses, with borrowings of £1 million, then a 'double' increases your worth to £3 million, but a halving of value destroys your entire wealth. The world has grown comfortable with the first part of this truth, whilst it seems quite unaware of the second – but at moments of crises, everybody discovers the truth at the same time. A flight out of assets into cash (in grown up talk this is 'liquidity preference') makes the market seize up completely. It is one of the eternals of the investment world, and can be found in most second division Victorian novels. It is dislocative, it is frightening, and it leaves the greedy immeasurably poorer.

The difficulty with accommodating a future catastrophe within a portfolio is clear. It might have been possible to have spotted the condition of the New Orleans' levees, but quite another to know when a hurricane might bring about the tragedy of their bursting. By the time that it was clear that Katrina was a threat, it was far too late. So, too, for us. We are preparing for an eventuality which might be a long time away, and which could take more than one form, and it will only be at that point that we will know whether the portfolios are built on rock or on sand. Our absolute preoccupation is to make every preparation that we can, and trust that our judgements are right. This judgement is built around the thought that the core of all financial crises is the domino-like mischief of default. Defaults are dislocative; as obligations fall due and are not met then reasonable expectations of future cashflow go begging. If such a default is on the cards, the burning question becomes: who will default? What will default? Developments over the last year have been the backcloth to our startling (at least it was so to us) decision to sell our fixed interest stocks which had served us so well over many years.

Our Summer investment review spelt out the reasons for this, and the argument is set out briefly below. It turns on the nature of the default which occurs in the aftermath of a financial dislocation. The historic pattern was that the burden fell on the borrower. When borrowers get into difficulties, asset values fall, and the crying need is for spendable streams of income. In such an environment, government bonds are the only satisfactory haven, as government bonds do not default.

But there is a circumstance when bonds do effectively default – when the currency is compromised, and here the lesson to be learnt is from the 1970s. The world today is very unlike that period, which was a time of chronic supply shortages and a labour force at the height of its economic and political power. Then, when the cake got smaller, the unions demanded the same calorie intake as before, and to everyone's amazement, especially the Keynesian economists, peacetime inflation erupted. Governments and central banks (the same thing in the UK in those days) were afraid to put interest rates up to levels unprecedented in a non-inflationary era: so they kept them low. A horse born to cowardice out of confusion: and the result was a racehorse. The default which had threatened the whole financial system had a resolution: inflation relieved the nominal damage done by the asset destruction, and negative real interest rates ensured that lenders shared the burden of the borrower for the egregious exuberance of former days. In the 1970s, it happened by accident: caused by excessive workforce demands and craven governments. Today, unions are flat on their backs with a world workforce which has roughly doubled in the last 20 years. Moreover the underlying problem is an overabundance of supply, not a supply shortage. This is deflationary, not inflationary. But, crucially, central banks now understand the mechanism to spread the grief of a default between borrower and lender. They know that a generation of young middle-aged would suffer all the pain of a housing price collapse, while their parents merely take fewer Saga holidays. The central authorities can engineer both the compromise of the currency, and the negative real interest rates; they can achieve by diktat what economic forces imposed on the world a generation ago.

The consequences of such a course would be profound for investors. It would mean that there is no protection either in equities in general, or in the fixed interest markets. Our response to this is to invest in Switzerland, in gold, in 5 year gilts and one or two other things. It would be extremely likely that, in this environment, high marginal taxation would ensure that the discomfiture of the lender was complete. In such an environment cash itself is far from riskless. With index-linked gilts yielding 1.1% real, there is little protection in this asset class either. At the moment, the portfolios are cantering along in a summer sun which feels distinctly Indian. In the hatshop, we are at the Sou'wester counter.

What Are We Aiming To Do?

January 2006

I have quoted the old jingle before: 'Aim at nothing in particular, and you can be sure of hitting it'. The purpose of this review is to explain what we are trying to do, and how we set about doing it.

Ruffer was set up in the autumn of 1994 to pursue a novel way of investing. Instead of trying to 'beat the indices', we set out to make money for clients. We advertised this eccentric approach under the banner, 'the difference between aiming at comparative and absolute performance'. For a number of years we appeared as quixotic as a car manufacturer who hopes that his vehicle will get you from A to B, while his peers are offering their customers a transformed social life, a symphony of engineering and *Vorsprung durch Technik*. When the bad markets came in 2000 the ability to get to a given destination seemed rather *à propos*. The phrase 'absolute performance' was an honest description of what was in the tin, but it subsequently became a financial cliché. Today, in so far as it has a discernible meaning, 'absolute return' is a synonym for 'high fees'.

Our meaning remains as it was then: the satisfying of what we described as 'the hopes and fears of real people who want to preserve their assets come what may, and to see them grow over the course of time'. To do this, there are two requirements: trying never to lose money on a one year rolling basis, and to produce a return sufficiently ahead of that available to cash on deposit to justify the risk and the cost.

The difficulty with this approach is that the requirement of not losing money points to investment in riskless assets, and, apart from cash on deposit, they do not exist. All investment is, by definition, an investment in assets that can go down as well as up. On the face of it, we are faced with an impossibility – the creation of a portfolio made up entirely of risk, which has the characteristic of risklessness.

The best way of getting good returns is by always being right. Alas, this is a manifest impossibility, but the complexity and diversity of stock markets creates anomalies, and these anomalies are magnified by the behaviour of investors whose passions and disgusts are very often irrational and routinely result in mispricing. It is like playing roulette on a wheel whose machinery is intermittently defective, and whose croupier is drunk. It's not as good as owning a casino, but it does change the odds: when the odds are wrongly priced you need to be right less often.

Which is just as well, as evidenced by our investment reviews stretching back to 1995, which we sent out to clients last summer in book form. In 1995, we were bearish, as we were in 1996, 1997 and 1998. In 1999 we were still bearish, the same pattern being noted for 2000, 2001 (very bearish), 2002, 2003 (quite bearish) and 2004. In 2005 we were also bearish. Over the period the stock market indices rose in eight of the years and fell in only three of them – we were wrong three-quarters of the time. And yet over those eleven years we have handsomely beaten these self-same stock markets, and we outperformed our target of twice the return over cash, doing so in each calendar year except three: 1999 (all square), 2001 (up 5.5%) and 2002 (up 3.0%). Being wrong eight times out of eleven sounds like a multiple failure of Lady Bracknell's lost parent test. But, if the odds are right, then the arithmetic of the performance will be right as well.

Nor should it be a surprise that our natural stance has been bearish. This is partly because caution is the best basis for preserving money, and partly because the underlying outlook is worrisome. Thus the bearish bias is a simple reflection of the fact that we are always looking at what could go wrong, not at what could go right for us. Part of this desire to protect the portfolios is, of course, to be bearish of being bearish – if you have too many investments in 'fear' then these will tend to go down, not merely stand still, in a bull market. (This is what caught us out in 1999, incidentally.)

The second reason, apparent to those who have waded through our collected investment reviews, is that we think that the US Federal Reserve's monetary experiment will end in maelstrom, and that it could have done so at any point in the last eight years. Greenspan is like the driver of a car whose brakes have failed at the top of a very long hill, and who has been enormously adept at keeping the car on the road through an imaginative use of the steering wheel. Well done him on the steering, but every successful negotiation of the bends leaves the car travelling that much quicker.

Central to the construction of the portfolios is to try to take the element of timing out of the risk of the portfolio – so that it will have enough things going well in the good times to keep it making money, but with enough protection in the downturn to continue this process. We therefore favour investments which are placid over those which are more exuberant. For instance, both the Swiss Franc and gold are stores of value in a financial hurricane: the Swiss Franc is the Fiat and gold is the Ferrari. But in the summer of 2005 gold shares were the only mining companies not to have gone up in a general commodities boom: this made them 'safe', notwithstanding their volatility, and so we bought heavily into them. Stock picking is also an essential part of the exercise. This is entirely the preserve of our research department whose job is to find specific companies in which to invest, given our views on the investment climate. In this they have been successful over an extended period of time. By picking good'uns our portfolios are somewhat protected in bad markets and punch above their risk-adjusted weight in good ones.

One of the things one looks for in companies is stability. Here one might quote an example of a stock which has not yet come right for us: Yamazaki Baking. We think that Japan will succumb in due course to retail price inflation, and this should be very good for retailers. One of the cheapest of these, judged by price to sales, is Yamazaki Baking, a rather downmarket and only adequately managed equivalent of Greggs the Baker in the UK. Nothing on the horizon suggests that there is any reason to be buying Yamazaki except its cheapness. The question for us is not the conventional one, 'why buy it?'; it is a question of risk-control: if it takes two or three years for conditions we expect to become apparent, will Yamazaki have drifted into trouble in the meantime? In this context, its dullness is a virtue. We are happy (at least, I think we are happy) to await events. Clients will have seen a nearly complete absence of US companies in the portfolios (except possibly mining and oil stocks), not much in the UK, but lots of it in Japan. Japan has suddenly become everybody's favourite market but, for us, the issue is not how much money we are likely to make there, but how much money are we in danger of losing if the markets turn sour. We made glorious gains in Japan last year, but we needed to because we had over two-thirds of our money invested in misery and dismay when the sun was out.

We are by no means alone in our sombre assessment of the outlook, but most of the bears are commentators, not practitioners whose actions are more important than their words. The significance of having participated in this explosive rally means that we can remain on the front foot as regards how to invest in the current climate. We go into 2006 with around two thirds of the portfolios positioned for a sharp financial setback. In all honesty, I cannot say that either we, or our clients, would have had the confidence to do this if we had largely missed out on the bull market. Moreover, this two-thirds position does not represent a sudden knee-jerk response to events, in the hope that we have just pulled our bets off the table in time. We have been running with this sort of percentage in 'fear' investments throughout the period. Good stock picking has helped, and our correct identification of some important 'each way bets' (long bonds denominated in Swiss Francs, the Japanese domestic market and gold shares in particular) have been responsible for this.

I am hesitant to write these words in a widely circulated review, since they are a hostage to fortune. By the time you read this we might well be drafting one of those heart-sinking letters well known in the industry which urge you not to lose your nerve despite heavy losses sustained – letters usually written when the evidence points unwaveringly to the opposite conclusion. Nevertheless, we have a great deal of latitude in what we do for our clients, and an explanation of the philosophy which underlies our actons seems to me to be an important element in the building up of trust between us.

Alas, Poor Eeyorick?

April 2006

The stock market rally is now three years old, and the exuberance of 1990s style money making is part of the financial scenery again. There is one big difference from last time – then, there was a theme, whereas today it is a case of 'prizes for everyone'. At the turn of the millennium new technology was the buzzword. If you believed the script, you not only knew what shares to own, but which shares not to own. There was no price too high to pay for Yahoo and Baltimore, but the same thought caused investors to fear that bus companies would never be the same again in this exciting world of inventiveness – and they went down.

Today it is not at all like that. The market seems to believe six (mutually) impossible things before breakfast, and almost all risk assets have responded positively. For those who believe that the economy is powering ahead, commodity shares and Far Eastern stock markets beckon and have offered the sorts of returns normally found only in Peru and Ukraine when the sun is out. For those who think the exact opposite, and that there are deflationary – and possibly depressionary – conditions ahead, long dated fixed interest stocks have been impressive performers. Fixed interest stocks of lower quality (whether sovereign debt, asset backed debt or corporate debt) have gone up by most, yet a fear of recession should widen these spreads, not narrow them. Cyclical stocks have done well, but an inverted yield curve (short rates higher than longer rates) gives a contrary message. Rising interest rates in America normally signal the end of a bull market in financials – but the bulge bracket banks have been stellar performers over the last year. At a time when leverage is at its highest and savings rates in the west at their lowest, all the traditional indicators of stress – volatility and yield spreads – are at generational lows.

Of all the impossibilities in the market place today, none is more marked than the savings conundrum. It is easy to see that the world is awash with money – it is the money which puts the purr into the fat cats (and also the purr into purchases), but there is a marked difference in view as to where the money has come from. The Federal Reserve, and several well-respected commentators believe that there is, to quote Dr Bernanke's phrase, 'a savings glut'. Although they concede that the savings ratio in America is negative – they are net borrowers – and is at the lowest level for decades in both the UK and Japan, they believe that this combined shortfall is more than counterbalanced by the flow of savings from the Far Eastern and other exporters whose surpluses are providing the necessary liquidity into the West. We emphatically believe that the liquidity is not a savings glut, but is a result of leverage – a pyramid of borrowing. The growth of US indebtedness has occurred independently of the savings preferences of Asia and Europe. Nobody in America asked permission of overseas investors to issue its bonds. It merely offered debt at rates that it knew would be considered attractive. The repackaging of US mortgages and home equity loans as securities was a triumph of financial engineering, credit enhancement and structured products. This issue is critical because savings can be spent, but leverage has to be repaid, or it defaults. We have declared our hand; the easy money is borrowed money, but an important aspect is that the market is backing both these diametrically opposed arguments. The purpose of this note is to analyse why this has been so, and what happens if the glittering prizes turn out to be chrome-plated.

This broad-church theology where there is no fundamental compass, is both a rare phenomenon, and a dangerous one. It sometimes feels that the world we live in is unprecedented, but a similar situation arose in the 1930s, and, while it was worldwide, it took its purest form in the UK stock market. The stock market had bottomed in the depth of the Depression in 1932, and then staged a remarkable recovery which peaked at the end of 1936. The parallel with today is to be found in the market's conditions of that year. Real interest rates were negative (by about 2.5%), and long dated bonds gross gave no real yield at all with inflation running at between 2.5% and 3.0%. It was a time when debentures traded almost inevitably above par, whatever their coupon, and preference shares of companies which were in profit were even more expensively priced, demonstrating that yield spreads were unprecedentedly narrow. The yield on the equity market went to a low of 3.4%.

The background to this was one of seemingly uncontrollable inflation some fifteen years before giving way to conditions where the opposite horrors of deflation became apparent. The Depression began in the spring of 1930 in the UK (not as badly hit as most other countries, thanks to Sterling's devaluation in September 1931). The Government started a policy of easy money from the autumn of 1932, so that three-month Treasury bill yields fell from about 2.5% to 0.5%; how many people know that in 1935 the Government issued a gilt with a 1.0% coupon: the Treasury 1% 1939/41? Commercial conditions remained poor in the mid-1930s, so the easy money which accompanied the low interest rates did not find its ultimate use in the commercial field (although the government did spend a great deal of money on building council houses through this period). Instead, the money found its way into the financial arena, and the deflationary conditions of the commercial world ensured that asset price inflation did not spill out into retail prices. Long-dated government bonds became the natural home for the cheap and easy money. Although the inflation rate had averaged –1.6% a year over the previous ten years, prices were on a clear rising trend from the latter half of 1935, and sharp commodity price rises meant that gilts were unattractively priced. Investors tried to 'finesse' their purchases by buying other assets with a higher yield, momentarily overlooking the concomitant danger that went with it. The mispricing of gilts resulted in a general mispricing of assets as the relationship between gilts and those other assets remained in place.

This seems to me to be a remarkable pre-cursor of today's position. Today we look back on the period fifteen years ago when inflation was very high and, in the early years of this century, when disinflationary forces looked as though they might get out of hand. Although the general populace never feared deflation, it is perfectly clear that Alan Greenspan absolutely did, and his Central Bank response at the Federal Reserve in 2002 was precisely that of the Bank of England in 1933: cheap money and plentiful money. Two factors are different in significant detail, but they happen to cancel one another out. The deflation of the early 1930s was real and terrible; the deflation of the early 2000s was feared, but never became anything more than a disinflation. This meant that the option of financial assets in the middle 1930s over commercial assets was overwhelming, much more so than today. On the other hand, pre-war monetary transmission was very much of the Austin Seven variety: simple but effective. Today, with securitisation and hedge fund activity, monetary transmission is massively more sophisticated and its force uncontrollable: the relative attractions of financial assets may be less, but there is a corresponding surge of purchasing power as opposed to a happy gurgle in the 1930s.

Those who study the Boys' Wonder Book of Financial Statistics will know that 1936 is the year which is quoted as the one after which investors suffered the longest period of time before they saw their money back in real terms: 49 years. It is true that world war, socialism and high taxation all elongated this period beyond its natural course, but it is nevertheless a testimony to how overvalued the stock market was. The unreality of 1936 was broken by the realisation that the conditions of over-easy monetary conditions had delayed the inflationary consequences, but had not extinguished them. In 1937 the UK inflation rate touched 6%. Such was the broadly based upward move in asset classes that many people, who had quite forgotten how good they were at investment, prospered whatever they did. The 'selection by pin' stock picker did pretty well (as he has done recently); the best stock pickers, now as then, have that wide eyed incredulity which bachelors sometimes get when dining alone with a newish companion.

The question that must be asked is whether 1936/2006 is a true comparison, or merely on a par with the observation that Hamlet and Piglet both sound pretty porcine, and have the same number of letters in them. It is certainly true that the financial system is as different today as the stealth bomber is to the wartime Lancaster. But markets still respond to the same stimuli, and there is enough of a 'rhyme' for us to see that today's pressures are likely to have a less than benign outcome. One doesn't after all, have to see a photograph of someone with the measles to know that one is better off without it.

Confidence and Credit: The Naughty Sisters

July 2006

O ur reviews have been increasingly shrill over the last year, because we have felt that the investment arena has been looking increasingly dangerous. This quarter a thunderstorm broke.

If any of our investors imagine that this is Ruffer's finest hour, they should read on – and examine the quarterly performance where they will (probably) see a smallish diminution in the value of the portfolio.

The market setback began on 9 May, and commentators are undecided whether this is an unwinding of some of the more speculative aspects of the recent bull market, or the start of something more sinister. We unhesitatingly opt for the former interpretation – this is emphatically not the first unravelling of a dislocating market. A bull market has a tendency to go up at a faster rate the longer it continues, and that was certainly a feature of world conditions in the latter half of 2005, and the start of this year. The more exotic the investment, the more quickly it rose: investor confidence provided the inclination, and easy credit provided the opportunity. These twin sisters of adultery always promise more fun than they deliver, and the subsequent decline was symmetrical in its operation: the markets tripped up, and those who had run the fastest had the worst grazes on their knees.

While this was happening, there was a kennel of hounds which did not bark. Credit spreads barely widened at all in the first month of the crisis. Market volatility, as measured through the VIX Index briefly doubled, and then settled back at the low levels prevailing in the early spring. Bank shares, representing corporations sensitive to any financial uncertainty, were not unusually weak. Debt issuance has not missed a beat, and – alas for our portfolios – investments which should do well in a financial dislocation were quite unmoved by the brouhaha. The Swiss Franc did nothing, nor the Norwegian Kroner: five-year gilts dropped a little and gold – a curious combination of commodity and currency – fell sharply. This latter development was costly for the portfolios.

And yet it is hard to feel that we are mistaken in holding these investments in fear. They have proved, however, to be insurance vehicles for the catastrophe, not for the routine mishap. The result is that the bent bumpers and scratched metalwork of portfolios are not covered by the insurer. We remain confident that these protections will work when it matters.

The irony is that the synthetic protection afforded by derivatives, which we think will be compromised in a dislocation, worked a treat in this latest squall. Many hedge funds, who through a combination of size, leverage and a policy of active trading are now the major swing-player in the world markets, have such protection in place. They have been reluctant to sell down the bullish risk that they have in their investment portfolios, and they have added to those bull positions protection through put-instruments on the market indices.

This provides us with an opportunity. If investors are, in the round, heavy in exotic 'special situations' with limited liquidity (ie, not easily sold), and short in index stocks (the big capitalisation stocks which are easy to deal in), then it is likely that the latter will do better than the former. We could be reverting to a situation seen ten years ago when shares in a handful of big companies did much better than everything else, and the indices were notoriously hard to beat. Big caps over exotica feels like a good bet – and has the advantage that if Vesuvius blasts off, the big caps offer, through their liquidity, a motorway to escape, which the scenic route offered by their smaller cousins does not provide.

We do not believe that the catalyst for the latest setback was a sinister one, but a number of factors have combined to make the medium term outlook less certain. There has been less liquidity – the Japanese quietly removed ¥22 trillion from the system between January and May – a lot of money even when measured in proper currencies. The United States persisted with interest rate rises against a consensus view that they had peaked at or below 5%. There is a worrisome backlog of unsold housing stock in America which might presage a fall in house prices – arguably the main asset which keeps the world afloat with borrowing. World economic growth prospects, which had been pushed higher in March, have been shaved back to the rates predicted at the end of last year. Any one of these might turn out to be pivotal, but it is a mistake to assume that the mere existence of such things will be enough to derail the system. There is always something to worry about if one's hobby is worrying.

One last word on gold and gold-shares. They had a terrific run over the previous year, and were clearly vulnerable to a setback. If we had been pre-occupied with month by month, or even quarter by quarter performance, we would have sold out of these – no doubt considerably too soon. But our belief is that, unlike copper mines or oil wells, or, indeed, all the other commodity plays, gold could turn out to be an essential part of a portfolio when conventional investments suffer. Our philosophy remains one where we always avoid the possibility of being absolutely right because we want never to be absolutely wrong. Our nervousness remains in place, and this is reflected in the fact that the majority of the money is invested in fear. Only time and, somewhat uncomfortably, arithmetic, will tell if we are right or not.

'Small Earthquake in Chile, Nobody Dead'

October 2006

This invented caricature of a non-story is a lampoon of the journalists' struggle to produce news when there's not much about. It comes to mind in the context of this investment review because our portfolios have been comprehensively battered in the last quarter by a series of adverse moves in our investments (the earthquake) – but the portfolios have emerged almost unscathed (nobody dead).

First, 'the story'. During the quarter, the broad solid investment counters such as utilities, food retailers and banks have moved slowly but steadily upwards. We missed these stocks – and missed them by a mile. We did not like them three months ago, and we still are fearful of their valuations one year out. Instead, we are heavily invested in gilts and other government bonds of four–five year maturities. There to capture falling interest rates, they have suffered at the hands of rising short-term interest rates in Europe and America. More serious has been an investment policy which has had comparatively little in Sterling at a time when the British currency has been rising in value, and this has been exacerbated by the choice of our favoured alternatives: the Swiss Franc and the Norwegian Krone (and the Yen, through our equity positions there). These have tended to weakness, as foreign speculators have borrowed in low yielding currencies. Nor has it been a good time for gold shares. But the 'non-event' is that the portfolios are barely changed over the quarter. We have lost a skirmish, perhaps we may lose a battle, but we are preparing to win a war. The rest of this review will spell out the nature of this war.

We believe that the imbalances in the world financial system will end in a financial crisis, following on from an extended period of exuberance fuelled by liquidity. Ever since Good King Wenceslas first looked out, the gravitational rules remain the same: on the way up asset prices support, and are supported by, higher borrowings: at the crisis, the asset prices tumble, but the debt does not. There is a rush to sell assets to repay the debt and markets which were thought to be continuous turn out to be exactly the opposite. The issue at the critical moment turns out not to be the fall in market prices, but that there are no market prices. The house, the share, the corporate bond may well have a value, but without buyers, this can be academic in an emergency.

It is one thing to claim that a financial system is on a war footing, but where are the troop movements? The chart below is eloquent: never has the ratio of debt to the size of the US economy been so great – it is now standing at the 315% level. There is no rule of economic law, of course, which says that the dam breaks at 315% – or even 415%. Nevertheless, the die is cast: the ratio will continue to degrade until the inflection point. A gradual reduction in leverage is neither psychologically likely, nor practically possible – more borrowings are needed simply to sustain the process of asset stability, let alone enhancement. This is most clearly seen in the overvaluation of streams of income, be they property rental, infrastructure-related or corporate debt. Nor is this mania wholly irrational. The riskier elements of structured synthetic debt (CDOs, CBOs) give an annual return which is extremely attractive to those managers who take a performance fee – provided, of course, that the capital value of that instrument remains constant. In many instances there is no two-way market in these things: provided the bond pays the coupon, they can be held at par according to model. The early and total demise of such an instrument acts on such a manager as the bailiff's notice does to a squatter in a mansion. It's sadly the end of the free ride, but the past benefits (for the hedge fund managers, the performance fees) are not forfeited.

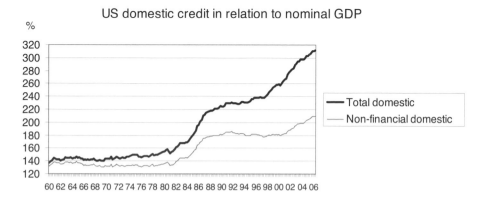

US domestic credit in relation to nominal GDP

Our investment strategy is intended to embrace a number of different outcomes in what is likely to be a fast moving and irrational marketplace, but our central view is that the US Federal Reserve – and, by extension, all central banks on a coordinated basis – will respond to the emergency with a surge of liquidity and very sharply reduced interest rates. This is what they've done every time there has been a crisis in the last ten years. It is the equivalent of Bruce Forsyth's 'nice to see you!' and the markets yell back 'to see you, nice!' That is the reason for the five-year government bonds – a very sharp fall in interest rates would result in the asset class moving decisively upwards in capital value.

Our second belief is that, in such an eventuality, the currency markets will not be shouting back to the Federal Reserve, 'to see you, nice!' The Dollar has had the ingredients of weakness for a decade or more, and its resilience has dulled holders of that currency to their potency. It has survived, and thrived, because it is the one truly liquid market in the world. We know that dislocations are frightening events, and that in such times, there is a wholesale destruction of wealth. Those who are overexposed must turn from their first planned intention (sell those assets which in the event prove to be unsellable) to a second course of action: sell those assets in which there is still a market: in currency terms this pre-eminently will be the Dollar. Some will want to sell the Dollar because its perceived weaknesses will be magnified when looked at through the prism of fear. Some will want to sell the Dollar simply because they can. Some will want to sell the Dollar speculatively to take advantage of a mismatch of buyers and sellers. This could add up to an instantaneous and powerful force to drive the Dollar downwards – and, as a by-product, with so much of the world's savings denominated in that currency, it will have the primary consequence which all crises bring about: wealth destruction. The opportunity for investors comes from the fact that a fall in the Dollar means a rise in other currencies. Sterling might well appreciate against the Dollar in this environment, but it will be weakened by all the same fundamentals which have caused the Dollar to degrade. We therefore prefer those currencies which are seen as boltholes – hence our love of currencies like the Swiss Franc. At the moment they are being weakened by speculators borrowing in those currencies to invest elsewhere – it will be exactly the reversal of those positions which will make these currencies impossibly strong in such an eventuality.

Going forward, it is a case of more of the same. Always the difficulty of times like this is to have enough investments in greed – it is easy to reinforce the fear in an attempt to be absolutely right if and when the crisis comes, only to find that the crisis is long in coming. (This has been an error we have made in the Investment Trust.) One answer is to buy undervalued stocks, but, as Mrs Beeton observed, 'first catch the hare'. Another is to favour 'megacap' stocks throughout the world, including America. Unsupported by speculative and leveraged takeovers, woefully overpriced at the beginning of the century, they have not been the right place in which to take risk. If the band plays on, we think that will change. The largest companies have a big representation in sectors which we really can't face – the financials particularly, but nevertheless the big'uns could produce healthy capital gains quite quickly while we await the force of gravity.

Plonk, Plonk, Plonk

January 2007

The 2006 vintage of Château Ruffer was not one to relish. The stock markets put in another barnstormer, but we were more barn owl than barnstorm. We had a good showing in both 2004 and 2005 (each of them recovery years in the stock market) but we were not able to repeat it in 2006. Why was this?

This last year has seen the second mania in ten years (the last was the dot-com boom). This is a most unusual phenomenon, since the disgust which follows the puncturing of a bubble usually lasts a generation and sometimes rather more. The reason, of course, is that the whole of the last ten years has been a period of an irrational exuberance of appreciating asset values, with various classes taking it in turns to bathe in the sun of investor euphoria. In early 2000 the top hundred NASDAQ stocks made, in aggregate, no profit and were valued at $6 trillion, the equivalent of the gross domestic product of the United States for eight months. (The last time that such madness had been seen in the investment community was in 1989 when Hirohito's tennis court [and accompanying palace] was worth more than California: astonishing when one considers that Hirohito wasn't even very good at tennis.)

The present manifestation is every bit as extreme as the technology boom of 1999/2000, and is considerably more pernicious since it is not so easily identified for what it is. In that earlier period even the bulls of Colt Telecommunications and Yahoo could see that these companies were not without risk, however attractive their long-term outlook. As a result they were largely acquired with saved money, or with minimal debt – all the risks were in the investment vehicle. Today we see the reciprocal of this – all the risk is in the funding of the investment, which means that the investments themselves have, in abundance, all the qualities of safety. The investment opportunity comes about from the availability of massive borrowing

136

at reasonable rates. A recent example has been the purchase of Thames Water for £8 billion, funded with £7.75 billion of debt, and only £250 million of equity. On this sort of financial structure, a fall of 3% in the value of the asset sees all your own money evaporate; from then on it eats away at someone else's – the lender's. The key is therefore to draw attention away from asset values, and onto cashflow considerations. If a target investment has a gross yield of, say, 6% and borrowings can be obtained at 5.5%, there is a 0.5% differential which, geared up thirty-fold, gives a return of 15%. Use it to pay down the debt, and the excess gearing recedes. After a few years, the debt has become manageable, so the key is to hope that the string bridge of positive cashflow holds steady over the initial period when the chasm of capital gearing makes the debt/asset value impossibly risky. Thus, the targets of this mania are built around stability and duration of the cashflow, not the capital value. The major beneficiaries of this phenomenon have been top quality property (Manhattan real estate selling on a yield of 3.5%, and in Piccadilly at 3.75%), utilities, infrastructure projects, good brand names of staple products (think Marmite) and long duration bonds of less than exceptional quality, whether corporate emerging market debt, or synthetic.

Synthetic? Once a mania is underway, naughty children find new forms of misbehaviour. The 'synthetic' bonds (assets backed by an index representing underlying bonds often with a total value only a fraction of the synthetic itself) have value only on the assumption that the underlying asset movements continue to behave in an orderly and predictable fashion. This cannot be assumed. It is a repeat of the velveteen scam of the zero coupon preference share debacle coming back in a different garb: me no lycra.

Another enormity is to borrow money in a foreign currency with a lower interest rate than the currency of the host investment. The benefit is a lower cost of debt, widening the differential on the net return in the investor's favour, but with a substitution of currency risk. Jim Grant of Grant's Interest Rate Observer cites how rampant and widespread this phenomenon now is: 92% of home equity loans in Hungary are Swiss Franc denominated, and 70% of housing related debt in Poland has such currency risk. Moreover, it transpires that the naughty child is not naughty at all, but a genius: the foreign currency risk has turned to be a currency reward as more and more 'investors' jump onto the bandwagon and drive these currencies downwards (see chart, overleaf).

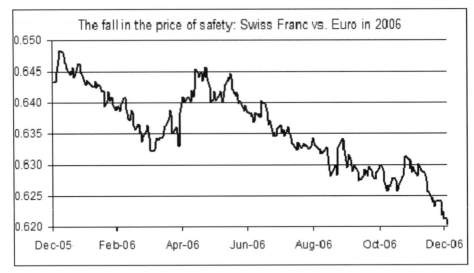

The fall in the price of safety: Swiss Franc vs. Euro in 2006

Source: DATASTREAM

This chart is a thermometer of the heat of this mania. The relationship between the Swiss Franc and the Euro is a stable one, since they have so much in common. One thing alone differentiates the Swissie – its reputation as a safe haven and for this 'insurance policy' its holders pay a premium in the form of a lower interest rate and less liquidity. Its movement is, in broad terms, a gauge of markets' fear and complacency; this most eloquent chart shows a decisive victory for complacency over fear.

It is a single example of a most worrying characteristic. Investments in absolute safety are all weakening, and the more absolute the safety (such as index-linked stocks, short dated government bonds and bolthole currencies) the more they tell the same picture of a retreat in value. It is normally the preserve of risk assets to fluctuate in value, since the sort of safety which comes about through risklessness rarely loses value comprehensively. This phenomenon is not, however, unprecedented.

It was the striking feature of 1999, when the rush into telecom madness sucked money out of safety to feed the frenzy. It is the dynamic of the tsunami, the first evidence of which is the retreat of the tide in the opposite direction from which the danger itself comes. Those who understood, knew that it was time to head for the hills. We believe that a similar move is warranted now.

We have long predicted a financial tsunami, but we always make it clear that its timing is uncertain, and that there was little point, and some mischief, in trying to pick the moment of its arrival. The prediction of a financial dislocation is a big enough investment call, without adding an overlay as to its likely timing. But, for the first time, we are calling the top. To us it is simply incredible that the big majority of forecasters do not even consider this relentless rise in leverage as worthy of consideration. In our view, we take our cue from the Michelin rosette: stock markets are currently worth a detour.

Commentary

2 0 0 7

The year started pretty similarly to the last three: onwards and upwards – but with little triumphalism. There were winners everywhere, to be sure, but at a less rarefied level. The middle classes remained squeezed by school fees and mortgages: Adair Turner, government-appointed chair of the Pensions Commission, announced that the gap between pensions savings and the requirement for old age was a whopping £57 billion.

The first sign of trouble came in February when the connection between mortgage defaults and the securitised instruments whose income stream was affected came to light. The expression 'sub-prime' entered the general language – but it looked as though it was a storm in a teacup. Early estimates suggested that losses might total $50 billion – or three months worth of banking profits. Alan Greenspan suggested a little later that the world might be looking at rather more – perhaps $100 billion. The markets quickly recovered their nerve, led by private equity – whose financing remained unimpaired in the light of the banking sector's appetite to lend to them.

The next shock came in June, when Bear Stearns announced that a couple of their seemingly anodyne funds, the Bear Stearns High-Grade Structured Credit Fund and the Bear Stearns High-Grade Structured Credit Enhanced Leveraged Fund, had been caught up in the crisis: owing to the leverage within the fund, one of them was probably worthless, and the other down by a half. The markets were stunned (particularly those players who had not taken the trouble to read the name of the two funds), but despite a weakening bias, held up well. The uncertainty took an altogether darker tone when it became apparent that Northern Rock might be in difficulties. Northern Rock had been established in the middle of the 19th century, and had become as much a pillar of the new aristocracy of the north-east as had Alnwick, seat of the Dukes of Northumberland, in the *ancien regime*. Their support for a wide range of charities, and their sponsorship of the local football team, Newcastle United, gave them a standing beyond their financial status. By 2007, though, the company was no longer a pillar of anything very much. Run on an aggressive basis by the affable bullet-headed Adam Applegarth, the youngest CEO of a FTSE company, it had concentrated too much on the type of business that it did (its mortgage book was of high quality) but had not shown a similar care as to the quantum and the source of its borrowings. The crisis broke on the evening of 17 September; an interviewer asked commentator Robert Peston whether depositors' money was safe. Never a man for the quick one-liner, Peston's eyes rolled, his arms waved, there was a mention of complications . . . and the next day the queues formed outside Northern Rock. The first bank run in Britain since . . . nobody could quite make up their mind. Was it Overend Gurney (1866), the City of Glasgow (1878), perhaps the Bank of England in 1914?

The darker implications of leverage were becoming apparent. Debt to GDP in the United States had gone up in a generation from 140% to 360% by the end of 2007. In the good times, this was a following wind – and, of course, the extra activity, extra profitability, extra volumes of transactions were self-fulfilling. But when the inflection point came, it would act in reverse. There was no knowing, ahead of time, when that would be. The defaults in US mortgages in late 2006 were an indicator that this inflection point had become a 'when' not an 'if'. The February hiccough confirmed – if confirmation was needed – that real events had financial consequences. The June crisis showed that these financial consequences, when leveraged, could cause investments to vaporise. The September collapse of Northern Rock further showed that the financial world was reliant on mutual interdependence – there was no obvious connection between the seizing up of the Certificate of Deposit market and the sub-prime crisis – but it *was* connected, and by the autumn of 2007, all the pieces in the jigsaw were on the table, face-up. It required only the master-hand of events to show what this meant in practice.

Cracking the Credit Code

Three months ago we described a full-blown investment mania which rivals – and in some way has surpassed – the tomfoolery of the technology boom in 1999/2000. Since then there has been a hiccough in the markets when the subprime mortgage market came to grief. The bears, somewhat short of straws to clutch, immediately seized on this development, but the stock market only managed an overall decline of about 7% before rallying. There is considerable nervousness that this may be the start of an unravelling of the excesses, but they are matched by those who see only the punishment of exaggerated exuberance in a peripherally small market.

The subprime market debacle is significant, in our view, for quite a different reason: it gives an insight into what is actually going on. Henry Maxey at Ruffer has just written an important paper on the state of liquidity in markets (see p188 *et seq*), and the remainder of this investment review draws heavily on his insights – the trade-off being: more analogies, less understanding.

It is easiest to see the mania at long distance – through its consequences: mortgages given to insolvent arsonists, sovereign spreads that can't distinguish between Che Guevara and Maggie Thatcher and growth rates in debt far in excess of either money supply growth or GDP increases. Securities issuance in 2006 was no less than $11 trillion, or 25% of world GDP: half of that was in bonds issued in the US. But, like London's fashionable 43 Club in the 1920s, what looked like a drunken orgy from a distance, on closer inspection presented as well dressed gentlemen having a 2am cup of tea with their young nieces. 'My club caters for those who like an early breakfast,' explained its proprietor, Mrs Kate Meyrick. In that case, the circle was subsequently squared through an examination of Sergeant Goddard's bank balance, which was on the high side for a police officer, and Mrs Meyrick was duly sent to prison for what seemed like the rest of her life.

Where, then, are the Sergeant Goddards of today's markets? They are to be found across a wide range of risk assets: the private equity market, the emerging market sovereign debt and other high-yield markets, but perhaps the most easily examined (not least from the light thrown on it by sub-prime), is the immensely important housing Mortgage and Asset-backed mania. Its importance in the fabric of the world economy cannot be over-emphasised. This is how Larry Summers described it in an article (FT, 26 March 2007): 'It is clear that the global economy has been relying on the US as an importer of last resort; that the US economy has been relying on the consumer for its primary impetus; and that until now consumers have been encouraged to spend their incomes fully or more than fully by being able to access the wealth in their homes.'

The mechanism by which the US consumer accesses this wealth is out of control, subprime being a single example (and which may or may not be the catalyst for its ultimate breakdown). This mechanism can be thought of as a motorway, one end of which is US consumption, which travels, via the householder, through the structured finance (Mortgage and Asset-backed securities) markets to the Collateralised Debt Obligation market to the hedge funds, and on to the general public via the fund of hedge funds.

This motorway carried over $2 trillion worth of structured finance paper last year, and it has to be asked, Why did the world oblige by taking on such an extraordinary amount of debt? It relies on two separate pools of investors whose appetite is whetted by the way these instruments are par-celled up. One pool is attracted to the apparent safety in the regularity of the income payments from the bonds, the other attracted by the multiplier inherent in the higher risk/higher yield 'junior' tranches of the bonds. These assets are layered according to risk – those which have more inherent safe-ty will have a correspondingly higher percentage in the 'absolutely safe' cat-egory, but even the subprime will have perhaps 75% of its issue in this 'safe' category: in this example 25% of the universe of subprime borrow-ers can default, impacting the junior tranche, before there is any default in the 'senior' tranche .

The safe investors, those buying the 75% senior tranche, provide the heavy lifting in terms of investment: powerful conservative investors throughout the world, including Far East government agencies, oil money, European pension funds and other non-speculative investors.

But just how 'safe' are they? The bonds they buy are often loosely packaged retail mortgages thrown together so that the Methodist minister, the bookie, the golf pro and the single mother of seven with a captivating smile are all thrown together in one. How does the risk manager of an Italian mutual take a view on that? The answer in this kingdom of the blind is to seek out the one-eyed king: the rating agencies, whose job is to put a grade on the security. Watch out for the moral hazard: the more you can squeeze into a 'safe' rating, the more you can sell, and the agencies earn prodigious sums from this source. So it is tempting for them to put a very high rating on a bundle of assets whose true risk is too opaque to be known. There are not enough investment grade bonds to go round, and it is therefore not surprising that investors will pay a high price for it, accepting only a small yield enhancement over the Pepsi and Glaxo-style 'safe' paper: arguably too small an enhancement.

Nor are the rating agencies quick to point out deteriorating conditions. It is not without significance that the subprime crisis only broke in the market in the third week of February, despite the fact that the underlying events were breaking news the previous November; it took that long to be reflected in the underlying asset prices. Why should it take so long? The answer is that the rating agencies are loathe to downgrade the status that they ascribe to their paper, and do so only when they are absolutely forced to by events. The structured products are too obscure for the layman to have an informed view as to the underlying risks, and therefore put great reliance on the rating agencies. But those agencies do not respond to deteriorating circumstances since it would effectively destroy this asset class. Their behaviour at the time of the collapse of Enron is a case in point, easily demonstrable because there was an active market in the bonds. In the final week of August 2001 the Enron 9.75% 2003 dropped from around 104 to 20, where it had a yield of just over 45%. Nevertheless they were rated as investment grade, and continued to be until 28 November. (Enron formally defaulted on 3 December.) In short, the rating agencies can delay the recognition of bad news, and, provided that the bad news is not dislocative, this can continue for a great length of time. But the subprime development shows what happens if the reality of a situation becomes sufficiently unambiguous to force a response. In subprime, a series of near hopeless borrowers actually defaulted, and that default could not be ignored.

The junior tranches are the playthings of the hedge fund industry. The overvaluation of the senior tranches means that, comparatively speaking, the junior tranches are undervalued, so that a long/short strategy can redress this anomaly in favour of the hedge funds. But it is only a relative play, and relative players are blind to where the absolute value may lie. Approximately 30% of the hedge fund industry – about $450 billion – specialise in opportunities arising from credit markets.

It may seem odd that the structured debt players are hungry to take on both illiquidity and danger when normally dangerous investments only make sense in liquid markets, from which one has a chance of escaping before the carnage. And yet they do. The reason is that these hedge funds are attractive to 'absolute return' investors who seek ideally, a 1% per month return with low volatility. For an investor in a fund of hedge funds, this equates to a 20% annual return before fees, and it is a real challenge to produce this without some considerable accompanying volatility. One way to provide this is for the fund manager to operate through leveraged spread strategies in illiquid assets. It is a variation on the theme set out in our January review: borrow up on a multiplier of the assets in the fund to take advantage of yield differentials which are, of themselves, pretty small. It has been suggested that a hedge fund with $10 million assets is able to have exposure (through a combination of quite modest borrowings and a much greater embedded leverage in the underlying assets acquired) to $850 million of residential mortgages. But the low volatility only holds if the assets are illiquid and therefore hard to value, because hard-to-value assets are marked to model, rather than to market; for as long as the input into the model holds, the performance fee can be claimed. There is no external monitor such as there was in Enron where disquiet weakens the capital value of the asset (but even that was not enough actually to change the rating) – therein lies the moral hazard in the junior tranches.

While there is no dislocation, the effect on this enormous motorway of issuance has been to ensure that consumer expenditure in the west has continued at a higher level than has ever been seen in the past. It also explains why private equity can appear so effortlessly generous in acquiring businesses at prices which conventional wisdom cannot justify. When the motorway is closed, whether by subprime, or one of a number of other surprises in this financial equivalent of the 43 Club, then, of course, there is trouble. The players disappear without trace, and holders of the very large senior tranches of structured debt lose money, and who knows where the eventual trail of junior tranche losses will fall? But these things are no more or less than the fun of the fair.

It is the narrowing of future borrowing-power, even for self-evidently safe loans, which will be the final mischief. The Federal Reserve can lower its rates as far as it likes, but a disgusted investment community takes a long time to recover its nerve. A world in which borrowings are commensurate with yesterday's mistakes, rather than tomorrow's opportunities, is not one in which economic prosperity abounds.

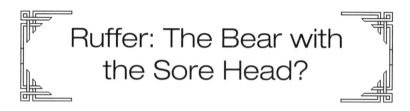

Ruffer: The Bear with the Sore Head?

July 2007

For our tenth anniversary (2005), we published ten years of quarterly investment reviews, and my secret hope was that they would show a dazzling array of insight and timing: cautious in danger, bold in opportunity – a kaleidoscope of investment wisdom mutating with the seasons of the investment climate. Instead, it reveals forty essays in pessimism: each one of them an anthem for an undertakers' trade association.

This is particularly relevant at the moment because our recent bearish reviews have coincided with dull investment performance, so that it looks as though we've made the mistake of becoming market timers, and, like all such investors, getting it wrong. The purpose of this review is simply to offer reassurance.

First question: why do the investment reviews read so bearishly? It stems partly from the natural humour of their author, more attuned to danger, fearful of its constant presence, and the extent of the damage which can be done when exposed to it. In a naughty world, it's sometimes known as real-ism, but in any event it is no bad thing if one is looking after money where preservation is at least as important as growth. But preservation is not enough – unless the assets are invested in genuinely risky assets -proper bets on the table -the preservation will merely be the brighter side of the three-penny piece of stagnant returns. No risk, no reward – not an attractive offer by a fee-charging institution. Yet a missed opportunity is by far a less-er evil than a botched investment.

It is worth recalling the long-term nature of the investment world, and the similarities of our clients' experience in 1999 to today. Then the dot-com boom was raging, and those who brought money to be managed in early 1999 must have wondered just what planet Ruffer was on – no money made at all in markets which represented the easiest investment opportunity since the sack of Rome. But what seemed an irresistible reward for embracing the brave new opportunities of the technological revolution ('has Ruffer actually heard of the internet?'), turned out to be another mania, with 'TMT' stocks joining the tulip, the bogs of the Mississippi, the railway and the conglomerate on the pile of busted investment opportunities.

Our pre-occupation is in the evaluation of risk: it is always the case that a mania in one area creates opportunities in others – but there is a price to pay while one waits. The subject of the mania is the overwhelmingly obvious place to be, and goes up, and up, and up, and the opportunities – whose low valuations provide safety – seem the opposite of safe: they go down, and down. In 1999, we could see that the move to growth had left the dull-dogs without a kennel. We made no money in that year, but we made good money in each of the three subsequent ones when the UK market dropped over 50%.

When the market bottomed in April 2003, and went explosively upwards, our investment review continued to be bearish. In that month, it stated, characteristically, 'Our roadmap tells us that markets are far from cheap and we remain concerned . . .'. But in the first six months of the bull market the portfolios put on 'better than market' gains. The catalyst for the market rally was cheap and plentiful central bank credit which did not destroy the imbalances that threatened (and still threaten) prosperity, but it did disguise them. It was not hard to see that Japan and commodity prices would be the unequivocal beneficiaries of that – we entered Japan for the first time in well over a decade. We did it as much to protect our 'deflationary' investments as to make money outright. It was not at all clear that Greenspan's reflationary initiative would succeed or whether it would be overwhelmed by the primary focus of overproduction. By 2005 it was clear that the leverage in the system was enough to continue the party, and to compromise the attractiveness of the long-bond market. We therefore exited it.

So where are we today? Facing danger, certainly, but 'twas always thus. What is overwhelmingly certain, in our view, is that we face the bursting of a bubble, the second one in seven years – more accurately a second manifestation of the same one: central banks' accommodation in the light of the deflationary forces of oversupply and world capital flows. Our response is much the same as it was in 1999. We have avoided the objects of the bubble, and this has condemned us to a difficult performance for the reasons already given. Just as the food and bus companies looked stupid in 1999, they looked great in 2000. So we believe it is with our defensive stuff today. Wheels come round in full circle, and it is the 'steady eddy' companies which today are as overrated as the internet stocks were seven years ago.

Our investments in fear are unchanged: short-dated government bonds, and bolthole currencies. Our investments for growth now have something of a dot-com feel to them. Commercial risk – the technology companies, pharmaceuticals and companies whose exuberant management can grow market share – has never been cheaper comparatively speaking. The benefit is that the money to be made in them – if the risks turn out to be reward – is considerable. Of all the opportunities, Japan remains at the top of the list. Fear and greed: agnostic as to whether one or the other is better, anxious always to get the odds right.

At the moment, we're not succeeding as we would like, but we're trying to do just what we always have, and we believe that by continuing to do so, we're on course to succeed.

A Storm or a Teacup?

September 2007

The last few weeks have given investors a real fright, but nobody is quite sure what the fright was, or indeed, whether it was frightening. Our investment reviews this year have identified the subprime danger and, thus far, events have played out as we forewarned. Have we, then, been vindicated? The answer is: no, we have not (not yet, we might add *sotto voce* – but the important part of the answer is the 'no').

'Subprime' is, like all generalisations, unhelpful in being merely a representative part of the dangers inherent in the asset-backed and structured product market, but subprime itself is nowhere near big enough to destabilise the financial systems of the world – its size, about $120 billion, is less than the four biggest equity buybacks this year. The power to dislocate owes much to the sophisticated packaging and reprocessing. Nobody knows where the securitised debt has ended up (they are finding out now) and the amount of leverage (borrowing) that many institutions have taken on means that a smallish loss can destroy the entire net worth of an investment vehicle – and, at one remove, fall on those who have a contractual or commercial imperative to stand behind them. The relationships are as close-knit and complicated as the royal families of 19th-century Europe; subprime is its haemophilia.

Central banks have been commendably alert, pumping in over $100 billion, and facilitating bail-outs when necessary. Liquidity is the antidote to the acute stage of the crisis, and the initial spiral downwards has been halted. The early dislocations have been dealt with, and the full weight of the Federal Reserve stands ready to put order back into markets made disorderly by future shocks. One must not underestimate this good work; the possibility of a vicious circle arising from that initial shock was a real one. The central banks will not do so well in the next phase of the dislocation, not from a lack of care or skill, but because the next phase will show that we are dealing with a credit crisis, not a liquidity crisis.

In the early stages the two are hard to tell apart. No economy can survive without borrowing, and it is interrupted by any disruption of the borrowing mechanism. There is, however, a world of difference between a lending crisis brought about through the fears of the banks themselves (too frightened to lend to one another) and one raised by fears of the depositors (no deposits equates to no loans to anyone). Central banks have learned to fight the first disease, tutored by Walter Bagehot in the 1870s – the lender of last resort (the Federal Reserve here) must lend generously and expensively. Interbank lending has resumed, if not seamlessly, at least effectively enough – and with the full weight of central bank intervention, not surprisingly.

But banks are carnivorous – they make their living by putting their money at risk. They have every incentive to put aside their fears and re-engage. But depositors are not carnivorous – they are the herbivores of the financial food chain. They seek, above all, safety, and take whatever returns the market place offers. They never seek risk; indeed try to shun it, but every so often they are seduced into taking a risk which they did not appreciate. In the nineteenth century the paramount problem was the failure of the bank in which the money was deposited, and that remains a real risk into the present day (eg, those local councils who were attracted by the rates that BCCI offered before they went bust). The nature of the compact between depositor and bank has, however, changed during the last decade or so. No longer is it the traditional banks who make the loans – the banking industry has mutated into investment banking and learned to thrive by acting as investment principal and by fees, much more than by lending. And the role of lender has passed to the originators' securitised debt – the loans are now owned by investors, not bankers. Our April 2007 investment review deals on the interaction of the pension funds, insurance companies and government agencies who have bought the 'senior' securitised paper, and the hedge funds who own the toxic stuff. Who invests in the relevant hedge funds, owning perhaps $500 billion of risky paper? The fund of hedge funds, whose investors' risk profile is essentially that of a depositor: safe capital, and a steady return which exceeds that available on cash deposits.

The events of mid-August have shattered the illusions. The early indicator was the Bear Stearns fund – a big one at $3.2 billion, which after 41 unbroken 'up' months, promptly announced it was worth only a few cents on the dollar. Two terrible days in the markets – 10 August and 16 August have been enough to persuade these new 'depositors' that it's a mug's game to chase a small extra income at the hazard of the capital value. And, as is often the way with herbivores there has been a stampede – with the inevitable consequences that vast swathes of perfectly safe commercial paper finds no buyers today.

This is the battleground. The optimists see dislocation increasingly contained, and against a backcloth of a sound economy, bargain hunters are returning to the fray – 12 August was, by coincidence, the 25th anniversary of the start of Wall Street's run (the Dow Jones closed at 776!). Buying the dips has been right every single time since then, so one doesn't need to be brave to do it again. But they forget the nature of the herbivore. Why should he return to securitised debt? He's now discovered that the AAA he owned wasn't the 'Simon says' variety, and is risky. He doesn't want risk, he wants whatever return is consistent with safety and he's just learnt that safety is harder to come by than he thought. The optimists are looking at the wrong thing and, even allowing for that, coming up with the wrong answer when they say the economy is robust. This is essentially backward looking: admiring the firm physique of the followers of the Mahdi as they mass to greet the clickety clack of the Maxim gun. The deterioration of the economy will be manifested in two ways – the borrowers' ability to convert their capital asset (US residential housing, car loans, credit card receivables, etc) into spending power has been impaired, and that in turn takes out the essential ingredient to support asset prices.

There are many in the UK who remember with dismay the split-level investment trust fiasco. There the depositors were the holders of the 'safe' zero coupon preference shares, structured to give a 'cash' return in the form of a capital gain, attractive to garner a child's capital gains tax allowance. They were invited to believe, technicalities aside, that the shares were riskless. Their acceptance launched an industry: the sum of the parts was worth more than the whole, and the city obliged by creating £2 billion worth of it, and keeping the difference themselves. The worldwide phenomenon of the securitised debt industry is the same, but around 5000 times bigger.

It is what happens from now on which will determine whether our analysis is sound.

Beware the Rock

October 2007

Thank goodness for a portfolio balanced between greed and fear! Stock markets have closed not far off all-square for the quarter, which comprehensively fails to convey the extraordinary convulsions in financial markets in between – it is as if Dunkirk and D-Day had all occurred in a three month period, leaving the Allies with the same toehold in France that they had at the beginning.

The purpose of this review is to try to understand what is really happening on the battle front. Nevertheless, a quick digression as to where Ruffer – and its portfolios – stand is in order. We think we have decisively left behind us the 'tractor on motorway' sensation which we had up until the summer of this year. (The smooth tarmac has given way to some potholes, and it could be that the investment path is somewhat more agricultural from now on.) Our defensive stocks, which sometimes seemed pointless or even perverse on the autobahn, are now more than earning their keep. It has been a real relief to see that day by day the values of the portfolios have been little changed, whether the market has slumped or soared, and the job ahead is to sustain the upward bias evident in recent weeks, so that long-term returns can be stapled to short-term stability. We achieved that for many years up until the summer of 2006, and we think we are doing it again.

We sent out an interim review in early September to address the nature of the dramatic events which were then unfolding. One month later, the fundamentals are little changed, except to say that equity markets are trying to break upwards into decisive high ground. The first question must be – how can this possibly be so, given the grave and frightening nature of the financial crisis which broke at the end of July?

Part of the answer is the very ferocity of the crisis. Top entry in the Investors' Wonderbook of Clichés is the adage, 'Buy to the sound of gunfire, sell to the sound of violins'. Since 12 August 1982 (the day Jonathan Ruffer got engaged) the markets have always rewarded the former – they have not, for 25 years, rewarded those who listen out for the violins. A variation on the theme, which is less easy to rebut, is the idea that Mr Market is cleverer than the individual players – everybody knows about the bad news and in the face of it the markets have been extraordinarily resilient. It is often a fair bet that even crises which look to be without res-olution turn out to be nothing of the kind. The 1998 LTCM/Russian debt crisis was exactly that – an opportunity to lose one's nerve just ahead of the biggest boom in the stock market of all time. The optimists believe that the bears have thrown their most powerful punch at the market in a genera-tion, and not landed a decisive blow – when the storm passes, then the mar-kets in 2007 can repeat the pleasure-dome of the dot-com boom – in other stocks of course, but the dynamic is essentially the same. This thought is given validity by the irritation evident in the bearish camp, which has sometimes been manifest in immoderate and extreme responses in asset allocation.

At the heart of the outlook for the economies is the question: has the funding mechanism which powered credit markets, and which did so out-side the traditional banking system, broken beyond repair – or will it bounce back and the carnival resume? Our answer is that it has broken, and will not resume.

At the moment, the market is concentrating on a crisis of liquidity – the queues round Northern Rock are a once-in-a-century event, testifying to the extremely unusual conditions in the marketplace. Two features should, however, suggest that this crisis is containable. The first is the massive strength of the financials' capitalisation – losses which look eye-wateringly large scarcely dent the annual profit of the financial giants, let alone com-promise their capital. And when those losses are concentrated into weaker companies, the central banks are alert to demonstrate that it's 'business as usual'. Given that they command unlimited funds, there is no bail-out too big, no underwriting too extreme. Of course there are consequences down the road of too overt a rescue, but down the road is . . . down the road.

Where do we go from here? The optimists see only an acute, and there-fore essentially short-term crisis. Get through that, and the world will be better for the salutary shock – a timely reminder that if you bate the fami-ly Labrador too much, even it will bare its teeth. This waggy-tailed approach to markets is considerably too sanguine, in our view.

First, the imbalances need sorting out. Opaque investments of uncertain value are not easily sold to investors when the credulity born of a long bull market evaporates. When the banquet comes to an end, those opportunities that have not found a permanent home sit, undigested, like some giant tandoori in the innards of the financial system. The last eight weeks have seen a game of pass the parcel, but there has been no reduction in the overall amount of borrowing (see the primary brokers net loans, still stuck at $1.5 trillion) – they might now be moving into the hands of the financially strong, but each billion of assets on the financial sector's balance sheet is a $1 billion less of firepower for future lending. And it is the outlook for future lending which remains our biggest worry. No economic system can keep going without the capacity of borrowers to borrow, and the crisis disrupted that capacity. Those who originated the loans are getting their nerve back. But you can't make loans without deposits, and the depositors have had a nasty shock. The holders of AAA bonds have found that they were the patsies, and so have holders of asset-backed commercial paper. Unsurprisingly, the latest issuance figures are coming through very weak. The asset-backed commercial paper market is down by $0.25 trillion in just seven weeks, and the asset-backed securities issuance is down by about two-thirds. The nonplussment of the Northern Rock depositors is a powerful symbol of the call to safety, and if this huge constituency of depositors – both in the form of investors and purchasers of commercial paper – behave as human beings usually behave in these circumstances, then all our financial well-beings are compromised. At the time of writing, there is still an appetite for leverage on those corporations with strong balance sheets. Not all depositors are yet in the bunker.

In short, stock market confidence might yet be the relief felt by those on the stern of the ship when they realise that it was the front which had hit the iceberg. *Titanic* or *Queen Mary*? That's the question.

Pig-Sticking a Panzer

January 2008

A year ago the investment review was headed 'Ringing the Bell' – a flamboyant attempt to call the top which, with hindsight, I'd never try again. True, the top came some five months later (we assume) – not far off judged by the timescale of market cycles, and the proximate cause was exactly – indeed alarmingly – the one offered as its nemesis. Why, then, was it a mistake? The answer was that it wholly underestimated the strength in the beast of the bullmarket. In the last six months, the asset-backed securities sector, worth some $5 trillion, has completely gridlocked. The US housing market is in freefall, and the European looks as though it is following. Commercial property is in stasis: the fifth biggest UK mortgage bank is beached, the European Central Bank has made available an extra $280 billion . . . yet the world equity market is down around only 5% from its peak. We posed as the pig-sticker and encountered not a pig, but a panzer, which has absorbed a fearful battering of bad news pretty much unscathed.

Never have market views been more polarised. The optimists see the Federal Reserve admirably responsive to the rolling financial crisis, and are encouraged that the European Central Bank has been flexible and decisive in its dealings. Economic growth has remained robust -tellingly, with the Far East coming in stronger than ever. The bulls hope that a problem contained in the West, with a brave new world in the East, is one with which the markets can live, particularly now that the credit crunch is no surprise – the thing the markets most fear and hate. 'Fully discounted' is the sister-in-law to 'decoupling' in their dictionary.

For the last 25 years, the betting has always favoured those who have underestimated the true nature of a crisis. Over that period there have been many things which looked overwhelmingly frightening – balance of payment deficits, the derivatives timebomb, the debt overhang – but the key to money making has been to ignore them. Those who had a true understanding of each of these dangers regularly made the mistake of disembarking from this generational gravy-train of asset appreciation. Best, therefore, not to enquire too closely of the danger, lest it cause a grievous loss of nerve. It is an inversion of the fairytale of the boy who shouts 'wolf!': this one keeps his eyes shut and never shouts wolf, even when it is biting his shoulderblade.

This time, the credit problem is *el Gordo* – the fat one. A quick recap. An enormous amount of money has been borrowed, some of it by people who were never going to be able to pay it back, and a lot more of it by people who needed the value of the assets to go up if they were to be able to pay it back. Although that first category has duly blown up, and both the quantum and the whereabouts are unknown, it does not look to represent a systemic banking risk – some hundreds of billions of dollars to be absorbed by a US financial system where the banks have a net worth of around $1.3 trillion. The hits to the big financial institutions have inevitably generated both uncertainty and a marked reluctance by the banks to make new loans, but the central authorities are doing everything they can to alleviate these pressures. The optimists pin their hope – almost an assumption – that this will succeed.

We think that this optimism is, by and large, soundly based, and we have no particular argument with those who think this battle will be won. Nevertheless, this victory will not be enough to avoid a severe credit rationing, and the consequent economic effects which flow from this. The credit rationing will have an unfavourable effect on asset values – and that will compromise the second, much larger, category of borrowing.

To assess the depth of the credit problem, one must understand the structural changes which have taken place in the financial world. Over the last ten years there has been a revolution in lending. By the summer of 2007, the majority of it had been done outside the banks, taking the form not of loans held on bank balance sheets, but of investments processed by those banks, and sold in the form of securitised debt to long term investors. Although these investors are well able to take the losses which are only now becoming apparent, they are by nature conservative, attracted to these asset-backed securities because of their security, first of cashflow and, by extension, the capital value. Many of these investments are now unsellable, and some are clearly worthless.

Our view, based as much on common sense as high economic theory, is that this 'non-bank' lending is impaired; the conservative investors have learnt their lesson – the lesson being that danger can lurk in seemingly safe opportunities. The good news is that the dislocation will remain largely where it falls. Those conservative investors will suck their teeth and take the pain – a myriad of portfolios, some government-backed, some representing pensions, some insurance money, some fund of funds: each will be worth a few percentage points less. If there are large losses to absorb, it could not happen to a segment of the financial community better able to wear it. The bad news is that the dislocation will have a much greater effect on the availability of credit in the future. Non-bank loan growth was running at nearly \$3 trillion annualised; it isn't any longer. Unless the banks can take up the running, the economic consequences of sharply reduced credit availability will be apparent. Alas, the banks are struggling to keep even existing commitments in place. Even if, as we think, they do remain open for business, their capacity to lend will be much reduced, owing to the failed investments which they will have had to take back on to their own balance sheet. The will to expand the loan book will be more than correspondingly reduced.

At the end of the year, a surprising amount of this has not yet been reflected in a reduction in consumer demand. Liquidity in vehicles which take consumer credit assets has dried up, issuance has stopped, but retail sales have held up remarkably well. One of the main reasons for this has been that credit card spending has gone sharply up, with double-digit growth in what is essentially the most expensive way of borrowing money short of the pawnbroker. Consumers in the United States seem to have kept their expenditures rolling along for another few months, but at the cost of borrowings at triple the rate available in the good times. Whom the gods wish to destroy, they first make mad.

These developments – or, more precisely, the lack of them – have meant that our investment positions remain pretty much undisturbed from three months ago. The long awaited weakness of Sterling has transformed the short-dated Swiss and Norwegian government bonds from little chalices of nausea into springtime celandines. The short-dated gilts are performing well, as there is an increasing realisation that the economic outlook cannot support interest rates at their current level. We remain of the opinion that only a sharp fall in the stock markets stands between interest rates at their current level and levels no more than half where they are today. We remain reluctant to grasp the nettle of purchasing index-linked bonds, despite the fact that we believe that they will be a formidably good investment over the next three years as governments compromise their currencies in order to palliate the effects of financial dislocation. There will be, we hope, time enough to do this. Meanwhile, we have substantial investments in both gold bullion and gold shares, which have exactly the right characteristics in a world where the major currencies are being compromised in coordinated fashion. Our view on equities is fairly conventional at the moment – favouring big capitalisations over smaller ones, and, less consensually, to favour nifty-fifty ideas in America at the expense of Europe. Food inflation is now a well-worn investment theme, and we have moved from the primary producers into the food processing companies, on the basis that commodity inflation is like a goat passing through a boa constrictor, and we think it is time to move away from the jaws towards the middle part of the snake.

Commentary

2 0 0 8 / 9

The year opened with a sense that the troubles in the financial system could be contained – Northern Rock was for sale, but still regarded as an asset more than a millstone. Nevertheless the surprises were mostly to the downside. Citgroup was discovered to have big losses; Soc Gen, which had been crowing about its financial prudence in a Gallic sort of way, was found to have been the victim of a Breton rogue trader

A French problem was regarded as against the run of play, since the problems were felt to be US-centric, and this was reflected in Fed monetary policy, which focussed on lower interest rates. As they came down, the Dollar weakened, and commodity prices rose – this in turn meant that Mercantile Asia accommodated the devaluation of the Dollar with domestic liquidity (to devalue their own currencies in harmony) – and this was the stimulus for commodity prices.

The early part of 2008 was therefore not free from worry, but the worries were boom-related: commodity inflation, exacerbated by hedge fund momentum trades, but given a sound basis by China's announcement of a massive infrastructure programme.

It was well known that China was not so much on a roll, as a somersault. Its economy had grown, compound, at over 10% a year since 1990. By 2006 its booming trade volumes had made it third only to the United States and Germany. On 14 January 2008, it was confirmed that growth had accelerated in 2007 to 13% – its gross domestic product pushed Germany into third place; the parvenu had arrived. While 130 million Chinese still lived on less than a US dollar a day, the sheer size of the country overwhelmed the West, and it was a shock to see China coming in as a purchaser, not a provider. Up until now, the role of China – at least as far as the West was concerned – was to produce a vast array of goods (and also services) at ever keener prices, to keep the US spending frenzy from becoming inflationary. That the Chinese authorities were prepared to take US dollars – and US dollar-denominated debt – was a happy chance, for it allowed a mechanism to develop where the West created and facilitated the growth of debt-instruments which journeyed to China (and other surplus countries in the East), as the goods journeyed from the East to Europe. (The map of this dual carriageway is well-described at the end of this book by Henry Maxey in his Cracking the Credit Code report.)

By June, global inflation had blasted through its target price ranges, with food, fuel and base metal prices all rising sharply. Housing prices in the UK had started the year with annual gains approaching 10%, but they, at least, were slipping away.

These problems took investors eyes off the ball as to the true nature of the deflationary collapse which was already unfolding. The credit rating agencies were for the first time viewed as the villains in the structured products markets. The bond insurers, it was quickly realised, had a battleship's worth of danger on board – it was the start of AIG's journey from a market capitalisation of $80 billion to next to nothing. General Electric was the next on the radar: meanwhile in the UK, Bradford & Bingley were reduced to their bowler hats.

Then the troubles really began. Decoupling became recoupling as markets everywhere responded to this new dynamic. The homebuilders collapsed – and Fannie Mae and Freddie Mac, who between them had issued half of all US mortgages were faced with bankruptcy. The full extent of the crisis became apparent when the ECB arose from a deep torpor and von Rumpelstiltskin began to consider an easier monetary policy. The crisis was reached on 15 September – Hank Paulson, the US Treasury Secretary, had rescued Fannie, Freddie, and several banks, but let Lehman Brothers through the slips: it went bust and promptly put AIG into a similar situation – to be bailed out by the taxpayers at enormous cost. Lehman was a costly blunder, but the truth is that the whole financial system was a spaghetti junction of cross-claims: it took only one missed catch for the system to break down.

The autumn was the time of the genuine financial crisis – the system held, but the Montgolfier balloon continued to jettison its inessentials: Latvia, HBOS, Citigroup, sterling and by extension the reputation of Gordon Brown. Down they went, as did G W Bush – the Republicans lost the US election resoundingly in November to Obama.

Real-life events quickly followed: led by the US domestic auto industry, whose finance subsidiaries could no longer fabricate new sales. Export figures collapsed in sympathy – the fourth quarter figures for Japan's visible trade showed that exports had halved. In a world where a movement of, say, 3%, gets the story onto the front page, a figure of 49.4% suggested that the world as we know it had come to an end.

The financial and commercial crisis was met by a vigorous burst of 'organised support'. Those who remember the aftermath of 1929 will recognise with chill foreboding the sound of such assistance. It consisted then of a number of New York worthies walking ostentatiously across the floor of the Stock Exchange and flamboyantly putting in place 'buy' orders for stock in bombed-out counters. (It was later discovered that many of them were short the market, and one or two ended in prison.) In short, it was a sham.

Not so in 2008. The banks were bailed out, along with AIG, the Troubled Asset Relief Plan, was launched, followed by a series of other initiatives which, like TARP, were organised in acronyms to form four-letter words. None of them seemed to touch the spot, but in total, they were to have a powerful effect on the world. Interest rates continued to go lower (the Bank of England's reduction of interest rate in December 2008 to 2% left the UK as a high-interest rate country).

By March 2009, markets were at distress levels, but there was an increasing realisation that money would be made available, and the first intuitive worries as to whether the money was there – or affordable – became as irrelevant as that same question as the Spitfires came off the production line in 1940. First win the war – and then there'll be time to worry about these things. At the time of writing, the markets have risen by some 40% from those springtime losses: the firefighters – better, actually to think of them as firelighters – have saved the day. The costs are discounted – a healthy economy will forgive all today's ~~excesses~~ successes.

At the beginning of 2008, the great mastodons of the financial world were regarded as too big to fail. By October even the mighty AIG, not so long ago the eighth biggest company in the world, was out for the count. In the middle of 2009, the losses, the dislocations, the initiatives – all are met from the resources of the great nations themselves. They pay off the overdrafts by writing cheques. The next year will tell us whether the depositors of these national banks – the external holders of their currencies will continue to honour them.

Index-Linked:
the Pathway to Safety

April 2008

A truth almost universally acknowledged often turns out not to be true at all. One of Roosevelt's best, 'the only thing we have to fear is fear itself', may just turn out right now to be one of them. Are we heading for depression, recession or near-miss? Who knows? But when the brakes have failed the appropriate response is fright. There's not nearly enough of it about at the moment, and what fear there is is concentrated into the banking, property, leverage and retail sectors. Since fear is a lagging indicator, there will presumably be time enough for a confidence-boosting Fireside Chat from a latter-day Roosevelt in due course. The key now is to grasp the enormity of the situation and to work out what is the best way to keep safe. We think that it is in inflation-protection: best of all are the index-linked government stocks. The purpose of this review is to explain why.

The key to the current crisis is the existence of massive debt. Even in the best-regulated world, there is always an element of it providing two lunches today at the expense of tomorrow's. When the time comes debt must be repaid, tomorrow's lunch is foregone, and both economic growth and asset prices take the strain. These features are very much at the forefront of today's economic world; Billy Bunterdom has reigned supreme, and now it's yarroo! time.

The world is slowly coming to realise the extent of the problem now that the failures are hitting the blue-chips: Bear Stearns was the fifth largest US investment bank. It's easy to appreciate the submarine menace when a U-boat happens to sink the *Ark Royal*, but leverage's destructive power has been apparent in theory for a long time, and the speedy work it made of Bear Stearns' hedge funds last June was its early manifestation. Yet, even today, there is a sense that if other capital ships can avoid the torpedoes, we can somehow return to the old order. That world is as passé as the Dreadnought, and we live with circumstances where, to quote economist Roger Bootle, 'The umpteen billions of dollars which have been magicked out of nowhere must return whence they came.' The losses have to be borne (the easier part) and, more worryingly, the world has to live lunchlessly.

This is a recipe for a deflation (Why index-linked then? Wait and see ...), but the Federal Reserve has as its Chairman the one man who has spent almost a generation assessing how to avoid deflation in these circumstances. What Bernanke has written in his theses, what Bernanke has spoken in his set-speeches, and what Chairman Bernanke has done to combat the deflation have been utterly consistent. It is a common cry that the financial world is in uncharted waters, but the captain of the ship is a man with a one-note trumpet: he sees his job as providing liquidity and resources to the embattled financial system in its day of testing.

This steadfastness has drawn a favourable response from the investment community, but there are worries whether the Fed has enough fire-power to continue. This concern is utterly naïve. In the 19th century, Jonathan Backhouse, the Darlington banker, had a row with the Duke of Cleveland. Backhouse challenged His Grace to a duel: who was the richer? Could His Grace, for instance, tear up five pound notes without even flinching? So they set to, and every time the Duke tore one up, he was five pounds the poorer, every time the banker tore up a note issued by the Backhouse Bank, he was at the expense of printing another one.

What's this got to do with anything? It highlights the difference between paper and money; the Fed sits in the Backhouse banker's seat, not the Duke's. Bernanke alone controls the quantity of dollars, and he is choosing, as he always said he would, to create as many as it takes to preserve the financial system. And when these crises occur, the amount needed to staunch them is huge. Northern Rock required backing of £100 billion, of which a fair proportion will likely not be recovered. This is the equivalent of more than 15% of the total government debt: an expensive hobby – the central bank equivalent of trying to breed a Derby winner. So large, in fact, that it compromises the currency – and that creates inflation.

A quick diversion to consider inflation. I've always regarded the French as being basically untrustworthy because they use the same word for 'straight on' as 'turn right'. There's a similar issue with inflation. Most of the time inflation describes the situation when we all want a bushel of wheat, and there's not enough wheat to go around and – hey presto – the price goes up! (And so does the price of bread.) But sometimes, for instance in South America in the 1980s, the price of bread doubles in a fortnight, although there is no shortage of wheat, and no unusual demand for loaves. The reason then, of course, was that the *peso* no longer acted as a store of value. In the golden days, a sovereign did not change its value – only the wheat price did. Today there are two moving plates – in this example, the wheat price and the *peso*. A fall in the value of the *peso* masquerades as a rise in the value of wheat – but that's to look through the wrong end of the telescope.

Money has three jobs to do – it acts as a medium of exchange, a unit of account and a store of value (how much spending power have I got in my wallet?). In 1923, it took a wheelbarrow of money in Germany to buy a week's groceries – a prodigious amount of printed paper. It is said, probably apocryphally, that all Germany's printers could only process a quarter of the necessary banknotes in that October. But a lot of paper added up to almost no spending power – and in that, crucial, sense although there were a lot of banknotes, there was almost no money as defined in its 'store of value' role. This failure to be a store of value is something which is most likely to be a problem in deflationary times – because deflation exacerbates the likelihood of default. The German Mark 'defaulted' as a store of value – yet it goes by the name of 'the great inflation'.

We are pretty confident that this is what Bernanke has in mind for the Dollar. Not a currency wipe-out – but a steady reduction in its true value which is manifested both through the exchange rate and through the retail price index. There is far too much borrowing about, and there is immense danger in the deleveraging process – it makes practical sense to effect some part of that deleveraging through the compromise in the currency. A million dollars borrowed can thus still be a million dollars outstanding several years hence – but if it only buys half a Cadillac, the effect is the same, economically speaking, as a repayment of half the debt. The crucial point is that this only helps the hapless debtors if interest rates remain below (well below) the inflation rate. We can be sure the Federal Reserve will oblige in this respect. The phenomenon was invented by the British in the 1970s (by accident, like all the best inventions) and observed by both Greenspan and Bernanke. To recap: inflation is both necessary and unavoidable if Bernanke's trumpet-tune plays out. If it does, interest rates will almost certainly remain low. There will be few places for investors to hide. It is the Britain of the 1970s – equities lowly rated, not much appetite for risk, and cash certain to lose value as the gross income (and *a fortiori* the net income) is less than the value lost each year through inflation.

Thirty years ago, investors had to buy a hole in the ground in South Africa (the gold producer Vaal Reefs was the preferred counter), to protect themselves from negative real interest rates since there were no index-linked, and gold ownership was disallowed. Today there are index-linked gilts (and similar instruments in most other major countries). They are already difficult to buy, and there are not nearly enough to act as a lifeboat for all. It's time for investment ungallantry – we're going for the lifeboat now, elbowing aside the women and children: *sauve qui peut*!

Monetary Stability

July 2008

Three months ago we sprang like a bathing belle from a birthday cake, proclaiming that the world was unequivocally in the thrall of inflationary forces, and that the investment mix – for mix it remains – should have the hallmarks of inflationary protection. The purpose of this review is to explore this theme, both in the light of another three months passage of time, and in the complexities which surround an assessment of the value of money. For years we have been warning against the dangers of deflation – why, one might ask, this 180 degree turn?

The key to its understanding is to know that inflation and deflation are both manifestations of monetary instability and their opposite is not each other, but monetary stability. Imagine a rowing boat, rowed by a gentleman, heavy in hock. When all goes well he sits in the middle of the boat and makes good progress. But imagine, too, that he unwittingly moves the *avoirdupois* somewhat to the right of the boat. The boat lurches to the right – but which way will our hero fall? If he does nothing, over the right side he will go. If he over-corrects and lunges to the left, he'll join the fishes on the left side of the boat. Which way he goes is more a finesse than a polar opposite, and so it is with inflation. Events are frighteningly deflationary at the moment – if nothing is done, then things will tip over into deflation. But it is our contention that something will be done by the central banks and the efforts they make to save the economy from its travails will release inflation, and this is the dominant theme of the review.

We will turn in a moment to our assessment of what is going on in the world, but first let us declare a plague on both the houses in the current inflation/deflation debate. The inflation camp is largely occupied by those who to a greater or lesser extent are optimistic about the outlook. The credit crunch, they concede, was massively dislocative, and has had a dampening effect on the economy. Growth has slowed, and may well slow further, but the dislocation is essentially behind us and we can look forward to better times. Alas, the inflationists acknowledge, the world must get used to a higher cost of food, of energy and of other forms of *materiel*; no longer will Chinese goods be a driver for lower prices. Inflation for them is the parrot on the shoulder of Captain Hook and his 3% growth per annum. The deflationists will have none of this. The credit-creation mechanism is broken they say, and 60 years of leverage must be reversed. This is the *mistral* feared by the shepherd-economists: a wind which freezes asset values, economic endeavour and threatens the very stability of capitalism. It is deflation which we must fear – and the excess demand for oil and other goods will soon wither away in the icy conditions. The deflationists are (as described) spot-on, as far as they go – but we have often observed that inflation can be brought about in deflationary times by a compromise of the currency. Paper currencies are not anchored to anything whose scarcity allows them to hold their value: trees grow a-plenty. If Bernanke chooses to compromise the Dollar, then it will show itself in a rise in domestic prices. This is the plan – for America. It is an attempt to reproduce on an international stage the 'stagflation' of Britain in the 1970s. Prices go up, interest rates stay low so that the over-borrowed are subsidised and the astute or lucky player who was in cash when the locusts appeared, finds that he is penalised by receiving less in interest payments than he loses in inflation. In short, the lender is the one who subsidises the borrower. This we articulated in our April review. The last three months have reinforced the thought that Bernanke is set on this course. But the European Central Bank and the Bank of England are not with him, and are indeed pulling in quite the opposite direction. Why should this be so? The twin fears of deflation and inflation rise up like a rock and a hard place at the moment. Which course to steer is, it seems, dependent on the folk-memories and fears of the helmsman. For helmsman Bernanke, the bogey-man is the 1930s depression in the United States, brought about by Central Bank inaction as deflationary forces multiplied and spread. The solution for Bernanke is therefore a world where interest rates can be held below the inflation rate, and inflation generated by currency compromise at a time when prices might be expected to behave in a deflationary fashion. Britain's secondary banking crisis showed the efficacy of negative real interest rates. For Bernanke therefore, Britain's stagflation in the 1970s is a solution. Alas, the bogey-man for the Bank of England is the self-same circumstance – a world where the English remember the wholesale incompetence of economists and bankers alike (Messrs Gordon Richardson and Jasper Hollom's lifeboat a shining exception to this). The present team will do anything in their power to prevent its recurrence. When Sir Mervyn King and his deputy governors talk of fighting inflation, alas, they mean it. The ECB plays the same inflation-busting tune, but less culpably: they do it to establish their credentials as warriors of free thought: battle honours are more important than the outcome of the battle itself.

International money flows are no longer favourable to a unilateral attempt by Bernanke to bring about this necessary result. In the good times, the oversupply of dollars which resulted from the Fed's loose policy was reinvested in the US fixed-interest market. Now the emerging markets, who are the recipients of excess dollars, prefer to recycle those dollars into 'real' assets like oil and wheat. Rising prices of such staples quickly change domestic inflation expectations in America, and compromise bond market yields. This worsens the squeeze in credit markets. This has meant that Bernanke has had to pause in his fight to use loose money to keep the economy in order. The rhetoric has increased: a table-thumping diatribe for sound money, although nothing has been done to restrain money growth or put up interest rates. Nevertheless, it has ensured that in the last few critical weeks, the economy has had no help and this has translated into extremely messy markets as the economy weakens sharply. This is the background to the world that we see going forward. In the short term, these developments are not supportive of our new-found enthusiasm for index-linked stocks as a weak economy suggests a strengthening of the deflationary conditions. Without evidence that the authorities will respond inflationarily, the deflationists could well come centre-stage. If this turns out to be the case, our philosophy of never having all our eggs in one basket will prove vital. If, in the early autumn, the world looks to be succumbing to deflation, then we would expect all three central banks to respond vigorously with expansive policies, and our primary view will swing back again.

It is a pleasure to be able to report that there is beginning to be some value in the equity markets. The opportunities are few and diverse – the old adage about glisters and gold remains true. Integrated oils, some telecom stocks, Japanese domestics, some food manufacturers and a range of debt-restructuring opportunities all look like they could provide good returns from here. We find nothing in the banks or the house builders: not much, either, in the retailers (except in Japan, and possibly the food retailers). We remain of the view that a deflationary scare will provide a last – and possibly the best – opportunity to put in place a full protection against tomorrow's challenge: inflation.

The Crisis

October 2008

Let's start with a confession. We wrote in an earlier Investment Review, "*The hallmark of the monetary merry-go-round has been a lack of fear of debt and the damage that it does to families and their dependents. A lack of rigour in Fannie Mae and Freddie Mac's accounting policies are to some extent reminiscent of the enormities of Enron, and they share a generally complacent attitude to the whole issue of debt.*" Bravo, Signor Ruffer – when did you write such wise and lapidary words? Um, in October 2004. Mercifully for clients, we didn't run for cover for nearly another two years – and we were still a year early.

Now that Fannie Mae, Snow White, and most of the other dwarves have been seen off (hey, ho), it's time to look forward, not back. The purpose of this Review, as always, is to explain to clients why we are investing as we are, bearing in mind that our overwhelming priority is to protect the value of portfolios in real terms.

The financial crisis which has engulfed the western world has shown, even to the ostriches, that the world has changed. What was thought to be a free lunch – increased borrowings resulting in increased asset values – has turned out to be a costly mistake: not a free lunch, but one in which the costs have merely been deferred. The crisis began over a year ago, but to begin with, the Maitre D's reckoning was not taken seriously – that figure must be in Lira! that bill's for the table next door! Now that the birthday boy and a couple of the party girls have been shot, the mood has, unsurprisingly, turned nasty. The only source of funds is governments, and, as we write this, there is a debate as to who really foots the bill when a government steps in and pays.

What is clear is that the US administration is alive to the dangers, and will do everything that is necessary to ensure that it bails out the system. Hank Paulson makes a somewhat creaky James Bond figure, but nevertheless he's the chap twiddling the knobs on the bomb's black box to stop an almighty explosion. If the film goes according to script, then Mr Paulson will be the hero of the day, with the clock stopped, showing 27 seconds from detonation, the world unaware of the narrow escape which it has had. Unfortunately, the script has been tampered with by one of those surreal producers who delight in the unexpected. Just as Mr Bond is unscrewing the lid of the black box, a janitor has wandered into the room, and is demanding that he fill in his name, car registration details, purpose of visit and time of entry into the building ('in triplicate, please') before he can get on with the job.

It seems that Mr Paulson, Dr Bernanke and team did rather too much of a good job in the early stages of the crisis. Furiously bailing out the financial system with measures which seemed technical, but were powerful in their effect on the monetary world, the script was that there was nothing really to worry about: a little local difficulty, which might result in moderation of economic growth, but all was well with the world. Perhaps none of us should have been surprised, therefore, when Congress, confronted with a gun to its collective head: 'give us $700 billion or else the whole world joins Atlantis as an underwater community' – chose not to take the threat seriously. It is probably bad luck that the crisis developed only weeks from an election, but it is certainly not bad luck that Wall Street is as popular as the defendants at the Nuremberg trials of 1945 – that is simply what happens at this stage of a crisis. More could perhaps have been done to make the bail-out seem less financially-centred, but it was always going to be difficult to persuade the politicians to go along with it.

The Congress debate has raised interesting questions. Has America got the money? Who is going to pay? Ordinary Americans see more clearly than the financial world that somebody picks up the pieces when commitments like this are made – investors have too often regarded a government bail-out as akin to holding a stock which is bid for, and the proceeds receivable in cash: never mind what it does to the bidder: the value of the original investment is rescued.

So, has the US got the money? Like most administrations, the United States government has no money at all – in fact, it has a deficit. What it does have is the ability to tax the nation's future wealth creation. It is the exact opposite of the typical borrowing proposition which created this leverage crisis. The US government is in a strong position in that a stream of income from taxes is much more reliable and stable than the artificiality of a 'market value' which, at a time of crisis, turns out to be either lower or non-existent just when it is needed. The taxpayers know that they are in line to pay.

It is this element of the deal which has struck the general public so strongly. There is a widely canvassed figure that this deal will 'cost' each US individual $2,333. Not surprisingly, Joe Sixpack sees that as a commitment over and above all his other financial problems, going straight into the hands of the hairy-knuckled charmers who run the financial system. On balance, they'd rather not oblige.

But it is far from clear that it is the taxpayers who foot this bill. Another feature of government bail-outs is that they are sourced in a quite spectacularly different way to anything else. They are created out of thin air: in Victorian language, the money is printed. There is never a short term difficulty in effecting a bail-out. $70 billion, $700 billion or a few trillion – they are simply figures on a cheque. The real issue is whether the bank on which this cheque is drawn will honour the payment. This buck does not stop with the taxpayer, as everybody imagines, but with the holders of the dollar. That's the true victim of a bail-out – every dollar thrown at the crisis is a bucket of cold water which compromises the entire universe of existing dollars, making the increased pool less hot, less desirable. There is, of course, a great overlap between them and the taxpayer, but the distinction is crucial. It is the existing holders of the dollar who determine whether the process has gone too far. Already only one thing holds the dollar in place as a serious currency: confidence. Indeed, the whole financial system is held together by confidence, a confidence which has been serially shattered across a wide range of financial assets. But it still holds for the major currencies of the world. It highlights how little understanding there is that a deleveraging process results in default, and it does not much matter to the arithmetic whether the default happens at the level of the small depositor, or the mighty governmental empire which stands behind this tsunami and is overwhelmed by it.

The Fed may appear to be the Excalibur of this mighty giant, but in truth it is in the lonely position of being the victim of a blackmail. As the provider of last resort, when the chips are down it must do just that: provide. It may huff, it may puff, it may snarl, it may let the odd Lehman go to the wall, but the US government, as all governments, will have to go on providing the cheques. Ireland has shown the way by guaranteeing all depositors' money. There is great pressure for the United States to do it, and we would not be surprised if, by the time you read this Review, most of those guarantees were in place. Who pays? Nobody if the guarantees are not called upon, but it will be the holders of the dollar if confidence is lost.

So, the flightpath is as follows: more bail-outs, more guarantees, more loans, more support, any of which through bad luck, bad judgement or the relentless force of arithmetic could result in a magnified financial crisis. All those guarantees will have bought the Federal Reserve time – but only time, and sooner or later, confidence in the dollar and other paper currencies will be lost. We can see from the pathology of runs on the banks how quickly this can spiral out of control. When confidence is fragile, it will be clear that the dollar has no fundamental asset backing, simply because that's not how currencies work. There is currently an acute shortage of dollars in Europe, which ironically is due to European holdings of impaired US securities, and this created a short term demand for dollars. Perversely any solution to the woes of the wholesale funding markets will reduce this technical demand and the dollar will be weak. Then people will remember a speech made by Dr Bernanke in 2002 when he made it clear that far from being reluctant to provide unlimited liquidity, the Chairman of the Federal Reserve actually regards the payment of this Danegeld as an appropriate action. It was such an astonishing thing to say, that we wrote a report on it which we circulated in December 2002. The speech was well received at the time because the problems then seemed to make this recipe an attractive one. It was a great mistake to articulate this, and we said so. Five years later, we stand by every syllable of what we wrote then.

The realisation that the economy is contracting sharply is making people understand that inflationary pressures caused by raw material price increases are abating. We think that this could be the last moment that people fail to see that deflationary forces brought about by default are likely to be the same forces which cause the compromise of paper currencies – which is, in itself, a kind of default. This currency compromise manifests itself in inflation, and that is why amid all the talk of deflation, recession and crisis, we are protecting ourselves against the very opposite: inflation.

The Crows are Counting

The events of 2008 have been so shocking and extreme that it is a brave commentator who ventures any prediction for this year beyond pious optimism. Nevertheless, the shape of the struggle to come has become clearer. In essence it is a battle as to the future value of money – are we facing a deflation, exemplified by the Great Depression of the 1930s, or an inflation, as governments and central banks man the printing presses to combat this deflation?

The consensus has been remarkably slow to pick up the possibility - indeed, the likelihood – of deflationary conditions. The highwatermark of inflation was more than 20 years ago, and the long bull market in government 30 year bonds has mirrored its reluctant acceptance. Lower interest rates encouraged borrowing, and this tendency was much reinforced by a Federal Reserve which, through policy, kept interest rates below their natural rate.

A shattered financial system has meant that borrowing has become expensive and difficult to obtain. A sudden adverse change in circumstances has made heavily borrowed businesses – or those reliant on a high volume of transactions – unviable in short order. Hundreds of thousands have already lost their jobs; millions fear for them. Individuals are going from living beyond their means to living within them, and paying down debt. This is a world where profits go down, prices in the shops go down, rents go down, and total incomes go down – through a combination of higher unemployment, and lower wages. Even the tabloid newspaper reader can see the domino effect of this – a never-ending circle of enervation, and eventual stasis.

This is why the central banks are throwing everything they can at the problem – buying troubled assets, guaranteeing deposits, standing behind institutions, giving tax cuts, pump-priming to keep expenditure going.

175

Bernanke, a student of the Great Depression, has spent the last 25 years working out what radical initiatives might be necessary in such circumstances – ironic, perhaps, that he didn't consider during that time that prevention is better than cure.

At the turn of the year 2009, the jury is out on whether inflation or deflation will triumph. Everybody now sees the deflation; everybody knows that printing money is inflationary. There is, however, a consensus, well expressed in a Christmas edition of the FT as follows: "Fortunately, today's economic guardians learned from errors made in the Great Depression. Governments throughout the world are now taking decisive action . . . a combination of vast sums of money and fast response time will prevent any 'rerun' of the Great Depression."

The key to this optimistic view is that however great the deflationary force, it is finite, whereas the monetary response, being made through paper-backed promises, is effectively infinite. The boxer's maxim applies: a good big'un will beat a good little'un.

If these things seem a little arcane, let's break – once again, I'm afraid – into analogy. The consensus view runs like this: the economic ship is holed below the waterline. This vast deadweight is sinking, and will undoubtedly be lost if nothing is done – as happened in the 1930s precisely because nothing was done. This time, the rescuers are pumping literally trillions of helium balloons into the hulk of the stricken vessel to restore its buoyancy. At the very least, the ship will sink more slowly – remember there's an infinity of helium, as against the finite features of the ship – and it is therefore not unreasonable to hope that the two will in due course balance out and the deflation will be at Of course, they will concede there is a possibility – a likelihood – that too much helium will be injected (here the analogy falls down a bit . . .) and we'll end up with inflation. But that's not the current problem. It's today's deflation which must be broken, they say, not tomorrow's inflation. Time enough for that battle in the future.

We think this is a mistaken way of analysing the battle between deflation and inflation.

The starting assumption is spot-on: conditions are frighteningly and comprehensively deflationary. The mistake, though, is to imagine that the central authorities' initiatives are an effective counterweight to these deflationary forces. There is a mismatch between the deflationary forces, which are real-world actualities, and the initiatives which have been rushed in place to combat them. The latter are virtual, and require the confidence that $1bn of created debt is commensurate with the $1bn diminution in the value of pre-existing assets. The fundamental word here is confidence. Just as the banking system depends on confidence, as the travails of 2008 demonstrated, so do paper currencies; if the confident consensus assumptions about the created debt turn out to be misplaced, the currencies through which the bailouts are being effected would be compromised. We fear that there will be a second loss of confidence – this time with money, which will play out through the currency market.

The nature of this dynamic is that it may well be sudden. The bank crisis is instructive. In its first stages, the fear was limited to the failing bank itself. Even when several banks were seen to be in difficulties, there was no general alarm. It was only when many banks became compromised that bank-deposit fears became universal. It was the thought-process of the crow, which can differentiate between 1 and 2, and 2 and 'many' – but not between 'many' and 'all'. Once many banks were in difficulties, as far as depositors were concerned, they all were. And the way human beings are hard-wired, the flashpoint seems to come from nothing: whether it is council tax riots, petrol riots or the banking-deposit crisis. To predict these, one must look for the ingredients, not the build-up of events. I set out in an article in *The Spectator* last month (see page 179) the inherent fragilities which can be found in a paper-currency, but the key is that it requires confidence that a $20 note (or £20 or €20 one) is a store of value. The deflationary force elementally swept aside the conditions which allowed confidence in the world's banking system – surely it's worth considering whether that same force could not destroy confidence in something inherently much more fragile: the currency system.

Let us in passing deal with one canard: that currencies are a zero-sum game – if one goes down, then the others, by definition, go up. Perfectly true, but that's to miss the point. When confidence is lost in a particular currency, it reflects primarily through the foreign exchange market, not (as often supposed) through the inability of a government to borrow money through the issuance of government stock. The thrust of the argument is that at first the wider implications of a sharp fall in say, first the Dollar and then, say, in the Euro is seen in the context of the currencies themselves. But the crows are counting . . . just as the banks got into difficulty one after the other, so can currencies. The logical next step is that confidence is suddenly lost in all currencies, bypassing the traditional sequence of events, where an appreciable lag occurs between the inflationary fundamentals, and the behavioural response to this new reality.

Ultimately, this inflation will be beneficial since the overhang of bad debts in a sharply contracting environment remains impossible to clear through conventional means. The history of America in the 1930s and Japan in the 1990s makes this abundantly clear. If inflationary circumstances can be created out of currency compromise, then a clearing system is possible. We are already seeing a world where savers are punished for the benefit of borrowers; if we do see genuine currency compromise, then this phenomenon will grow considerably in strength. Negative real interest rates are the ultimate answer to the world's deflation. This situation presents an extraordinary opportunity to investors. The index-linked market could provide an eye-wateringly interesting return on capital. This is something of an eldorado – and, of course, the or in eldorado – gold itself – also has a place to play. We continue to hold Yen in case HMS Deflation does go down with all hands, but a good proportion of that Yen is invested in financial stocks, to protect from a US/Japan entente – where Japanese savings bail out the West in return for much needed income streams: the Mitsubishi UFJ/Morgan Stanley deal writ large. That's how we are placed for the start of 2009.

BUSINESS

The global currency crisis is still to come

Jonathan Ruffer argues that state bail-outs in response to the credit crunch
could lead to yet another massive shock: a widespread collapse of currencies, and a new inflation

Now that businessmen from Kazakhstan to California speak a single language, it's perhaps not surprising that we endured a Babel of borrowing over the past ten years. And like all towers which reach too high, it fell — and great was the fall of it.

So great, in fact, that the financial world was overwhelmed. The debris of dislocation and default rained down upon the fortress of the financial system, smashing it to matchwood. Shocking: but all, it seems, is not lost. With screeching tyres a jeep has come into view. Who's that at the wheel? Why, it's King Canute! And with him, Gordon Brown, Ben Bernanke, Hank Paulson and the Prime Minister of Iceland, together commanding that all will be well; all must be well. The onlookers cheer at such a spectacle of initiative and timeliness.

There is certainly no doubting their energy. Promises have been made, enterprises underwritten, depositors guaranteed, expenditures accelerated, taxes and interest rates cut. These bold actions have, however, the character of a response to blackmail. Only when things were unequivocally on the edge of disaster have they been proffered. And in this case the highwayman has demanded 'your money or your life' but has been happy to accept payment by cheque. A cheque for a billion is as easy to write as a cheque for a million — just remember to replace the 'm' with a 'b' (or possibly a 'tr') and get your Treasury people to tell you how many noughts to put in the box.

In naive minds this raises an important question: which is the bank on which the cheques are written? When Hank Paulson selected $700 billion as a good round number for a bail-out, Congress asked the question but gave itself the wrong answer when it concluded that the taxpayer would underwrite the deal. The true answer is

that it is the existing holders of the currency who bear the burden. The totality of holders of a currency can be thought of as a vast lake of value, in which the heat of that lake is its store of value. When a pension is magicked into existence to reward a crony, a bucket of ice-cold water is thrown into the lake. *De minimis:* it couldn't matter less. But if the buckets proliferate and become a vast network of pipes forcing the ice-cold water into the lake under great pressure, sooner or later there is a tipping point. The interesting question is when that tipping point is likely to occur.

Milton Friedman: blamed the Depression on lack of action by the Federal Reserve

Events unfolding today are almost exactly similar to the backcloth of the 1930s. This is not such a surprise, since there are not many variables to a deleveraging process. There are, however, many different policy responses to it. The Great Depression is America's equivalent of our Battle of the Somme: an event too horrible to contemplate. It was not until a generation after the event that Milton Friedman established what is now the accepted causology of the disaster. He asserted as its true cause a failure by the Federal Reserve to take the necessary action to combat the destructive forces. This

failure, he thought, stemmed from a moral infantilism, and an almost complete lack of imagination by the authorities — and it is true that period newsreel films of Herbert Hoover and Ramsay MacDonald reinforce this explanation. Dr Bernanke, the chairman of the Federal Reserve, has made it his life's work to study this failure, and he vowed to Milton Friedman on the latter's 90th birthday that it would 'never happen again'.

The Americans allowed a depression to develop in the 1930s because they were afraid of the consequences of losing the principles of sound money. In an effort to avoid a re-run of the 1930s, the Western world is imposing the opposite, equally unbalanced and intemperate solution. We might thereby avoid a depression — but the bad stuff which follows currency compromise will crash down upon us with great vigour. This is the one and only one, and probably last, shock that the credit crunch has yet to impose on a still unsuspecting world.

It is instructive to see today's crisis in the light of a 1930s mindset. When Britain left the gold standard in July 1914, there had been a sharp theological debate between the smart alecs, led by Maynard Keynes, who thought that paper currencies were the 'frictionless' way forward. The greybeards would have none of it. Human beings could not be trusted; too many trees would mean too much paper and valueless currencies. A century later, we can see that the smart alecs were right. The world has survived and thrived under a paper regime. But the greybeards were right, too. Within 15 years, the currencies of Russia, Germany and Austria were worthless. France's had dropped in the eight years up to 1926 by 86 per cent, Portugal's was down by 93 per cent and by 1930 only six had held steady against the 'gold exchange' dollar of 1918. The rules were understood by all.

www.spectator.co.uk

If you were going to have an incovertible currency, you had to behave impeccably: deficits were dangerous and there must be no growth in the money supply.

There is a terrific vignette of the power of this thought in the memoirs of Hugh Dalton, who became Labour's chancellor of the exchequer in 1945. As a member of the 1929 Labour administration, he was active in the row which broke out within the party in 1931 about whether the dole (unemployment benefit) was affordable. The bulk of the Labour party argued that it was already at subsistence level: to save £22 million this way was immoral. Ramsay MacDonald, the Labour premier, disagreed, and called an election on a national ticket combining with the Conservatives in a pledge to reduce the benefit. Dalton recalls that in the election campaign, MacDonald, high up on the dais of the town halls which he toured in that away September world, would hold up a one million mark note from the 1923 German hyper-inflation and wordlessly set fire to one corner. When the votes were counted, Labour scraped just 59 seats out of more than 600.

Why are these obvious truths so forgotten? It is 50 years since a first division currency almost went bust (France in the late 1950s). Bad behaviour has certainly devalued currencies in the last half century, as holders of sterling well know. Nevertheless, the loss of value expressed itself in chronic form, not by way of sharp default. The dynamic was always that of a rubber currency — behave badly, bend it a bit more, lose a bit more. When there is no inflation, rubber currencies become like chrome. Bad behaviour puts them under pressure, and they snap. Today's deeply deflationary conditions have de-rubbered the currencies and turned them again into chrome.

We have seen a parallel dynamic in ordinary people's attitude to banks over the last year. To begin with, people feared whatever bank happened to be in difficulties. Then, quite suddenly, as the number of troubled banks grew, so too did fear of the entire banking system. The collective wisdom of the crowd was essentially that of the crow, which can count, but only on the basis of one, two, many. Once many banks were in difficulty, the corvine conclusion was that they all were, and none could be trusted. This could be what will happen to currencies, played out to begin with through the forex markets. There can be one currency crisis, there can be two, but many crises means that confidence may well be lost in all currencies. Predicting the level of an inflation in this environment is a bit like predicting the size of the baby born to the housemaid who explains away her indiscretion by noting that it was only a very small one.

We have had a lot of frights in 2008. Everybody is frightened. But the danger of currency compromise is almost completely ignored, at least at the practical level of policy-makers and the investment community. It will catch many people out. Alas, the lugubrious dad's army of gold bugs will soon have their day. They have been waiting for this moment ever since the guardsman nearly dropped Queen Victoria's coffin. We will all have to sit through their cock-a-doodledo of self-congratulation. Oh dear, it never rains but it pours.

Jonathan Ruffer is chief executive of the investment management firm Ruffer LLP.

My thanks to *The Spectator* for permission to reproduce this article.

A Team – and a Service

April 2009

Human beings have a great capacity to accommodate extraordinary events, and come to regard them almost as normal. The slowdown in world trade has been absolutely eye-watering – Japanese exports in the three months to February 2009 dropped by 49.4%, traffic volumes on the A14 (the one which serves Felixstowe docks) are down by 49% on a year ago and scrap metal thieves in the USA are only getting 35% of what they received for their work in mid-2008. These random examples could be expanded ten thousand fold, and are a graphic demonstration that the failure of a single commercial entity (in this case, Lehmans) can have a disproportionate consequence on economic realities. The response from the authorities has been equally startling. New York last month asked members of the public to write down $1 trillion in figures (the correct answer is $1,000,000,000,000). What became clear is that these figures are too big for people to get their minds around, let alone their pens. The authorities are not yet running out of acronyms, but since each one has four letters and gobbles up at least $200 billion, this is unlikely to be a brake on their issuance.

World trade has had a heart attack, and the paramedics have applied their shock therapy. Wild events are rampaging through the world of money, but every morning in London the sun rises a little earlier, and shines for a little longer, taxi drivers still moan and the commuters go about their business as they always do. We at Ruffer while away the day by deciding whether the US railroad stocks are due a decent bounce in the market, or perhaps whether the Swedish Krone is somewhat oversold. It reminds me of the 1963 report and accounts of Gamble-Skogmo, a US retailer, whose report began with a trundle through their revenue growth, their dividend policy in the light of the revenue growth, and a couple of other housekeeping trivia. Then the report went on (I paraphrase): 'Some people have asked how Gamble-Skogmo would fare in the event of a nuclear holocaust. With stores in Alaska, Hawaii, Caracas and Fiji, we believe that Gamble-Skogmo is well placed...' Now that the Cuban crisis is a distant memory, the bathos is quite amusing. But we should not lose sight of the enormity of what is going on, and the moral inadequacy of believing that a moneymaking wheeze is a sufficient response to the crisis that the world is facing.

It is striking that the first property crisis comes a mere ten chapters (in Genesis) after the creation of the world. The judgement on Babel was not that some Old Testament Fred Goodwin had recklessly leveraged the enterprise, but rather that human beings have a moral warble fly which in certain conditions will breed a collective hubris of exuberant wealth creation. Now that we are mired in the inevitable consequences of its aftermath, it is hard to avoid the feeling that the authorities' attempts to present themselves as the Master Problemsolvers of the Universe demonstrate a similar hubris, since the money which they inject into the system, directly or indirectly, is money which has been created at the will of the authorities, not represented by any corresponding wealth. In the days when government bailouts needed gold, you either debased the currency (effective for about five minutes until the coins start rubbing against one another) or you couldn't do it. Today, the power of money creation is infinite, and so, in a sense, are the stakes. Just like weapons of war as the decades have gone by, so their power of destruction has increased.

The enormity of this is more easily seen by the common man than the sophisticate – so it was with the emperor's clothes. The clever chaps know that money creation does not require collateral. They know that when money usage declines – as it does precipitously in dislocative deflation – then you can print more of it to maintain its old equivalence. If business is crashing, and bad debts are destroying money, is it not desirable – no, essential – to create it in wholesale proportions? The honest answer is that we just don't know, but the ordinary man knows that a banquet is inclined to be followed by the bill. He can sense that his £20 is not the store of value that it was before tens of billions of new ones were created. He doesn't perhaps know how to express his uneasiness. One day he will – and on that day, money will begin its journey of inflation.

It is our task to build the core of the portfolios around this priority, and to reinforce that inflationary 'centre' with a wide range of assets whose primary job is to protect its value in the event that we are either wrong or too early.

Over the years these investment reviews have been the expression of my own idiosyncratic views, but I would like to introduce the reader to the team who are primarily responsible for the wholesome ingredients of the portfolios. Robert Tamworth runs the partnership effectively, and on a tight budget. It has earned him the nickname 'Discount Tamworth'. He has been there from the beginning, along with Jane Tufnell, herself a stockpicker, friend and strong tower to those whose lives here are dedicated to the lonely task of stockpicking. I am thinking especially of Tim Youngman, whose ability to find value in Europe has been quite literally second to none in London – no, Europe, and Alex Grispos who should really be Warren Buffett's right-hand man, but luckily works with us. At the epicentre of our investment process sits Henry Maxey, whose insights and technical understanding of the arcane world that we live in caused him to write 'Cracking the Credit Market Code' in April 2007, which will remain for its insights and timeliness one of the great predictive calls since the Captain of the *Titanic* cried 'abandon ship'. I have forgiven him for being better than me. Peter Warburton, whose economic understanding and judgement has been recognised by his membership of the Shadow Monetary Policy Committee has meant that we have two tigers burning bright on our 'big picture' calls. We are already indebted to the cautious boldness of Kentaro Nishida, our Japanese specialist. It is hard to know how we could possibly have steered our way through this opaque market with such stock-specific success without him. Trevor Wild, James Heal and James Verdier have recently joined the partnership, and make a really valuable contribution in their analysis of the equity universe. A determination not to be bound to any one asset class be it bonds or equities has led us to bring in the previous Global Head of UBS' Credit Repo Operation, David McClean. Mary McBain runs our Hong Kong office, and from there she continues her enviable ability to spot safety and success. And this is not an end to it on the research side: I am jolly proud of them, as the lawyers would say, 'jointly and severally'.

Above all, what I want to provide at Ruffer is a *service*. Although half the world seems to work in a service industry, the idea of being a servant seems rather Gosford Park and not at all what the doctor ordered in the twenty first century. I think it is a question of defining one's terms. To me, being a servant is not a matter of the forelock, but rather it is seeing a situation from the other chap's point of view. This is what I believe it is humanly possible to do all the time. To produce constantly good performance is, alas, not always possible, and I hope you will be gentle with us when we fail on this latter point.

Foreword to Cracking
the Credit Market Code

Henry Maxey

September 2009

One of the more colourful memories of an otherwise grey first year of engineering at Oxford was a mechanical engineering lecture in which the tutor described excited letters he received from members of the public containing their designs for perpetual motion machines. He briefly displayed some of the more intriguing designs on the giant overhead projector screen before pulling them apart in a frenzy of intellectual ridicule. My own distinct recollection is of being unnerved by how long it took to spot the source of internal inconsistency within these machines. Like Escher's impossible staircase (remember the stairs that seem go up forever), the imperceptible skew of each cog, drive belt, or fluid flow can delude even the consciously rational mind.

I am reminded of this because I believe it captures the paradox of the latest credit bubble: it was a product, not of wild animal spirits or exuberant expectations, but multiple layers of attempted rationality- models, theories, rules and regulations. Only by understanding the slight skew in each of these 'cogs' and the resultant incentive structures could one see the internal inconsistency, or what I describe in technical terms as a fallacy of composition. It was the financial world's own perpetual motion machine, yet the ridicule was reserved for those who questioned the legitimacy of 'almost rational' components and warned about the absurdity of the output.

And it was absurd. How could an 'efficient market' allow subprime mortgage-backed securitisation issuance to accelerate in the second half of 2006, when it was clear that the US housing market had peaked in the Summer of that year with delinquencies in the subprime mortgage market spiking higher?

Cracking the Credit Market Code was my attempt to unpick this fallacy of composition.

The conceptual cogs of the report had been the focus of much of my thinking over the preceding 5 years. Subjects included: the impact of derivatives on risk transfer; the effect of performance fees and the alternative asset revolution; the behaviour of central banks, rating agencies and regulators; global flows and the savings glut debate; and the evolution of securitisation. Each independently provided a reason for caution, but none was sufficiently skewed to be wholly responsible, hence the long gestation period for the report.

Integral to this investigation was a detailed understanding of the key institutions and credit instruments. For an equity focused fund manager, this wasn't a simple task, not least because it meant spending considerable time in the basement laboratories of credit markets, where English comes a distant second to Greek in the communication stakes.

I will leave readers to judge, with the hindsight of Warren Buffett's naked swimmers on a neap tide, the report's effectiveness. What I will point out upfront is the report's main 'miss'. At the time of writing, my expedition into the world of securitised credit had not led to any encounter with structured investment vehicles (SIVs) or conduits. Perhaps constant proportion debt obligations (CPDOs) finished me off before I reached the banking undergrowth which hid these bank off-balance sheet vehicles? While inconsequential to the conceptual argument- these were the banks' own hedge fund-like structures, i.e. part of what I labelled 'hedge fund banks' and what convention now calls the 'shadow banking system'- the effect of this missing cog was significant to the ordering of events. I had deduced that banks would be brought into the crisis through the failure of the 'hedge fund banks'. As it turned out, the actual hedge funds themselves were able to close the gates on investor redemptions, preventing a run by their investors, while the shorter duration funding schedule for SIVs and conduits immediately precipitated a wholesale funding crisis for banks. So banks suffered first and hedge funds followed later as the banks, as opposed to investors, pulled funding.

A brief rereading reminds me how far and how fast we have travelled since the crisis began. Statements, which seemed extreme at the time, now lower eyebrows rather than raise them. The provocative tone feels gentle, even kind, rather than insulting and worse. This is all the more stark for me personally, given the response to the report from one of the big rating agencies in June 2007. An article by John Plender in the FT had alerted them to the report. The promise of its presentation to the Centre for the Study of Financial Innovation seemed to fan the flames, and their displeasure could only be placated by giving us a good 'duffing up behind the bike shed'. In a face-to-face meeting, the head of ratings services in Europe told Jonathan and me, "It's easy to make the mistake of thinking you can judge something you are not in a position to understand. We suggest you think carefully about changing your wording".

The unfortunate effect of this was to mothball a second, more detailed report focusing on rating agency methodology, the monolines, and private equity. Better, we thought, to focus on managing client portfolios. Luckily, we didn't have to wait many weeks before Ohio Attorney General Marc Dann weighed in with words rather more weighty than ours: "The ratings agencies cashed a check every time one of these subprime pools was created and an offering was made. They continued to rate these things AAA . So they are among the people who aided and abetted this continuing fraud". (We just said they might be unwittingly overrating securities).

We took further flak in July after expressing our 'fallacy of composition' concerns in an FT Insight column. The CEO of Fisher Investments thought the idea of subprime contagion sparking a widespread credit crunch was "demonstrable nonsense" and called investors to 'be bullish and watch the bears impale themselves'. We begged to differ but judged by equity markets, and testament to the power of bull markets, we were still the eccentrics.

Very deterred and in need of a friend, I visited Bill White, the then head of research at the Bank for International Settlements in Basel. Now rightly credited as one of the prescient few amongst the central banking community, he was at the time sneered at by peers and, for that matter, colleagues because of his premature warnings and consistent bearishness. It's a thankless task being Chicken Licken in a Cocky Locky world. So Bill White really does deserve honour for standing up against the central banking crowd, as he did in his Jackson Hole speech in 2003, and continued to do so in the years up to the crisis. At the end of the meeting, he asked, "Do you think this is the big one?" – the glint in his eye betraying the rhetorical nature of the question.

A short time later, I was asked by the Committee of European Securities Regulators (acronym CESR, which sounds like 'seizure' if you say it with a Swedish accent), to present to their taskforce on rating agencies. The process was demanded by an angry Charlie McCreevy, European Commissioner for Internal Market and Services, to 'clarify the role of the rating agencies'. I found out subsequently that there had been only four presentations to the Stockholm based taskforce; three from rating agencies and one from me. 'After the Cracking comes the CESR'

That was in September 2007. It took another 12 months before Lehmans failed and the financial world experienced acute seizure. Keynes famously said, "Worldly wisdom teaches that it is better for reputation to fail conventionally than to succeed unconventionally," For an internal document written initially as a roadmap for portfolio managers, the turbulent trajectory of Cracking the Credit Market Code was a telling example of these wise words. More importantly though, it is a reminder that markets always offer opportunity to investors robust enough to withstand the discomfort of the journey.

Cracking the Credit Market Code

by Henry Maxey

April 2007

Introduction

Anyone with a cautious disposition has a sense that there is fragility within the US centric financial world: too much debt, excess consumption, record deficits, carry trades, ubiquitous hedge funds, monstrous derivatives markets...

Yet complexity in the interrelationships and instrumentation confines most cautious commentators like us to broad statements about the obvious dangers that these symptoms present. The facilitating mechanism appears to be, to quote Churchill, "a riddle, wrapped in a mystery, inside an enigma".

But now the subprime mortgage "pop" has knocked the lid from this "black box" and we have had our first opportunity to observe the mechanics of history's most excessive credit binge. It is our contention that the *magic* of the mechanism is nothing more than fallacy of composition, wrapped in moral hazard, inside Myopia Hedge Fund Partners LLC. Hence this report.

Structure

This report is a "whodunnit", or more appropriately "whosedoinit", rather than an exhaustive review of all the dicey elements of credit markets. We want to identify the serial killer, not the dodgy vicar or the crafty great aunt. It is divided into six chapters. The appendix contains a primer on structured credit which should be read first by anyone unfamiliar with the basics of these markets.

Abundant Liquidity"

This ill-defined, 'warm and cosy' concept is an apposite starting point given its proliferation in all sanguine market commentary. We find funding liquidity, and in particular, non-bank funding liquidity to be the most dominant feature of today's liquidity landscape.

The Anatomy of Funding Liquidity

We present our hypothesis that structured credit, hedge funds, and rating agencies are the key facilitators of the funding liquidity boom. We consider the incentives, the strategies, and the logic to support our hypothesis. Herein lies the key to the credit market code.

The Evidence

We examine some visible numbers and behaviours which support our hypothesis on funding liquidity.

"Hedge Fund Banks"

Given the evidence in Chapter three, we toy with the idea that hedge funds have become the real banks of the US financial system.

Fallacy of Composition

We address the question of how it is that a sophisticated financial system can allow such inefficient outcomes to occur.

Endgame

Having identified the key mechanics, we suggest the chain of events which would put an end to the "abundant liquidity" we considered in Chapter one.

Dot-to-Dot Review of the Argument

We link the argument together over two pages

Conclusion

Appendix

A primer on structured credit (CDOs etc)

"Abundant Liquidity"

The Asymmetry and Abuse of "abundant liquidity"

The term "abundant liquidity" is probably one of the most abused expressions of today's markets. It is rather like being told to eat muesli "because it's packed full of goodness". I am sure it is, but what on earth is 'goodness'? In the absence of an accepted framework of definitions, it is completely meaningless. In fact, worse than meaningless, it is deceitful: how much 'goodness' is there in a bowl of muesli if you have a nut allergy?

Our thesis is that the wave of purchasing power hitting asset markets is self-reinforcing, unstable and asymmetric.

I use the word purchasing power deliberately because, unlike liquidity, it isn't associated with any technical definitions; it merely refers to the aggregate ability of anybody to purchase assets through whatever means they have at their disposal – their firepower. Understanding what drives purchasing power is the first step in testing our thesis.

When we talk about purchasing power, we are dealing with three concepts (ignore any technical definitions for a moment, and think conceptually):

1 Money – gives you the ability to acquire assets that you can afford now with no external assistance. I have £1000 in my pocket, I can buy the £1000 bike in the shop window immediately.
2 Credit – gives you the ability to acquire assets which you can't afford with the money you have now. I don't have £1000 in my pocket, but I have £100 for a down payment and I can convince the seller that I can pay £50 a month for the next 2 years.
3 Leverage – gives you the ability to use what you have as collateral to acquire even more. I have bought the bike, I use the bike as collateral for a scooter, I use the scooter as collateral for a motorbike...I go home in a Ferrari (clearly a contrived example).

The difference between credit and leverage may appear unclear. Think of it in balance sheet terms; you don't necessarily need a balance sheet to get credit (I am an insolvent arsonist with no assets to my name, but the US mortgage system gives me a loan at 100% loan to value, and so I go out and buy a house. I now have a balance sheet: an asset/house valued at $x, and a loan/liability valued at $x). The point is I didn't need a balance sheet to get the credit. Leverage on the other hand requires, a priori, that you have a balance sheet since you are using an existing asset as collateral to acquire other assets. Perhaps the best way to phrase this is that credit is extended on the basis of what you can (or are perceived to be able to) deliver in the future, while leverage is extended on the basis of what you can deliver now.

In practice, of course, there is often an element of both in transactions, e.g., if I have a house worth $500k and I acquire $750k to buy a second home, some of this purchasing power is down to the house I already have (leverage) and some of it is down to perceptions about my future income/asset prospects (credit). Where we can identify leverage more clearly in its own right is in financial markets, e.g., hedge funds acquire purchasing power several multiples of their equity purely on the basis of the assets they present as collateral.

Where does liquidity sit relative to purchasing power?

Liquidity is a consequence of the combined firepower of spenders, be it money, credit or leverage. But the interesting question is not really whether it is credit or leverage, but rather 'who' is making the liquidity available. Money (as defined above) can come from anybody or anything with savings – this is balance sheet liquidity. But credit and leverage need the cooperation of a third party – traditionally a bank, but crucially nowadays, quite likely from someone other than a bank (or from a bank acting "off-balance sheet" and therefore outside its banking *persona*). The first of these are defined as "monetary liquidity", the latter as "funding liquidity". The three constructs are:

1 Balance sheet liquidity (who: anybody with a benign balance sheet) is about the relationship of cash to debt and equity on the balance sheets of non-financial entities. This essentially refers to the money purchasing power that non-financial entities have access to now. This relationship changes quite normally and predictably with the business cycle for companies, while maybe less predictably for households.

2 Monetary liquidity (who: banks) refers to the expansion of the balance sheets of central banks and commercial banks. Central banks alone can create high-powered money, which is mostly in the form of bank notes. Commercial banks create broad money (deposits) as the counterpart liability to their lending to the public and private sectors, including financial corporations. This includes lending via subsidiaries and affiliated companies to trading and underwriting in securities markets.

3 Funding liquidity (who: non-bank financials too) refers simply to the

means of financing a transaction and is influenced by both banks and non-banks. This will include bond and equity issues, unused lines of credit, and the use of collateral and leverage. Typically, there will be an element of the financing which is provided by banks in the form of overdrafts and lines of credit.

So references to liquidity should, if used precisely, tell us more about the who than the how, e.g., funding liquidity may be Goldman Sachs providing leverage to a hedge fund, or it may be its warehouse line of credit to a subprime lender. One is leverage, the other is credit, but both are funding liquidity from a non-bank financial institution.

The "abundant liquidity" we hear so much is really referencing funding liquidity. It refers to the ease and capability of financing an asset purchase by whatever means (credit or leverage) and is associated with a loose credit environment. It may be loose in the sense of being offered cheaply and/or loose in the sense of being plentiful in supply. While commercial banks provide some of the financing for these transactions – in financial instruments, business acquisitions and property – they are not alone in funding transactions. A high proportion of that funding liquidity is credit and leverage from non-bank financials.

Why does it matter if funding liquidity comes from non-bank financials?

Funding liquidity is far more pro-directional, fast footed and unstable than balance sheet or monetary liquidity. In a crisis, balance sheets need to be reduced by exchanging assets for cash, as only cash is safe. The liabilities of banks can be quickly exchanged for cash because central banks are forced to buy from them whatever exotica they hold in order to keep the banking system secure. Non-banks do not enjoy this buyer of last resort support, and are forced to attempt to sell their assets (probably no different in quality or type) into hostile markets.

History is littered with financial smashes and in the last 200 years governments have tried to control and dampen these excesses. They do so in two ways: by controlling how reckless the players can be, and by providing liquidity to rescue them when they have nonetheless overdone the exuberance. Economists call this high powered liquidity because it is directed at the commercial banking system where $1 does $10 of work as a result of the multiplier of the fractional banking system. The regulations tend to be backward-looking in that they firmly close the stable door from which the last horse has bolted, but, *autres temps, autres moeurs*, and the next crisis emerges from a new stable. So we should not be looking to the banks to be the source of the next crisis.

Banks in today's context represent genuine monetary liquidity: as we said above, if the banks have any sort of problem providing depositors with their cash (à la 1930s) because their more exotic assets are illiquid, the central bank stands ready to provide the necessary high powered liquidity to avoid a confidence crisis. This doesn't theoretically stop a bank going bust, but there is an umbilical cord to the Fed and realistically speaking the Fed will not allow a major bank to close down as a result of a run on deposits. This 'insurance' provokes moral hazard, another economists' term to describe excessive risk taking because someone else suffers the downside consequences. To mitigate this moral hazard, banks have to operate under constraints governing how much risk they can expose themselves to. (Ignore for the moment the effectiveness of these constraints – banks try to by-pass regulation through off-balance sheet activity).

In other words, the banking system represents liquidity through lender of last resort backing and security against serious moral hazard/malfeasance through lending constraints/regulation. The same framework clearly does not apply to non-bank institutions which extend credit or leverage.

Take non-bank credit: I have bought my car on credit, the credit has been provided to me by a non-bank credit company which has managed to raise funds in the bond market by selling a collection of other car loans to willing investors. Better still, if there are lots of willing investors, it is possible for the cost of finance on my loan to fall. However, if I fail to pay my interest and then default, the credit company has to foreclose on the loan, reclaim the car and then attempt to get cash back by selling the car. There is a high probability that the cash realised from the sale will not match the principal of the loan, i.e., the liability is not readily and reliably exchangeable for cash. In fact, it can be worse, because it is likely that the point at which the car needs to be liquidated is a time when others are also trying to liquidate foreclosed loans, e.g., if there is an economic downturn. Therefore, non-bank credit is very different to monetary liquidity, and far more pro-cyclical.

Take non-bank leverage: we tend to look to the financial sector for pure-play examples of leverage. An example would be a hedge fund which uses its assets as collateral for leverage provided by a non-bank (usually via the repo market). If the margin requirement is 20%, the fund could be 5x leveraged. However, if the assets of the fund fall in value, more collateral will need to be posted or assets sold to maintain margin requirements. Of course, when lots of investors are leveraged and adverse price dynamics require asset sales, then the prices and 'market liquidity' (defined in the footnote above) decline quickly, forcing further sales etc. So again, the purchasing power conveyed by leverage creates pro-directional influences on prices: on the way up it feels like there is "abundant liquidity", on the way down it feels like there is a deficiency.

In Summary

Although non-bank funding liquidity (credit and leverage) confers purchasing power, there is no certainty that the assets which collateralise/underpin that lending will be marketable at the value against which they are currently collateralised. Provision of funding liquidity is therefore determined, in large part, by risk appetite: when providers are comfortable with the asset price environment, funding liquidity will tend to increase. By its nature then, funding liquidity will tend to be pro-cyclical to the economy and pro-directional to asset/risk markets (as the collateral increases in value, you can leverage up more), and this creates asymmetry in aggregate liquidity (more on the way up than on the way down). It means there is more fragility than if purchasing power is conferred by monetary liquidity or balance sheet liquidity.

The Anatomy of Funding Liquidity

Today's funding liquidity boom

For several years now, we have marvelled at the capacity of credit markets to accommodate ever more ludicrous developments: mortgages to insolvent arsonists, a leveraged buyout of "the world's 'crappiest' steel company", sovereign spreads that don't care whether you are Che Guevara or Maggie Thatcher, AAA rated Icelandic banks, derivative market growth rates that make your eyes water ...

We have heard such developments rationalised away with equally ludicrous new paradigms, and repeatedly been reassured that even if there are risks, credit market innovation has allowed risk to be dispersed more healthily around the system.

Despite our scepticism, it has been very difficult to penetrate the technical innovations of these more opaque markets to pinpoint what the frailty of the mechanics might be. Now, with the subprime debacle unfolding, we have been able to get a better look under the bonnet of the machine and increase the precision of our understanding. This has allowed us to refine our instability hypothesis as follows:

The funding liquidity boom has, at its heart, explosive growth of structured credit markets. The development of structured credit markets has more to do with the models of ratings agencies and the incentives of hedge funds than the arbitraging of pricing inefficiency out of credit markets. The players involved are behaving as if they have discovered a 'perpetual motion money machine'. The result: an unstable surge in non-bank funding liquidity and rapid expansion of debt into a very benign part of the credit cycle, which means that any inappropriate debt creation will not become apparent until the cycle turns down.

The story begins with moral hazard...

The macro monetary conditions of negative real interest rates created by the US Federal Reserve to fight the post 9/11 deflationary forces are responsible for setting off the current pro-cyclical wave of funding liquidity. Fed Chairman Alan Greenspan had already established enormous credibility in bailing the system out of stress situations (the Greenspan equity market put), and when Bernanke delivered his November 2002 speech in which he promised unconventional measures to stave off deflation, we got the Bernanke credit market put. This provided credit markets with the necessary confidence to begin recovering from their Enron/'corporate malfeasance' malaise, and with that, the positive momentum of this stage of the credit cycle began.

Coinciding with the turn in the credit cycle, was the emergence of the alternative investment focused, absolute return paradigm within portfolio management and developments in structured finance, which led to changes in the mechanics of the US credit system. The rise of hedge funds and ratings agencies as key players in these new mechanics has, as we will see below, introduced moral hazard into the credit system at the micro level.

The aim now is to explore the mechanics of how a system saturated in macro and micro moral hazard has released this surge in non-bank funding liquidity into capital markets. And what better place to start than with "the hedge funds".

Boo for "the hedge funds"

It has become fashionable to blame any market woes on "the hedge funds". So, let's start by saying that the term hedge fund is only marginally more useful than the term liquidity. All it really tells us is that we are talking about a fund which charges a performance fee, has access to leverage and is usually unregulated. When talking about hedge funds we should identify the investment strategy being employed. For the sake of this report, when I talk about hedge funds I am referring to those funds which are active players in structured credit markets – about 28% (or $420bn) of the universe (see Chapter on Evidence).

We believe that these funds have become critical players in the credit system, but it is their influence rather than their size that is important.

First consider the forces driving the growth in credit related hedge fund assets, the preferences directing these flows, and the incentives these produce.

The making of hedge funds

Post 2002, hedge funds are the answer. It was the 2000-2002 bear market which brought the hedge fund opportunity into the mainstream. Factors driving this change were: the poor performance of stock markets post the TMT boom, a rejection of the relative return approach to fund management, and the acceptance by asset allocators that alternative assets should make up a more material portion of portfolios. Hedge funds as part of the alternative asset world appeared to offer the nirvana of positive absolute returns in all markets. (The overall universe of hedge fund assets has grown from c. $350bn in 2000 to more than $1.4tn today).

Fund of funds are the conduit. Because of their specialised, opaque and diverse nature conventional investors could only cope with them (like Medusa and the mirror) at some remove. Encouraged by the success of early hedge fund investors, such as Yale's endowment fund, investors and advisers rounded on the fund of funds hedge fund model. As such, the fund of funds management model has quickly become the key driver of asset flows into the growing hedge fund universe.

Smoothed returns are the goal. The fund of funds model is heavily biased towards funds that generate low volatility, positive absolute returns (usually of c.1% per month, net of fees), both because that is what the overall fund of funds aims to achieve and also because leverage is often applied by the fund of funds too (so they don't want leveraged downside deviation). Emphasis in fund of fund asset allocation is on 3 to 6 month performance statistics, and risk management necessitates the culling of funds which under-perform over this time frame. Of course the fund of funds usually charges fees on top of the underlying fund fees so, suppose the hedge funds in the fund's portfolio have a decent year and make 20% before any fees. After the standard hedge fund fee of 20% of the profits plus 1.5% of assets, your gain is down to 14.5%. Then the fund of funds socks you for an additional 1.5% of assets and 10% of profits, so your 20% gain has shrunk to a return of a little more than 11.7%. Looked at another way, the fund of funds need its underlying funds to produce 20% gross return each year to get its 1% per month.

But 20% returns imply capital risk. According to Dimson, March and Staunton (ABN Amro, 2006), the best performing asset class between 1900 and 2005 was equities. The annualised percentage real return on US equities was 6.5% over this period (Swedish equities were the best with 7.8%). This implies that to achieve consistent nominal 20% annual returns requires:

(i)   a fund manager who can deliver consistent alpha and/or
(ii) high inflation and/or
(iii) acceptance of higher risk (e.g., use of leverage)

The first of these is exceptionally rare, the second is not currently relevant, which leaves the third as the most likely candidate.

This is fine for hedge funds 'genetically' predisposed to volatility. The embedded call option-like payoff structure of hedge funds (big fees if performance is good, no personal loss if performance is bad), and the limited liability legal structure, provide incentives to take more risk than if the payoffs were more symmetrical. As we know from Black-Scholes pricing models for options, the value of an option increases with the volatility of the underlying asset price. It makes sense therefore that hedge funds should look for assets with high volatility, since this maximises the value of their '12 month call option' by increasing the chance of their big pay-off. Herein lies micro moral hazard.

But funds of funds aren't tolerant of capital risk. High capital volatility is bad as far as the fund of funds risk management assessments are concerned, and these assessments operate on shorter time horizons than hedge fund performance payouts. This means hedge funds have to balance the incentive to take more risk with the need to satisfy 'capital volatility scared' investors, in order to retain assets.

This leads us to the theoretical holy grail of hedge fund strategies: leveraged spread strategies in illiquid assets.

Illiquidity in the assets is essential. The danger with liquid assets is that market forces can change prices for both fundamental and haphazard reasons. Ordinarily holders of assets expecting a 20% return will accept commensurate volatility, but in a world demanding smoothed returns, this is unacceptable. Consequently, it becomes key that the capital value is not left to the vagaries of the market place.

Without a liquid market to price an asset, pricing is supplied by, for example, models. These frameworks tend to be self-serving because they are developed by players, such as ratings agencies and investment banks, who are more incentivised to give investors what they want than to ensure the price is an accurate reflection of the fundamentals. Prices, therefore, don't change until the fundamentals, e.g., default rates, force a reassessment of the model inputs.

Everything hangs on default and downgrade. Actual default or downgrade become the critical events rather than markets' forward looking pricing of that event, so problems are withheld until discontinuous pricing events occur rather than being anticipated in a continuously priced market. The capital prospects for the asset beyond 12 months are not of primary importance while the leverage yield spread provides the necessary return/volatility performance figures. Such a strategy is encouraged by a lack of visibility of the underlying portfolio (strategy secrecy), and a lack of regulation. To see this in action consider the following:

In a Morgan Stanley piece on high yield equity tranches, the probability of exceeding the breakeven loss rates for the 0-10% tranche is calculated using historical patterns of default rates as being>95%. "Despite being much "thicker" than their investment grade brethren and offering all upfront cash flows, the high yield tranches represent much riskier plays on credit" ["thicker" being a technical term to describe the % size of the equity tranche, rather than a descriptive one].

Why on earth would anyone invest in something which has a 95% probability of 0% IRR? The answer is that the attraction of a big upfront premium (in this case 79% to cover 5 years) is overwhelming for players who can afford to ignore the lifetime returns of the asset because they are rewarded for the premium which they calculate to have been earned over

12 months. By the time this 'earned premium' proves not to have been earned because backend loaded losses wipe out prior year premiums (to give the 0% IRR) the performance fees on the prior years' 'earned premia' have been taken and are not refundable.

Which leads us to the perfect hedge fund asset. The junior tranches of structured credit are nicely formed to offer the ideal combination of attributes (and a few additional ones too) to satisfy the needs of hedge fund operators themselves, if not their clients. And within the universe of structured credit, CDOs, CMOs, and CLOs are the most distilled vessels of credit risk, because they tend to buy the junior tranches of other structured credit instruments or subordinated debt/loans from debt financing deals. This process of distilling credit risk gives the junior tranches of these structures a very high yield, an impossible to model price, and maximum illiquidity: they are the perfect hedge fund asset.

So what exactly do the hedge funds do?

The real answer is: it's difficult to know for sure since there are multiple strategies. But generically two broad approaches are possible:

1 *Long bias* credit risk strategies- funds buy junior tranches of structured credit (CDOs, CLOs, CMOs, MBSs, ABSs, etc) to express a positive view on credit and enjoy the high yield these leveraged instruments provide. It is tempting to think from the incentives described above that this is the main game. But I think it is also disingenuous to suggest that the hungriest and ablest people in finance would be doing something so vanilla. Especially so, when we consider they have to persuade fund of funds, who are risk management driven, to invest their money. So while I am sure that there is some long bias money playing in credit markets, I think the majority of money is in much more sophisticated relative value strategies.

2 *Relative value* credit risk strategies – funds arbitrage the theoretical difference in value between different tranches of a structured credit, and between tranches of structured credit and other assets. A simple example of this would involve being long the junior tranches and short senior tranches (all beta adjusted) to give a much smaller net credit exposure but still providing a positive yield spread, which can be leveraged up to provide the required return. This approach keeps the risk police happy because the net credit exposure appears more limited and with it the capital volatility risk.

Intra-tranche relative value trades are known as correlation trades because the effectiveness of the trade relies on the tranches moving together in a correlated fashion. Holders of equity tranches are said to be long correlation since the risk they cannot hedge effectively against using other tranches is the risk of specific, rather than generalised defaults (see GM/Ford example below). If the predicted correlation breaks down then the short postions in the more senior tranches will fail to offset the long postions in the junior tranches as envisioned, disrupting the trade. This is exactly what happened in 2005 with the GM/Ford debacle.

When GM and Ford were being downgraded this was a negative event for equity holders of CDOs since a specific default by one of them would have likely wiped out the equity in CDOs that held either company's debt. Many hedge funds had shorted mezzanine tranches to buy equity tranches as a bet that any defaults in the CDO would be correlated (a general economic event) and so what would be lost on the equity would be more than made up for by gains on the short mezzanine position. The auto downgrades caught these players out, and because there was so little liquidity in the mezzanine tranches they could not cover their shorts. Instead they shorted the auto stocks to hedge out the long equity tranche exposure. Unfortunately, Kerkorian's bid for 10% of the equity then squeezed this hedge, inflicting double whammy pain. This was a good example of how variable tranche liquidity can catch 'sophisticated' hedge funds out.

So while it is tempting to suggest hedge funds are just punting risky credit to take performance fees on high yield spreads, I think it is wrong to do so. More likely, while there is probably still a net long credit risk position being run by the funds, there is a very much bigger gross credit risk position being achieved via relative value/correlation strategies.

Cosmetically, too, relative value strategies hold within them a theoretical grain of truth which allows the believers to hold their faith.

Grains of truth, agencies of deception

At the heart of every mania is a grain of truth to support the believers' faith in the fundamentals supporting the bubble. For TMT it was the very real opportunity of the digital revolution to change/improve so many processes, e.g., booking airline tickets, auctioning esoteric objects, etc, that formed the basis of the euphoria. In this case, the argument is that credit derivatives and structured credit allow players to arbitrage the pricing inefficiencies of what was previously illiquid credit. The standard line from the central authorities goes something like this:

> By spreading risk more broadly, providing opportunities to manage and hedge risk, and making it possible to trade and price credit risk, credit market innovation should help make markets both more efficient and more resilient. They should help make markets better able to allocate capital to its highest return and better able to absorb stress. Broad, deep and well-functioning capital markets complemented by strong, well-capitalized banks, able to provide liquidity in times of strain, make for a more efficient financial system: one which contributes to better economic growth outcomes over time. (Timothy Geithner, Chairman of NY Fed, March 2007)

There are two potential levels of inefficiency:
i) Aggregate/whole structure absolute price inefficiency, i.e., the cost of credit is, in aggregate, too high.
ii) Inter-tranche relative price inefficiency, i.e., some tranches are more expensive relative to others.

The theoretical argument for structured credit goes that by tranching up credit risk that was previously only saleable in whole part, one can release absolute value, i.e., lower its cost. The tranching process opens up the available market for the aggregate risk to a much bigger pool of potential buyers (e.g., institutional buyers for rated paper, specialists for the lower tranches), which maximises potential demand for each tranche of risk and minimises pricing inefficiency. It's rather like a French butcher selling Wild Boar. By cutting it into different parts he can get a better overall price because different customers prefer different cuts and anything the leftovers make is a bonus. By getting more in aggregate, the butcher can pay more for wild boar to the hunter which encourages hunting. Higher wild boar prices are equivalent to lower cost mortgages.

Relative value trades should be an integral part of this arbitrage process. If buying demand is weighted in senior tranches then those tranches can be sold more expensively, i.e., at lower yields, leaving junior tranches with more residual cashflow, i.e., at higher yields. Buying is then encouraged for these other tranches which should drive their price up/yield down, hence bring the aggregate cost of credit down.

In today's credit markets, the argument to support relative value is derived from the idea that the weight of money still favours investment grade tranches (liability matching by pension funds, foreign dollar surpluses), and the buying power for junior tranches is much smaller being specialist players such as banks and hedge funds.

In theory these arguments are robust. Even in practice, I am happy to believe there have been some genuine efficiency gains to be made. However, the frailty of the argument has been laid bare by the development of aggregate price inefficiency of the opposite extreme – too low a cost of credit for subprime mortgage borrowers.

A genuinely efficient market would not allow this absolute pricing inefficiency to occur. The conceptual reasons for this failure are obvious; efficient market theory assumes liquid, transparent markets for structured credit, in which everyone has complete information. False, false, and false again. Try pricing a tranche of structured credit whose underlying assets are tranches of asset backed securities. I quote from Morgan Stanley's primer on CDOs:

> The complex waterfall structures and the potential for diversion of cash flows because of structural protections and coverage triggers imply that analytical models have to take into account the default probabilities as well as the determinants of the different coverage ratios in mutually consistent fashion. This, coupled with the optional redemption feature of most CDOs, calls for the modelling of interest rate risk in conjunction with the default risks of assets. Since the underlying collateral pools are managed, albeit according to predefined guidelines, the impact of future trading activities of collateral managers is difficult to model. Some analyses model the trading provisions assuming that the managers will trade at the extremes of all possible trading constraints, which has the effect of painting all managers with the same brush, constraining relative value judgment. Trading further complicates the already difficult problem of modelling and parameterization of correlation.

Modelling is monstrously complex, and there is not a liquid market on which to base the valuations, which explains why rating agencies are the Willy Wonkas of the US credit factory, helping to create the illusion of the 'everlasting relative value trade'– "You can suck 'em and suck 'em and suck 'em, and they'll never get any smaller".

Ratings agencies and moral hazard

The rating agencies assign ratings to different tranches of structured credit. Many investors invest on the basis of the rating alone, because they don't have the tools, information or inclination to analyse the underlying collateral in the pools. More people will buy a given risk than an uncertain risk; by creating "certainty", the rating agencies are incentivised to maximise flow as they are paid fees by the issuers of the paper – this creates the second micro level moral hazard. By ensuring that the upper tranches offer a yield premium over similarly rated instruments in other assets' markets, the agencies guarantee that there is sufficient demand for these tranches. Because demand is generally blind to the underlying fundamentals, instead dependent on the guidance of the agencies, the rating and yield on this paper may not fully reflect the risks, i.e., it can be priced expensively. This implies that the junior tranches would get way too high a residual cashflow, offering correspondingly better value – we are robbing Peter (or more likely Mrs Watanabe), to pay Paul (at Myopia LLC).

One thing we should be clear about here, we are not saying rating agencies are maliciously deceiving senior tranche investors. They are very likely doing their best to balance sensible modelling with the demand they face for the paper in the market. The trouble is the heritage of these agencies is in rating non-financial corporate credit, they simply don't have the historical experience to back up their modelling of today's more complex structured credit instruments.

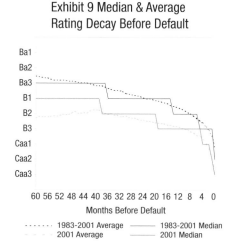

Exhibit 9 Median & Average Rating Decay Before Default

Source: Moody's, Default & Recovery Rates of Corporate Bond Issuers, February 2002

In conclusion, the rating agencies have pandered to the market for yield enhancement by assigning investment grade ratings to instruments that do not deserve them. By so doing they have endangered their own business and wilfully misled the investing public.

The reason that this deception can persist is that the poor/expensive absolute value of the upper tranches is not exposed by the fundamentals (i.e., actual defaults) in the benign phase of a credit cycle, so buyers of this paper are oblivious to the deception. In fact demand for this investment grade, premium yield, paper is high enough to absorb as much as is offered. Equally demand for the junior paper is limitless while the rating agencies ensure this relative value trade (junior tranches over senior ones) persists, and illiquidity of the junior paper means its price doesn't adjust up. *So herein lies the perpetual motion machine of collateralised credit.*

With demand for both senior rated and junior paper seemingly limitless, issuance proliferates, and the 'machine' is theoretically only constrained by the volume of underlying collateral origination (i.e., the volume of loans actually being given to the house buyers etc).

Now even this constraint is by-passed through the creation of synthetic products, a dynamic highlighted by the numbers emerging from the sub-prime market (but evident across many other areas of the credit market). In the year to November 2006, c\$420bn of subprime mortgage backed securities were originated. Hypothetically, if all of these were pooled and then tranched up (most of them were, but obviously into a number of smaller pools), UBS calculates that 75% of the pool would be rated AAA, 14% would be in tranches rated AA+ to A-, 3% would be in tranches rated BBB+ to BBB-, 2% would be lower rated tranches, and 6% in the unrated equity tranche. This implies \$12.6bn of BBB+ to BBB- paper was created out of subprime mortgage origination. Mezzanine ABS CDOs had been focusing on this paper (primarily to achieve their return on equity require-ments), and it made up 65% of their collateral over the same period. So if they had bought all \$12.6bn it would suggest that the issuance capacity for this flavour of CDO was \$19.4bn (\$12.6/64%). In fact, \$42bn of mezz ABS CDOs were issued. The additional \$22bn of paper was originated using synthetic BBB+ to BBB- paper, i.e., demand outstripped cash market origination by at least 2 to 1. With demand pressures like this, is it any wonder that mortgage brokers were handing cash out to anyone who could sign their name?

Headline commentary on the subprime affair has argued from a starting point of lax underwriting standards. It would seem to me that the relaxation of mortgage origination standards was not an ill considered decision by the mortgage originators, but a perfectly rational response to extraordinary demand pressures created by CDO activity. To increase their volumes, originators could have reduced the cost of the loan, or reduced their underwriting standards. Given the yield hunger of the CDO buyers, relaxing standards was the most rational response.

Why exactly does the efficient market fail?

If an efficient market really were operating, then this relative value opportunity would be arbitraged out since the price of the higher rated 'expensive' paper would fall, and/or the price of the junior paper rise. Without obvious relative value, the aggregate demand for collateral should normalise at natural levels and absolute prices should be less prone to distortion. However, because rating agencies control the demand for individual tranches via the rating and demand for highly rated paper is seemingly limitless (Asian surpluses, Western liability matching, oil, dollars, etc), overrated upper tranches sell expensively, allowing junior tranche investors to continue their arbitrage.

Ratings agencies are able to do this because the actual riskiness of a senior tranche of a CDO is greater than a correspondingly rated conventional bond: thus there is additional yield, commensurate with that actual riskiness, some of which can be used to provide a tiny yield uplift, sufficient to attract rating constrained, yield hungry buyers. Meanwhile, the junior paper is illiquid and so is priced by model rather than demand, so its price does not 'mark to market'.

The result is that the relative value trade persists because it cannot be arbitraged out. Demand for more of the same trade increases, ensuring that CDO issuance balloons. As CDO issuance balloons, demand for favoured CDO collateral (MBS paper, leveraged loans, emerging market debt, etc) balloons as well, and distortions in absolute prices proliferate.

Even as absolute prices for the underlying collateral become irrational, i.e., insolvent arsonists getting 100% loan-to-value mortgages, the persistence of relative value and continued confidence in ratings ensures demand remains strong very late into the cycle. This is why subprime loan demand remained strong into the second half of 2006 even though the fundamentals of the sector were already signalling bad times ahead.

Of course as absolute prices of collateral continue to increase, a net long bias is encouraged, and the popularity of credit related strategies attracts more money in, which fuels the credit machine further until actual defaults expose just how absurd absolute prices have become.

In Summary

The absolute cost of credit is driven to inefficiently low levels because relative value trades do not arbitrage the rating agency induced pricing distortions out of the market, with the result that demand for the underlying collateral increases.

In the olden days, banks generally tried to make good loans because it was their balance sheet that was hit if the loan went bad: banks acted as principals. Now, the argument goes that markets are better able to price credit risk than individuals at banks, so the growth of structured credit and credit derivative markets is an improvement. Yet, it is perverse that in this supposedly market driven system, demand is actually determined primarily by rating agencies and the rating they, rather than any market, deems appropriate. So we have taken one off-market system (banks credit departments) and replaced it with another (rating agency models). By doing so, we have introduced moral hazard because ratings agencies have only income, rather than capital, to lose if the rating turns out to have been misleading, but lots to gain while any mispricing keeps issuance high. So until market forces are allowed to act on the setting of ratings (i.e., the rating reacts to a market analysis of the underlying collateral, or there is a proper competitive market in ratings), the rating agency driven system appears inferior to the old bank credit officer one.

The Evidence

It sounds a neat theory, but are we correct to make the assertion that non-bank funding liquidity, particularly from alternative investment vehicles, is a dominant feature of the financial system?

The figures are public knowledge, and are big

Charts of primary dealer net repo positions give us a good proxy of leverage being employed by their prime broker counterparties, i.e., hedge funds. This chart shows a parabolic move up over the last 5 years to c$1.3tn or c.10% of US GDP. We should note that this data only captures primary dealers, so it doesn't capture the leverage of all prime brokerage arrangements but it captures most of it (and Greenspan used it as a reasonable proxy). Some studies have indicated the average leverage employed by the hedge fund sector is 1.5-2.0x, which given hedge fund net assets of c.1.4tn, would imply leverage of $2.1tn to $2.8tn.

Not only is this a huge figure in absolute terms (20% of US GDP), but two other factors make it considerably more toxic. First, it is the distribution of this leverage rather than the average across all funds that matters, and some funds are more leveraged than others. Second, the development and innovation of structured credit has yielded paper with high levels of embedded leverage which isn't captured in the leverage numbers above. This final point is the killer. The ability to achieve high multiples of leverage via investment rather than explicit leverage, makes it much harder to draw comfort from data on explicit leverage alone.

For example, a $10m unlevered hedge fund might leverage up 5x to achieve $60m of purchasing power. Then by buying the equity tranche (3%) and BBB tranche (4%) of a residential mortgage backed security it can achieve capped first loss exposure to $850m of residential mortgages. (This example is taken from a 2005 Fitch report discussing the influence of hedge funds on the market liquidity of credit markets). The jump from $60m of purchasing power to $850m of exposure is achieved because junior tranches benefit from residual cashflows after the higher rated tranches have been paid their coupon. At the same time they suffer the first hits if there are payment delinquencies or defaults within the underlying pool of collateral. So by buying the last 7% of the MBS structure, the hedge fund has used the cheap funding of senior tranches to acquire residual cashflows on a huge pool of collateral. The leverage multiple is $1/0.07 = 14.3x$.

If explicit and embedded leverage are facilitating rapid credit expansion we should see it at the aggregate level, and we do. A global GDP of $44tn and global savings rate of 20% give us c.$8.8tn of savings. Savings are obviously used for various purposes, e.g., financial investment, replacement capital, and fixed asset investment, so it is unlikely that more than $1/3^{rd}$ of savings, i.e., c.$3tn finds its way into financial markets. Yet, $11.5tn of securities, mainly fixed income, were issued last year. Now some of this issuance will be related to the rolling over of maturing securities, i.e., investors in the original security use their maturity proceeds to fund the newly issued one, but this would not make up the difference between c.$3tn and £11.5tn. So not only does this make a mockery of the global savings glut thesis, it implies huge additional purchasing power is available from somewhere. Money supply figures are nowhere near high enough for monetary liquidity to be involved. Therefore, the shortfall has to be accounted for by balance sheet and funding liquidity.

My thesis is that non-bank funding liquidity provides the firepower to fund junior tranche issuance, and global balance sheet liquidity combined with yield hunger in a low yield environment is sufficiently large to fund the higher rated paper.

Hedge fund participation in credit markets is material

In terms of attitudes towards strategies, Charles Peabody of Portales Partners characterised the US hedge fund world as being spread driven, in contrast to the UK being directional. Given that spread strategies are more likely to involve credit, this illustrates an important cultural bias which is undoubtedly reflected in the activity of funds.

Hedge funds, according to one recent survey, account for 58% of the volume in credit derivatives in the year to the first quarter of 2006.

Given that credit instruments may be used in a variety of hedge fund strategies, it is impossible to say exactly how much of the $1.4tn of hedge fund assets are allocated to credit markets. Jacob Schmidt, head of Allenbridge Hedge Info said, "at least 25% to 30% of the estimated 9000 hedge funds that exist in the world are concentrating on credit in some way now". Recent industry data from HFR, a hedge fund industry market research firm, supports this through its estimated allocation of $1.4tn of hedge fund assets:

8.0% or c.$112bn	=	Fixed income (MBS, High Yield, Convert, Fixed Income arb, diversified).
4.6% or c.$64bn	=	distressed debt
3.3% or c.$42bn	=	Convertible arbitrage
11.9% or c.$166bn	=	relative value

In other words, 27.8% or c.$390bn of hedge fund assets could be involved in leverage credit spread strategies.

The CFA journal recently stated that dedicated structured credit funds had grown exponentially in the last three years and now controlled $42bn of assets. It doesn't seem much until one considers the leverage that can be achieved as we showed above.

Probably most telling when it comes to the influence of hedge funds are the numerous speeches that T Geithner, Chairman of the New York Fed has made in which he specifically references hedge funds as being key players in the US credit system:

"Hedge funds, private equity funds and other leveraged financial institutions control increasingly large shares of aggregate financial capital and play very active roles in many asset markets and in credit markets. Although assets under management in hedge funds still represent a relatively small share of total financial assets, their relative share has increased significantly and their ability to take on substantial leverage magnifies their potential impact on financial market conditions. These private leveraged funds have become an important source of protection to regulated institutions by being large sellers of credit insurance in the rapidly growing market for credit default swaps" (Sept 2006)

Influence does not require size

A different approach is to ask how much participation is needed, given what we know about structured credit. Collateralised vehicles (CDOs, CMOs, CLOs) often invest in the junior paper of the MBS, ABS and leveraged loans. Let's say this tends to be from the last 15% of any structure/deal. Hedge funds investing in these collateralised vehicles tend to invest in the junior tranches or equity, i.e., the last c.10%-15% of these structures, in order to generate the 20% gross returns they need. This implies embedded leverage of 44-66x [1/(15% x 10-15%)].

Last year funded CDO issuance hit $488.6bn (Structured finance = $292, high yield loans = $165bn, investment grade = $22bn, high yield bonds = $2.7bn [from SIFMA 02/2007]). This represented 11.5% of the $4.21tn issuance of MBS, ABS and corporate debt in 2006. Using the 10%-15% ratios above, *it would only need buyers of $49-73bn of junior paper to support this CDO issuance (assuming the senior rated tranches are easily sold), which itself provided support to $4.21tn of bond issuance.* Such embedded leverage means that smaller pools of capital are able to determine the fate of much bigger pools of borrowing.

We have already seen from an earlier example that demand for BBB- subprime residential mortgage backed paper from managers of mezz ABS CDO funds was c.2x greater than the actual amount originated ($42bn versus $19bn). In other words, although 20% of last year's mortgage origination, or $420bn, was in subprime, this was still not enough to satisfy CDO requirements for junior paper. This shows the leveraged impact that these investors can have on overall markets.

The ratios above work at the MBS level too. Non-agency MBS issuance was up 15% last year at $743bn, ABS issuance was $1.23tn (Home Equity Loans, credit card receivables, auto loans, student loans, leases). Structured finance CDO issuance, based on MBS and ABS was $293bn, or 15% of non-agency MBS and ABS combined.

Beyond what is retained by the CDO issuers, hedge funds are active in the junior tranches of structured credit

We can see their footprints all over the place even if we can't see their faces. Various commentaries on CDO equity identify hedge funds as major participants: "Hedge funds buy them as a way to be levered in the underlying assets via the CDO vehicle rather than via their own debt financing. Some insurance companies and banks purchase CDO equity. In the past two years, several asset managers have started funds that specialise in CDO equity" (UBS credit strategist, Douglas Lucas, responding to the question "who are the buyers of CDO equity?").

The 20% required return of hedge funds (for the FoFs to make 1% per month) makes the high yielding junior tranches of CDOs very attractive. A UBS research piece shows how a mezz ABS CDO equity tranche yields 21% – bingo! (The underlying paper in this example is BBB and BBB- subprime mortgage paper.) Manufacturing paper that yields c.20% is likely to find buyers.

In another piece of UBS research, the authors were exploring why BBB tranches of synthetic ABS trade tighter than the same tranches of cash ABS. Bear in mind here, that a synthetic ABS is made up of credit default swaps, i.e., contracts in which the seller insures the buyer of protection against payment default, and therefore the seller of protection only has to put up a margin requirement against the contract rather than needing cash to buy the underlying securities. As such "If the marginal buyer is a real money account, with a choice of (1) buying the cash bond or (2) buying the synthetic and investing the money at LIBOR there is no reason for any spread differential. However, marginal buyers are rarely real money accounts; they are more typically hedge funds, basing their analysis on a risk-adjusted return on equity." In other words they fund the margin requirement, 7% in this case, because it is more favourable than financing the purchase of the cash bond with a less favourable haircut, 20% in this case. The calculations that followed showed how a synthetic position achieved a 14.3x leverage, versus 5x for the cash position, and hence a better return on equity. The bottom line is that synthetics trade tighter because hedge funds are the major players in these junior paper markets.

There are signs that ratings agencies are manufacturing relative value in structured credit

Objectively judging what % of a pool of collateral should be investment grade versus non investment grade during the benign phase of a credit cycle even if we could see the underlying ratings models (which we can't) is incredibly difficult. What we can observe is that yield premia over equivalently rated paper seem to be used to attract investors looking for yield but constrained by ratings parameters.

A telling proxy of distorted pricing in any market is a sustained period of super-normal sales growth. In this respect the 28% compound annual growth rate of Moody's structured finance revenues has exceeded their total revenue growth of 22.5% pa every year for the last five.

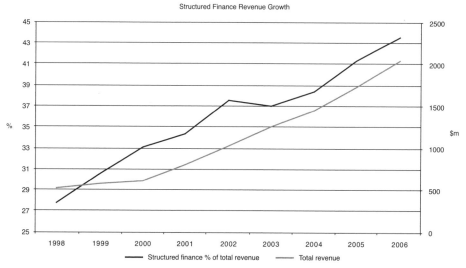

Structured Finance Revenue Growth

Source: Moody's

The mortgage market will give us a trial of our overrating thesis. Only once the subprime problems have damaged the rated paper in the structure will we be able to assess whether those upper tranches were more risky than the price/yield suggested. However, the early indications don't favour those 'safe' ratings:

"Assuming 40% of the assets of structured-finance CDOs are sub-prime bonds and all were downgraded by four levels, the credit ratings on some of the CDO's AAA securities would be lowered by two levels, Moody's said.

If 80% of the collateral are subprime bonds and are downgraded by four levels, even "super-senior" AAA bonds, the least-risky portion, would be lowered by two levels, and the other AAA bonds would be cut by six.

It would take downgrades of at least three levels on the collateral to affect the less-exposed CDO's AAA bonds and downgrades of two levels to affect the AAA bonds of the more highly exposed ones, Moody's said.

The amount of subprime mortgage-backed securities on 31 December in structured-finance CDOs issued before last year totalled 47% for ones issued in 2005, 49% for ones issued in 2004 and 41% for ones issued in 2003, Moody's said.

Standard & Poor's said in a report yesterday that mezzanine structured-finance CDOs' average exposure to subprime mortgage bonds grew to 74% of assets for ones created in 2006 from 42% of assets for ones created in 2003." (Bloomberg, March 27 2007)

A new index called the TABX was launched in February 2007, and as explained in the April 2007 issue of Grants Interest Rate Observer, it is already pricing in material downgrades of senior tranches of CDOs:

"Starting on Valentine's Day, a new, CDO-like set of derivatives began to trade. Suffice it to say that the TABX.HE 07-1 06-2 triple-B-minus index is a kind of synthetic CDO. It is authentic even down to the article of tranches, for it comes equipped with six subindices. The senior-most of the six tranches is, in the nature of these creations, the one that is protected by the five beneath it. It's called the 40-100 tranche, because the first 40% of the losses are borne by the junior five. Where would you guess the 40-100 tranche is trading now? The answer is available on Markit.com. The price is 83.8, which implies that the cost of a year's default insurance would run you seven full percentage points. Remember, this is the seniormost slice in the index, one that, if this were a rated structure, would carry a triple-A imprimatur – not because of the inherent strength of its assets, of course, but because of the supposed protection afforded by five tranches of padding."

Having listened to a conference call with Fitch which was hosted to address the subprime issue, it is clear that they are not going to act pre-emptively. They didn't with Enron – still investment grade when the bonds yielded 45% and only 3 months before Chapter 11.

No clear guidance of how downgrade decisions would be made was given, and any feature of the structure which could put off the tranche downgrade would suffice to delay this. So it will require the full impact of the cycle to be manifested in actual underlying defaults before downgrades occur. There appear to be plenty of delaying tactics available too, e.g., structural features such as over collateralisation tests, so delay and obfuscation until it cannot be contained any longer is how the ratings agencies will play it.

Although the integrity of ratings behaviour in structured finance is difficult to assess, the potential for distortion can be observed from strange rating agency behaviour in more obvious areas. Take for example, the March 2007 Icelandic banks' upgrade debacle. Moody's decided that it would upgrade 3 Icelandic banks to AAA rating on the basis of its new JDA modelling tool (JDA stands for Joint Default Analysis). The main driver of this model was the assumption that the government would rescue the companies if they had financial difficulties. Another beneficiary of the JDA model was a Hungarian lender OTP Bank, which received a three step boost to AA1, four steps above the rating of the government that Moody's said would rescue it. Although Moody's was forced to U-turn on these decisions, it is clear that they are quite happy to use perverse and the moral hazard enhancing assumptions in their modelling. What chance is there then that they are rating opaque structured credit tranches on the basis of underlying credit quality rather than what the market will bear?

It's not just agency's default modelling which seems a little strange, correlation assumptions too appear to be ad hoc. The following is from Arturo Cifuentes, former head of credit at Wachovia, in an article for the CFA digest – CDOs and Correlation: A Few Modelling Misconceptions.

"My personal opinion is that correlation based on geographical location is not very accurate. For example, just because Chile and Argentina share a common border does not mean that they share the same economic fate. In fact, their economic systems are fundamentally different, as are their political systems. Nevertheless, and despite my own misgivings as well as those of many other market participants, the rating agencies and monolines (insurers of debt) continue to believe in the validity of geography-driven correlations."

Probably the most compelling evidence for ratings malfeasance is just how extremely inefficienpot absolute pricing has become in exactly the areas you would expect it to if demand dynamics for the related collateral were being fuelled by a relative value trade which is blind to absolute prices. It must be highlighted that this pricing inefficiency is manifested primarily through falling underwriting standards, because if yields on the underlying credit were to fall too much it would reduce the attractiveness of the structures to yield hungry investors.

We saw the insanity in subprime loan origination, which continued unabated even after objective forecast measures of likely future performance were signalling problems ahead. We can see it in leveraged loan origination where *'no covenant' or 'cov-lite' loans are really to leveraged loans what 'no doc option ARMs' (Adjustable Rate Mortgages) are to mortgages.* It is the same underlying dynamic except it's fuelling private equity activity rather than mortgage origination. Look at the prices of any other of the collateral which is popular with CDO managers (eg, high yield bonds, emerging market debt) and you will see irrationality.

The predominance of relative value trades is suggested by the emphasis that 'correlation' as a variable receives within market commentary. Again from Arturo Cifuentes, CDOs and Correlation: A Few Modelling Misconceptions.

A fundamental flaw frequently seen in the modelling of CDOs (collaterized debt obligations) – that is, the variable most discussed [correlation], is the variable that is least relevant to the performance of the transaction.

The credit performance of the collateral pool depends on three factors whose behaviour is difficult to predict: probabilities of default, recovery rates, and correlation.

Default probability. By varying the value for the default probability by 20% (higher or lower), the mean of the portfolio loss changes by 20%. Thus, the estimation of the probability of default affects the model's estimation of portfolio loss in a significant manner.

Recovery rate. The variations in the mean and the standard deviation that result from the change in the recovery rate variable are both 13%. Thus, if an investor makes an error estimating the recovery rate, that error affects the expected loss, although not as much as a mistake in estimating the default probability.

Correlation. Investors can make a 20% error, up or down, and the mean loss calculated by the model shows almost no change (0.1%); likewise, the standard deviation changes by only 1.4%. Correlation, therefore, is far and away the least important factor in estimating the credit losses of a portfolio of assets. Probability of default is the primary driver – not correlation.

It is absolutely rational for correlation to be the focus of attention if relative value/correlation trades drive the decisions of the most active players in the market. This becomes even more relevant once absolute prices are implying unrealistic default probabilities and recovery rates.

Private equity both benefits from and fuels the process

Private equity transactions rely on credit markets to finance their deals, so heightened demand for junior tranches of collateralised leveraged loan obligations has allowed private equity/M&A deals to be financed at ever higher multiples of EBITDA.

Private equity funds also have skewed incentives (as well as their well documented tax advantages) in as much as they only have a chance of collecting performance fees if they do deals in the first place. However, they only get those fees once the fund has exited or realised its investments, which lies in stark contrast to hedge funds, who can take their fees annually. Because the private equity business model involves retaining a small slither of leveraged equity in acquired companies, their activity serves to increase the supply of debt/loans into the market and should, if anything, put upward pressure on spreads. However, demand for the high yield loans issued from the buyout financing has been so high that spreads have continued to narrow to record lows.

This can be partly explained by the rapid growth of CLOs (collateralised debt obligations typically backed by high yield loans), $165bn of which were issued in the US last year. If we assume that c.25% of the debt for a leveraged buyout is funded in the high yield loan market (a very rough estimate from a corporate financier), this suggests that c.$660bn of buyout activity was thus supported. Total US M&A value was $1.47tn, so our rough estimate suggests that nearly half of this activity received critical funding support from CLOs. Given that banks want to retain some of the paper, and hedge funds have become very active in buying whole loans directly, the CLO influence is significant. (General interest note: Total global M&A value was $3.7tn in 2006.)

Increased demand for corporate loans has resulted in underwriting standards dropping. According Morgan Stanley, the proportion of debt labelled senior in a LBO has increased from 37% of the capital structure to 59% between 2003 and H1 2006.

Demand for corporate loans has also allowed private equity to engage in recaps, i.e., early dividends, when the IPO market has been quiet, again with the help of hedge funds. These early dividends artificially boost the per annum return of the private equity fund.

A popular instrument to fund recaps has been PIK (Payment In Kind) bonds or loans. These are highly subordinated, unmarketable and do not pay interest for several years, but hedge funds can price them at book and accrue interest (15%-20%) annually even though the cash interest won't be paid until much later assuming no default. Defending a mark to model (even when it is indefensible) is easiest when you hold an ultra-high yield bond at book cost on the basis of: "it's paid the dividend, so it's worth what it was last year". In the case of PIK bonds you don't even get the dividend in the early years. The hedge funds obviously take non-refundable performance fees on this virtual interest annually.

The 'tag team' of hedge funds and private equity is particularly powerful. The hedge fund banking system creates super benign credit conditions, which allows cash flushed private equity funds to deal hyperactively. The apparent success of this alternative investment machine serves to attract even more money into these vehicles. Returns have been competed down, so the leverage needed to produce 20%-25% returns has necessarily increased. So far the credit cycle and credit mechanism have accommodated it.

In Summary
Non-bank funding liquidity is a hugely influential force in credit markets. Hedge funds are key to this liquidity, and their activity begs the question: are they banks? Unregulated, undercapitalised, wild-western BIS-free banks?

"Hedge Fund Banks"

Are these hedge funds unregulated banks?

Playing "leveraged spread strategies in illiquid assets" is essentially what a bank does. Banks take the spread between more liquid short term liabilities (deposits etc) and longer term, less liquid assets (loans) which usually carry credit risk. This liquidity gap is why they have to hold certain levels of regulatory capital relative to their assets, which are risk weighted (e.g., cash holding have 0% risk weight, unsecured loans have 100%).

So let's see how far can we take this "hedge fund bank" analogy. The new collective wisdom of the actuaries and investment consultants acts like the monetary policy of the central bank, and the new alternative investment focus is like a change in monetary policy. The asset allocators with this new alternative investment paradigm reallocate assets to hedge funds (often via funds of funds) and particularly to those demonstrating a historically successful spread strategy (which hasn't been too difficult over the last 5 years). These new investors entering the "hedge fund bank" model represent the 'depositors' of the system, the term of these hedge fund liabilities are determined by redemption periods, usually monthly, i.e., like short term bank deposits. Of course 'depositors' in a "hedge fund bank" do accept more capital volatility in their assets than depositors in commercial banks, however, their risk management techniques, which fund of hedge funds use to justify their fees, ensure that they will react as if they can't tolerate any capital volatility. In this sense they are apt to behave just like frightened depositors to a banking system scare, and run for the door if their capital is threatened.

Commercial banks can lever up their core capital provided they meet their capital adequacy requirements. "Hedge fund banks" have no core capital, but they can lever up their 'depositor'/asset base. In order to do so, they have to post margin (initial margin and then variation margin if underlying asset values change). Like the capital adequacy requirements, margin restricts the multiplier that can be achieved on the funds' asset base. It also assumes that the providers of leverage act like regulators and properly assess the risks of the hedge fund portfolio:

> "The ability of funds to take on risk and leverage is constrained by two external sources of discipline—the returns required by their investors [discussed above], and the terms on which their deal-

ers/financers are willing to extend credit. In other words, the fund is constrained by the willingness of outsiders, collectively, to take exposure to the fund. The willingness of banks and investment banks to take on exposure to hedge funds is in turn influenced by the capital and supervisory framework that applies to those institutions and the discipline imposed on them by the market."

But

"Funds typically deal with several different banks and investments banks. The desire to maintain the confidentiality of their trading strategies has traditionally led firms to be quite opaque to outsiders and reluctant to give their banks sufficiently detailed information on a real time basis about the risk profile of the overall fund. Without that information, individual dealers or banks have a difficult time evaluating the probability of default of a leveraged counterparty and the potential covariance with other positions of the firm." (NY Fed Chairman, T Geithner Sept 2006)

For commercial banks: "In the United States, for example, tier-one risk-based capital ratios have stabilized near 8.5 percent" (NY Fed Chairman, T Geithner Sept 2006). For hedge fund margin, it is difficult to ascertain since it is determined by the relationship between the prime broker and the fund, however, I have seen figures ranging from 7% to 20% depending on the collateral. What we do know is that competition for hedge fund business is intense (with fees and commissions accounting for up to 4% it's not surprising), hence margin requirements have been loosened to the extent that Geithner considers it a risk:

In market conditions where initial margin may be low relative to potential future exposure, the self-preserving behaviour of leveraged funds and their counterparties may be more likely to exacerbate rather than mitigate an unexpected deterioration in asset prices and market liquidity. As financial firms demand more collateral, funds are forced to liquidate positions, adding to volatility and pushing down asset prices, leading to more margin calls and efforts by the major firms to reduce their exposure to future losses. In the context of the previous discussion of externalities, firms' incentives to minimize their own exposure can amplify the initial shock and impose on others the negative externality of a broader disruption to market liquidity.

We believe that the major dealers, as well as the large commercial and investment banks, should take a cold, hard look at financing conditions and margin practice, particularly with respect to hedge fund counterparties and in OTC derivatives.

The effect of loosening margin requirements for the banks is to exchange counterparty risk for high upfront fees. The effect for the system is that the only supervisory mechanism on hedge fund balance sheet expansion is relaxed, rather like a relaxation in reserve requirements. A natural consequence of this is that hedge funds extend their advantages over regulated banks, allowing them to bid higher prices for credit and still achieve the required return on equity.

Fed Chairman Ben Bernanke justified the current regulatory regime in an April 2007 speech, Financial Regulation and the Invisible Hand, by saying that hedge fund investors are sophisticated and less likely to run than unsophisticated depositors of commercial banks. As we said above, fund of funds' risk management models force these sophisticated investors to behave more like scared depositors than long-term sages.

If capital adequacy requirements and margin requirements are the brakes on the balance sheets of commercial banks and hedge funds respectively, then shouldn't we compare the core capital of the banking system with the asset base of the credit related hedge fund world to assess whether hedge fund influence might be significant?

We can, but it would provide false comfort because much of the leverage achieved by these funds, as we saw with the mortgage example above, is embedded in the assets they buy. Because the funds are opaque, to both investors and leverage providers, there really is no regulation of asset risk beyond the self discipline of the fund itself, and that is likely to be *loose* beyond the 12 month performance fee horizon. This market failure encourages excessive risk taking and regulatory arbitrage.

Is it gross or net credit risk that matters?

Ultimately, the problem may or may not be that hedge funds are assuming too much net credit risk, but we can be certain that there is a concentration of instrument liquidity risk in hedge funds as they hold most of the illiquid, toxic, junior paper, and then hedge it with more liquid instruments (index products, higher rated paper, VIX, etc). So it is gross credit risk that matters since these relative value strategies expose them to the risk that liquidity is variable between instruments. And in gross credit exposure terms, they do look very much like banks.

In Summary

Conceptually, it appears reasonable to say that hedge funds which are playing leverage spread strategies in illiquid credit investments using short duration funds are copying the banks' business model. And when looked at through the prism of gross credit risk, it would appear that hedge funds are usurping it.

It is frequently said that today's banks seek to remove credit risk from balance sheets, preferring to collect fees on originating, servicing, packaging and passing on loans (rather than interest income). In other words, they prefer to be agents rather than principals. Trends in banking income distribution away from net interest income, particularly for the big commercial banks, support this thesis, and the rapid growth in the credit derivatives market (now $25-30tn) has allowed it to happen with little friction.

"Hedge fund banks" have stepped into the vacuum, accumulating leveraged credit instruments, acting as the new high-powered money, or actuators, of the US credit system. Relative value trades, supported by rating agency deception, have been the means by which this has happened – and it has happened without anybody really noticing. *With no regulation, portfolio opacity, model based asset pricing, distorted time horizons, and skewed performance incentives, there are no safeguards against poor distribution of credit risk or mispricing of credit risk.*

Fallacy of Composition

How does a system become so distorted?

It's a bit like seeing a newspaper picture of a fat bloke in a Batman outfit sitting on the Queen's bedroom window, you ask yourself, how on earth could a high level security system let that happen?

So why is it that a regulated financial system largely composed of sophisticated, intelligent people acting rationally can become so irrational from a systemic perspective – everybody knew that Option ARMs at 100% LTV were an insanity yet they continued to be originated? Surely there must be some stabilising feedback mechanisms to provide discipline?

What we have is a fallacy of composition. Everyone behaves rationally given the incentives and payoff structures which are presented to them at the micro level, but this does not translate into a rational outcome at the system level. Consider the table overleaf which relates to attitudes of the main actors in the expansion of structured credit and credit derivative markets:

Actor	Rational Motive	Issues leading to absence of 'safety valves'	Who exactly
Regulator	• Establish more complete markets • Reduce cost of credit • Theoretical boon to mankind • Don't pre-empt a bubble	• No proper recognition of market failures when overseeing the market • Counterparty risk not effectively monitored	• SEC and Fed
Servicer/Originator	• Satisfy demand from the market • Generate deal flow and fees • Generate gains on sale • Balance sheet optimisation • Competitive pressure to maintain market share	• Very little residual risk retained- 'originate, sell, forget about' model- increases problems of moral hazard and adverse selection	• Commercial banks • Investment banks • Brokers and servicers of loans, i.e., the distribution network
Collateral manager	• Increase funds under management, i.e., create more structures while they can be sold	• Secondary markets are illiquid so pricing is model based and can be discontinuous	• Investment banks • Specialist managers
Ratings Issuers	• Fees on business driven by business volumes, so maximise volume • Let demand for various tranches lead supply • Model driven ratings protect credibility	• Ratings set to meet demand not to reflect underlying collateral prospects • No standard pricing model • No market aggregated inputs for models • Ratings are discontinuous	• The rating agencies (there are only three big ones)
Buyer of rated debt	• Access to other markets/geographies • Diversification benefit • Get a yield premium over equivalent rated bond • No shortage of liabilities to match	• Yield premium drives demand. This probably reflects illiquidity, lack of detailed analysis of underlying collateral and difficulty in valuing embedded options in equity tranches, i.e., rating doesn't reflect true risk	• Liability driven institutional investors • Other Fixed income investors in need of yield • Holders of $ surpluses abroad
Buyer of junior tranches	• High yield • Relative value arbitrage with higher rated tranches • Pricing administered, reduces volatility • Front end loaded cash flow yield • Efficient financing for long term leverage	• Pricing administered by models not market • Performance fees earned annually rather than on total holding period return	• Investment banks • Hedge funds • Specialist funds • Insurance companies • Pension funds
Ultimate owners of junior tranche	• Alternative asset class for diversification • Low volatility, positive absolute returns over recent history	• Underlying funds are opaque • Liquidity risk not properly appreciated	• Fund of funds and their investors • Individuals via pension funds • Individuals via direct hedge funds • Insurance companies

Why are the custodians of the system not policing financial stability?

Because of this fallacy of composition, over-arching regulatory mechanisms, like central banks, should act as the system disciplinarians. Unfortunately, as we have seen, their preference for inaction justified through "grain of truth", market efficiency arguments only fuels the moral hazard of the system.

Central bankers believe that 'picking up the pieces' is a better policy than attempting to pre-empt speculative excess. Certainly from a personal political perspective it is, no one is going to thank/vote for you if you stop a party before it ends of its own accord. As we said previously, Greenspan and Bernanke have both fuelled the macro moral hazard fire, and even Timothy Geithner, who we can see clearly has the best understanding of the risks, ends his most recent speech with the following:

> Ultimately, though, ex ante judgments about leverage, concentrations and liquidity risk will continue to prove elusive. Our principal focus should therefore be not in the search for the capacity to preemptively diffuse conditions of excess leverage or liquidity, but in improving the capacity of the core of the financial system to withstand shocks and on mitigating the impact of those shocks. And, as always, central banks need to stand prepared to make appropriate monetary policy adjustments if changes in financial conditions would otherwise threaten the achievement of the goals of price stability and sustainable economic growth.

Through such post crisis action, Bernanke is, in effect, offering the balance sheet of the banking system as the shock absorber of malfeasance in the non-banking system, i.e., monetary liquidity to support evaporating funding liquidity- clearly an A-grade pupil of the Greenspan era. It is a very good job those US banks are "well capitalised".

In Summary

An inefficient and unstable macro economic outcome in US credit markets is being sustained through a fallacy of composition. Financial stability is a public good and should be policed by the custodians of the system. US financial custodians are both denying that there is an issue and, at the same time, saying that even if there were they would not look to act pre-emptively.

Military failures are often blamed on generals fighting the last war. The generals of the US monetary system seem to have gone a step further:

"Observe the belligerents but avoid admitting that any battle needs to be fought until you have a gun to your head". Perhaps they are taking a lesson from Iraq's former information minister, Mohammed Saeed al-Sahaf, infamous for his statement made to the sound of American M16 machine guns: "There are no American infidels in Baghdad. Never!"

Endgame

There are two routes to the endgame.
They are not mutually exclusive.

The Junior End

What caused the banking crises of yesteryear was a run by depositors on banks who could not liquidate loans fast enough to pay out the cash. In today's hedge fund banking world, I bet it will be a quasi-banking run by investors (direct and fund of funds) on the hedge fund banks which impairs the structured credit funding mechanism (CDOs, MBSs, ABSs etc) and precipitates the crisis. It might not bankrupt the commercial banking system but the supply shock to the US credit system will be sudden and aggressive: if you lose the buyer of junior tranches of MBS and CDOs (just as risk on those tranches is being reassessed and remodelled), issuance of these securities will hit the sand, and thus closing the valve on the whole credit mechanism.

The Senior End

Holders and buyers of the senior rated paper suffer downgrades as defaults threaten the safety of their paper, which causes them to lose confidence in the ratings system and to demand a bigger risk premium. This impairs the attractiveness of the relative value trade and slams the brakes on CDO issuance. Reduced demand for underlying collateral causes prices to correct and imposes a credit price & supply shock on the system.

Potential credit supply shocks like these have very serious negative implications for the real economy. It will be incredibly difficult/impossible to kick start the system once the moral hazard fuelling it has been revealed, since all new activity is done under the shadow of the newly revealed risk, which implies higher credit costs. In this case, who will be willing to buy CDOs exposed to non-conforming mortgages when historical models are breaking down, and the old structures are imploding?

It has to be emphasised that the direct losses of funds left holding the toxic waste are largely irrelevant; what really matters is that their absence leaves a vacuum in risk appetite which results in credit costs tightening throughout the credit system.

Anyone looking for concentration of risk by organisation in the financial system will be deceived into thinking that all is well. The concentration is not likely to be in an organisation like Long Term Capital Management, it is in the risk appetite of a particular group of institutions for a particular set of credit instruments, institutions who, collectively, will behave as if they were a single organisation under stress. If there is any concentration of risk at all, it most likely lies in the rating agencies who have been key facilitators in the structured finance boom since they provide the models by which the rated paper are priced. If the ratings system was sufficiently discredited by poor performance, legal action or regulatory sanction, then the outcome above would be the result.

Parallels to other market failures

There are clear parallels between the issues in structured credit and prior market failures. The Lloyds reinsurance problems of the late 1980s and the split capital trust debacle of 2002 provide good examples where vertical tranching of risk in illquid markets led to malfeasance and ultimately disaster.

Parallels of current issues to previous market failures

Lloyds reinsurance spiral: reinsurance basically involves tranching of insurance risk. The Lloyds debacle occurred because syndicates found they had reinsured the same risk many times over. The Piper Alpha loss of $1bn apparently resulted in $16bn of losses for Lloyds syndicates. A similar problem seems to be emerging in some CDOs:

> Moody's also said it's concerned that the "growth of synthetics", or credit swaps, may leave more CDOs invested in other CDOs exposed to the same bonds as they are.

The company said its models "were developed using the data that was available at the time", such as transactions backed by cash collateral. Moody's is now working on a research project to reassess the correlation between CDOs at a time when exposures can be "infinitely replicated', it said. (Source: Bloomberg)

The same risk can be insured multiple times using the synthetic market. Split capital trusts: these vehicles were found to have been investing in each other. The cross holdings were illiquid and when the unwind came, the mark downs were aggressive. Worrying then to see CDOs investing in each other:

> 'Some collateralised debt obligations that invest in subprime mortgage bonds, related derivatives and other CDOs may be less diversified than they appear, raising investors' risks, according to Moody's Investors Service.
>
> Greater use of credit-default swap contracts is creating more situations in which CDOs may be doubling up on exposures to the risks of specific bonds, either through multiple direct investments or purchases of other CDOs' bonds, according to a report this week by Moody's.' (Source: Bloomberg, April 2007)

Note: CDO squared instruments are explicitly designed to invest in each other.

So where are we now?

We have seen the effect of CDO and hedge fund activity on the provision of funding liquidity to the subprime mortgage market. Their insatiable demand for higher yielding, junior tranche subprime paper effectively imposed the decline in underwriting standards on mortgage lenders.

The problems in subprime have already caused liquidity to be switched off to this area of the housing market- demand for origination has dried up overnight. The next phase of this process will be the downgrade/default in the underlying collateral and the negative impact of this on the prices of CDO paper. Downgrades should pre-empt default, but the agencies are no more likely to pre-empt the crisis that the central authorities who preside over them, and as the Fitch conference call made clear, the downgrade process will be as slow as it can be. As this filters into hedge fund pricing, we should see redemptions which create liquidity issues in underlying collateral markets – what price a BBB-subprime tranche or CDO equity when there is no reliable model to price it?

Funds that cannot sell their most toxic paper will resort to selling their more liquid assets, which could cause contagion. We are starting to see this in the commercial MBS market where spreads have continued to widen despite calm returning to other markets. Meanwhile, CDO managers are likely to be desperately trying to reallocate their collateral away from residential MBS to more palatable areas of the credit markets (remember, CDO managers actively manage their pool of collateral). This will unfold over the next three to six months.

At the macro level, the rapid withdrawal of funding liquidity from this area of household credit market is likely to accentuate the damage done to the housing market in general. Housing inventory is unlikely to be shifted with the pool of buyers reduced (by up to 14%, according to Bernstein, if subprime mortgage costs increase by 3%, which they are doing) through tightening underwriting standards and the prospect of foreclosures flooding more properties onto the market. This obviously has serious implications for house price appreciation, US consumer demand and the real economy. Central authorities are likely to try to mitigate this by forcing the Government Sponsored Enterprises (Fannie Mae and Freddie Mac) to direct lending at non-prime areas of the mortgage market. Unfortunately, these efforts are unlikely to be able to pick up the reins as quickly as they have been dropped, and can only really be a palliative. They will not stop mortgage costs increasing.

As for the ratings agencies, the most likely outcome is that the inaccuracy of ratings models and a lack of pre-emptive action by the agencies will be revealed by the current mortgage market malaise. The fact that the ratings agencies will be subjected to regulatory pressures/legal proceedings will force them to act more conservatively and increase the cost of credit. Moody's stock price action will give us the best gauge of how this is developing.

While this whole digestion process goes on, we have to assume the manias in other areas of the credit markets continue. Equity markets could, in this time, be subject to leveraged demand as buyouts continue on even more insane credit terms, and asset managers reallocate their leveraged buying power away from the household sector. It is therefore possible, even likely, that we get a final hurrah in equities.

For equity investors, having actual call options, warrants, or instruments that behave like them is the best way to play it (upside participation with little capital risk).

Dot-to-Dot review of the argument

- Confidence in financial markets based on "abundant liquidity" is a dangerous deception created by a procyclical surge in funding liquidity, credit and leverage from non-bank financials.

- An economic and financial system which is supported by the purchasing power that non-bank funding liquidity confers, is more fragile than one which is supported primarily by balance sheet and monetary liquidity.

- The current credit cycle was kick started with macro moral hazard (Bernanke 2002) but has been driven to unprecedented extremes by a micro moral hazard overlaid on financial innovation to produce a surge in non-bank funding liquidity.

- The forces shaping behaviour at hedge funds should, theoretically speaking, mean there is a real attraction for these players to migrate towards a banking business model of taking leveraged spread on illiquid assets.

- The rapid growth and development in structured credit has allowed credit risk to be distilled, providing credit instrumentation with the necessary embedded leverage to allow this migration to happen. We believe it has.

- The visible symptoms are all around us: insane mortgage underwriting standards, the tightest emerging market spreads in history, leveraged private equity transactions on multiples that imply no business cycle, explosive growth in credit derivatives, credit players who themselves admit that credit risk is being mispriced.

- The specific mechanism we highlight as the turbocharger at the heart of this funding liquidity boom is hedge fund demand for junior tranches of structured credit, which appears to be encouraged by a relative value opportunity created by ratings agencies.

- Evidence to support our hypothesis can be seen by the issues emerging from the US subprime mortgage market. Rampant demand for junior RMBS paper by CDOs 'encouraged' the lapse in underwriting standards over the last few years. Rapid growth of CDO issuance has been facilitated by hedge fund demand for junior paper in CDO, the senior rated paper being easily saleable. Whether for relative value trades or straight credit bets, this demand has had a magnified impact on aggregate mortgage origination, particularly in subprime.

- At the heart of every bubble is a grain of truth to support the believers' faith in the fundamentals supporting the bubble. In this case, the argument is that credit derivatives, structured finance and structured credit allow players to arbitrage the inefficiency in the pricing of credit.

Relative value trades are part of this arbitrage process. However, distortion of absolute prices in subprime highlights the frailty of the efficiency argument.

- There are clearly various market failures which disrupt the efficiency argument. These include: inconsistent regulation (banks versus hedge funds), changing regulation (Basel II), discontinuous credit ratings systems, pricing inconsistencies (marking to model), informational asymmetries (originators of credit risk versus ultimate owners), hedge fund incentives (skewed payoffs, limited liability, and short time horizons), and rating agency incentives (paid by issuers on the basis of transaction volumes).

- Ratings agencies help create relative value through their model, rather than market driven ratings system. Static discontinuous ratings and illiquidity prevent the relative value from being arbitraged out, which simply encourages further origination of the underlying collateral, e.g., subprime mortgages. With apologies to Roald Dahl, no matter how hard they 'suck' the funds can't arbitrage out 'the everlasting relative value trade'.

- However, relative value trades in a market for credit risk that has become absolutely mispriced are vulnerable to variable market liquidity between instruments when reality breaks in and prices are forced to correct (what price a loan which has actually defaulted?). Therefore it is gross credit exposure of hedge funds that matters for considerations of financial stability.

- A fallacy of composition has allowed this inefficient outcome to persist and central authorities have not intervened to protect the public good of financial stability.

- The game can end from either the junior tranche or senior tranche side. The 'hedge fund bank' analogy provides a clue as to how the mania might end from the junior end. Capital loss sensitive investors (funds of funds) redeem en-masse which precipitates distressed selling/unwinding of fund assets. With little liquidity in these assets in the first place, forced sales will target the most liquid assets first. This creates conditions ripe for contagion right across the credit spectrum.

- From the senior end, investors in the higher rated paper lose confidence in the ratings system which underpins their demand. This is likely to be precipitated by downgrades which are held back as long as possible by ratings agencies. With reduced demand for senior paper, prices have to adjust, relative value trades evaporate, and the demand for junior paper disappears.

- The off-market nature of structured credit allows the ratings agencies to hold back the downgrades until actual fundamentals (i.e., delinquencies and defaults) force a reassessment of key model inputs: default probabilities and cumulative default rates, default correlations, and recovery rates. This is the phase the US non-conforming mortgage market is in, so there will be many funds which really are "walking and talking several months after their heads were chopped off".

- A forced withdrawal of CDO demand from this area of the RMBS (Residential Mortgage Backed Securities) market has already happened. This is likely to create headwinds for the assumed recovery in the US housing market, and consequently poses a threat to US consumption growth. One potential mitigating force against disruption in non-prime is a redirected effort by Fannie Mae and Freddie Mac, the Government Sponsored Enterprises, to lend into this area of the market. This will play out over the next 6 months.

- The more pressing question then is whether disruption in this area of CDO funding transmits to similar structures focused on different asset classes, such as leveraged loans and commercial mortgages and whether this distress causes a general reassessment of CDO funding. So far it hasn't, because of the delayed downgrade process, and this allows the mania to continue in its other markets, particularly corporate loans.

- While corporate credit conditions remain unaffected, equity markets may enter a 'last hurrah' phase, but only until the impact of housing on the real economy feeds back into real prospects for the corporate sector (remember the news can be bad for a long time before the mania responds to it; subprime issuance continued well into the back end of 2006 despite worsening fundamentals).

Conclusion

Today's credit markets reflect an unreal state of perfection. They do so because of the existence of four 'perfect' factors:

1 The perfect calm – courtesy of the US Federal Reserve's monetary policy and its attitude towards financial stability.

2 The perfect product – structured credit instruments with their off-market, leverage, and yield characteristics.

3 The perfect trade – persistent relative value created by rating agencies overrating the senior tranches.

4 The perfect buyers – performance hungry hedge funds for junior tranches, yield hungry and rating constrained institutions for the senior tranches.

This is not an efficient market phenomenon but a composition of market failures and distorted incentives.

The aggregate picture is one of leveraged, mispriced credit markets in which "hedge fund banks" are exposed to liquidity risks, the banking system is exposed to hedge fund counterparty risk, and rated tranche debt holders are exposed to mispriced default risk.

Don't be fooled by equity market complacency. Unlike other recent credit scares, e.g., the GM/Ford issues in 2005, we now have a situation of deteriorating fundamentals. Default, when it happens, is a painful fact; it cannot be relieved by changing market psychology. We are now at that point in the subprime market, which is why the subprime issue has significance beyond that implied by the size of the asset class.

Discussions as to whether the rest of the world can decouple from the US are interesting but irrelevant. The US credit super-cycle has driven the global cycle. The development and innovation in credit markets is a US-centric event, and the majority of liabilities are US-focused. In other words, it is not good enough that other economies might have positive momentum into a US slowdown. If the US economy slows sufficiently for the credit cycle to turn then US credit markets will encounter severe problems, which will translate into financial system problems, and hence global problems.

The only way we could avoid this is if the US credit system manages to overcome current headwinds and continue expanding. This requires that asset prices, and in particular house prices, continue rising and the funding mechanism retains credibility. Neither seem very likely now that the actual, as opposed to the modelled, probability of default is reasserting itself. Housing is the start of this process but its feedback into the real economy through consumption will cause this reassessment process to percolate right the way through credit markets going forward.

It is quite possible that equity markets stage a last hurrah rally as the M&A fervour drowns out the sound of gunfire in structured credit. This makes it a very difficult time for cautious investors. Our aim should be to find assets which provide call-like optionality, i.e., geared participation to the upside with little capital at risk. To monitor the condition of credit, we need to watch for signs of contagion, and reactions to the drip of bad news from CDOs and housing to judge when the next major stress point for markets will be. Of course, these tactical thoughts are a finesse. The end game might take time to play out but it cannot be avoided.

Post Script

There is a probable twist in the tale. As confidence in US structured credit begins to wane, Fed Chairman Bernanke will make good on his promise to 'go unconventional' and provide monetary liquidity support to this area of credit markets. First though, we need a credible deflationary threat, which the housing market can provide and bond markets will quickly accept, before a truly inflationary response can be unleashed. The dollar represents the only pool of liquidity large enough to prevent a serious discontinuity and Bernanke has made it very clear that he will use this pool, compromising the dollar for the sake of the financial system.

Appendixes

Glossary of acronyms

ABC	Asset backed securities
ABCDS	ABS credit default swaps
BIS	Bank of International Settlements
CBO	Collateralized bond obligation
CDS	Credit default swaps
CDOs	Collateralized debt obligations
CLO	Collateralized loan obligation
CMBS	Commercial mortgage backed securities
CPDO	Constant proportion debt obligations
CRECDO	Commercial real estate CDO
LCDS	Loan credit default swaps
LTCM	Long Term Capital Management
MBS	Mortgage backed security
MEW	Mortgage equity withdrawal
MFIs	Monetary financial institutions
OFIs	Other financial institutions
OTC	Over the counter
RMBS	Residential mortgage backed securities
SPV	Special purpose vehicle
SFCDO	Structured finance CDO

Structured Finance and Structured Credit

The structuring world draws the distinction between structured finance, e.g., asset backed securities and mortgage backed securities, and structured credit, e.g., CDOs, CLOs, CMOs. Instruments defined as structured credit will often have structured finance assets as underliers. The following illustrates how structured finance, in this case a subprime residential mortgage backed security, and structured credit, a CDO, interact.

A primer on structured credit

Subprime RMBS structure

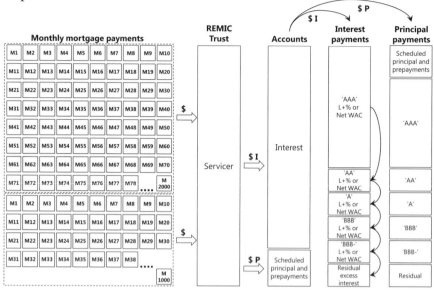

The lower tranches of this RMBS structure then feed into the CDO structure as follows.

Structured Finance CDO structure

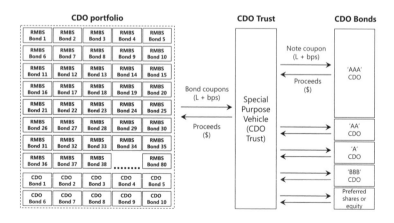

So the overall process goes like this:

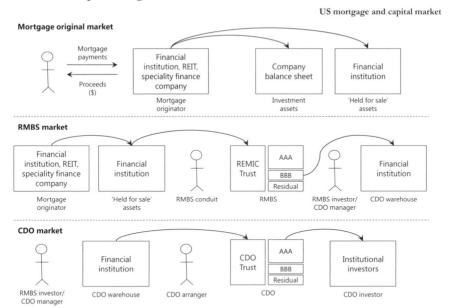

When it comes to thinking about any credit related instrument, it is important to be clear in your mind whether it is:

i) Cash market based – those that involve transactions in and structuring of the underlying cash credit market (CDOs, CLOs etc).

Or

ii) Derivative market based – those that utilise credit derivatives (CDS, CDX and synthetic CDOs).

This is important because cash based instruments are constrained by the dynamics of the underlying asset (market size, liquidity, etc), while derivative based are only referenced to the underlying asset and therefore can develop their own market dynamics. (Note: derivatives may have liquidity in their own right, but they do not increase the liquidity of the underlying asset).

What is structured credit?

It is defined by Morgan Stanley as *the process of taking plain vanilla credit instruments and "structuring" them to meet certain goals*, which can include diversification, loss or payment redistribution, hedging, principal protection, achieving ratings targets or stability, and altering a portfolio's sensitivities to spread movements and defaults.

Instruments

Specific instruments: Credit default swaps (CDS) are single name derivative instruments, focused on specific corporate credit risk. They are essentially an insurance policy that protects the buyer against the loss of principal on a bond in case of a default by the issuer.

Portfolio instruments: There are a variety of portfolio instruments, all with their own TLAs (three letter acronyms): CBO – collateralised bond obligation, CLO – collateralised loan obligation, CMO – collateralised mortgage obligation, CDO – collateralised debt obligation, synthetic CDO, FTD – first to default baskets, and CDX – tranched credit indices. They are generally variations on the same theme: slicing up pools of credit risk into different tranches which will appeal to different investors.

Some portfolio instruments are derivative market based, e.g., synthetic CDOs and CDXs, while others are cash market based, e.g., CDOs, CLOs, CMOs, FTDs.

CDOs

Introduction

Since 1998, the CDO market has experienced an average annual growth rate of 150%. The current size of the market is estimated at c.US$2.5tn (the credit default swap, CDS, market is estimated to have a gross notional size of $US26tn).

While the CDO market started as an efficient mechanism for managing credit risk on bank balance sheets and for obtaining regulatory capital relief, CDOs have evolved into complex instruments to achieve leveraged returns to investors with a wide range of credit risk appetites. Today's CDOs encompass a vast array of underlying assets ranging from unsecured debt instruments such as high grade, high yield and emerging market bonds; secured debt instruments such as middle market and leveraged loans; subordinated instruments such as trust preferred securities, to all forms of structured finance obligations and finally CDO tranches themselves.

What are they?

CDOs are stand alone special purpose vehicles (SPV) that invest in a diversified pool of assets. These investments are funded through the issuance of multiple classes of securities, the repayment of which is a function of the performance of the pool of assets which serve as collateral. When the SPV purchases the pool of assets outright, as opposed to acquiring risk exposure using credit derivatives, the CDOs are called cash CDOs.

Cash flows from the assets are used to pay the manager and trustees of the transaction and make principal and interest payments to the note holders in the order of seniority – senior notes first, followed by the junior notes. Preferred shares (the so called equity tranche) are the residual of the transaction and receive a current coupon out of the residual interest proceeds generated by the collateral.

How a typical cash CDO works

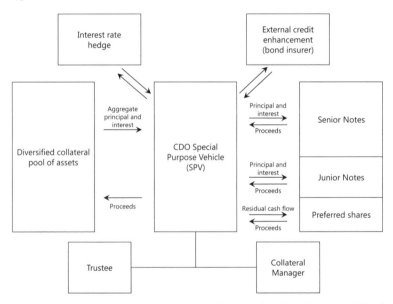

Source: Morgan Stanley, Structured Credit Insights

Understanding the structure of CDOs

The best way to dispel confusion and understand the different types of CDOs is to analyse a CDO based on four attributes:
1 the CDO's underlying assets
2 the liabilities of the CDO
3 the purpose of the CDO
4 the CDO's credit structure.

Assets

The collateral underlying a cash CDO falls into one of six primary categories: high-yield loans, high-yield bonds, high-grade structured finance, mezzanine structured finance, capital notes, and emerging market debt.

Today, about half of cash CDOs are backed by high-yield loans, another 40% are backed by structured-finance assets, and 10% are backed by such asset classes as emerging market bonds, corporates, sovereigns, bank capital notes, and so forth.

Liabilities

All CDOs make use of tranching to place their debt and equity obligations in strict seniority to one another – from the most senior tranche, typically rated AAA, to the unrated equity tranche. Beyond that, a CDO's tranches can incorporate various structures, such as a fixed- or floating- rate coupon, a pay-in-kind (PIK) facility, short-term or long-term debt, a guarantee by a monoline insurance company (i.e., insurer of debt) and a delayed-draw or revolving note.

Purpose

The two most common are balance sheet and arbitrage purposes. A third, less common, purpose is termed "origination".

A balance sheet purpose for issuing a CDO occurs when the sponsoring organisation wishes to remove securitizable assets from its balance sheet to reduce required regulatory or economic capital or achieve cheaper funding costs. In this situation, the sponsoring party sells assets to the CDO.

The sponsoring organisation of a CDO with an arbitrage purpose, typically an asset manager, is motivated by the desire to add assets under management. The investors in this type of CDO wish to obtain asset management services. The assets underlying the CDO are purchased in the marketplace (or in the case of a synthetic CDO, are other CDS, i.e., it can be created with no need to trade in the underlying market). Arbitrage cash flow CDOs represented 87% of total CDO issuance in 2005.

Morgan Stanley is little more candid about the motivations of arbitrage transactions:

> "Arbitrage transactions are motivated by the aspirations of the equity tranche investors and the collateral managers. The former seek to achieve a leveraged return as the spread between the post-default yield of the collateral pool of assets and the cost of financing the assets

through the issue of the debt tranches. This spread, also known as the funding gap, is the arbitrage that the equity investors are seeking to capture. The collateral managers seek to expand assets under management in order to realise fees for the management (acquisition, trading and monitoring) of the collateral pool of assets."

In the case of an "origination" purpose for a CDO's issuance, collateral assets are originated specifically to be purchased by the CDO. In particular, this situation occurs when bank capital notes from a large number of smaller-sized banks are sold to a CDO coincidentally with its issuance. The collateral-issuing banks participate in order to gain cheap equity-like funding from the CDO structure.

Credit Structure

The fourth, and final, structural attribute of a CDO is whether it has a market value or cash flow credit structure. In the former, CDO debt tranches gain their credit quality by ensuring that they can be retired by the sale of CDO assets. The market value of CDO assets must at all times be a multiple of CDO debt par. If the market value multiple is violated, CDO assets are sold and CDO debt is retired.

In the more typical cash flow structure, after default cash flow from the collateral portfolio is expected to repay CDO notes, which, of course, relies on assessment of how bad defaults and recoveries on the CDO's underlying assets can be.

Leverage

A key determinant of a CDO structure pertains to the amount of leverage within a structure. Leverage refers to the size of the equity tranche relative to the total size of the transaction. For example, if the equity tranche is $100 million in a CDO of $1 billion, it is said to have a leverage equal to 10 times.

Arbitrage cash flow transactions generally have a higher degree of leverage than market value transactions (8-12 times versus 4-6 times) and balance sheet cash flow transactions have much higher levels of leverage (25-50 times).

Policing the Capital and Cash flows: Performance Tests in Cash CDOs

Protecting senior tranches from deterioration in underlying assets requires a set of rules to govern the distribution of cash flows and how they relate to the protection of capital. In some early CDOs, the manager was also tended to be the owner of the equity (unrated and difficult to sell). This brought about a conflict of interest in that if cash flows deteriorated, the manager would sell higher quality assets trading around their par value to buy lower quality assets below par which had a higher yield, i.e., trading the capital of senior tranches to protect the cash flow of the equity tranche. Tests and protections now aim to prevent this sort of practice.

Senior notes in a cash flow CDO transaction have a priority claim on all cash flows generated on the underlying collateral pool and are protected by subordination, overcollateralisation and coverage tests, which serve to accelerate the redemption of the senior notes if the tests are violated.

Overcollateralisation (O/C) and Coverage Tests: The mechanisms most used to ensure the priority of payments are various collateral coverage tests. If $100 of par assets are available to service $80 of senior notes, the ratio 100/80 = 125% suggests that the senior notes are overcollaterised by 25%.

If the par coverage test for the senior tranche is breached, the senior notes will be redeemed until the test comes back into compliance. Likewise, if interest coverage tests are breached, all interest payments will be redirected to the senior bonds until the trigger is cured. In general, interest coverage tests are relatively less onerous than par coverage tests.

Interest waterfall of a sample CDO

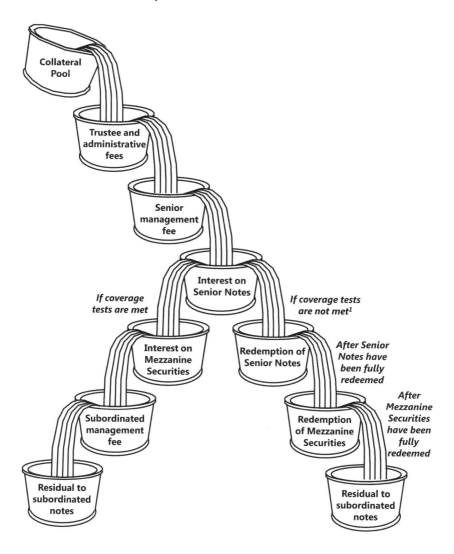

Source: Morgan Stanley
Notes:
[1] If coverage tests are not met, and to the extent not corrected with principal proceeds, the remaining interest proceeds will be used to redeem the most senior notes to bring the structure back into compliance with the coverage tests. Interest on the mezzanine securities may be deferred and compounded if cash flow is not available to pay current interest due.

Interest waterfall of a sample CDO

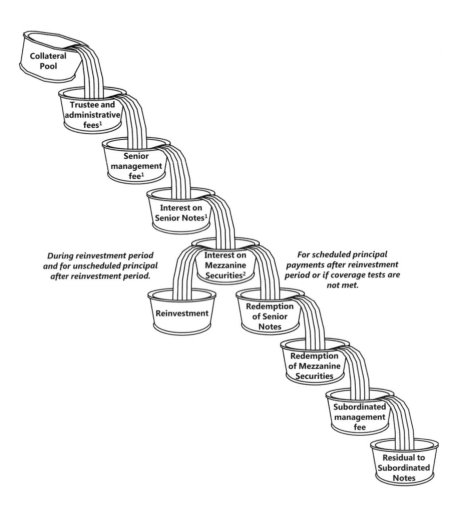

Collateral
Pool

Trustee and
administrative
fees[1]

Senior
management
fee[1]

Interest on
Senior Notes[1]

*During reinvestment period
and for unscheduled principal
after reinvestment period.*

Interest on
Mezzanine
Securities[2]

*For scheduled principal
payments after reinvestment
period or if coverage tests are
not met.*

Reinvestment

Redemption
of Senior
Notes

Redemption
of Mezzanine
Securities

Subordinated
management
fee

Residual to
Subordinated
Notes

Source: Morgan Stanley
Notes:
1   To the extent not paid by interest proceeds.
2   To the extent senior note coverage tests are met and to the extent not already paid by interest proceeds. If coverage tests are not met, the
    remaining principal proceeds will be used to redeem the most senior notes to bring the structure back into compliance with the coverage tests.
    Interest on the mezzanine securities may be deferred and compounded if cash flow is not available to pay current interest due.

Credit Quality

CDO debt credit quality is determined by both asset risks and structural protections. Two main types of structural protection exist for the cash flow

CDO investor. One is related to subordination, and the other, to cash flow diversion.

The cash flows generated by the collateral pool are largely probabilistic (or stochastic); in short, there is uncertainty as to what those cash flows could be. In contrast, the distribution of those cash flows to the different tranches is totally deterministic (i.e., it is governed by the waterfall or priority of payments- see above).

The credit performance of the collateral pool depends on three factors whose behaviour is difficult to predict: probabilities of default, recovery rates, and correlation.

Probability of default is the likelihood that the underlying assets will default. They can use information from the rating agencies; they can use Moody's KMV; they can use credit-default swap spreads to infer default probabilities; or they can rely on "fundamental analysis".

Recovery rate is, in essence, the amount of money the investor is likely to recover if an asset defaults.

Correlation is the stochastic variable that typically receives the most attention. Like volatility in option pricing, it tends to be backed out from market prices and used for relative value trades. The correlation that counts is not the asset correlation (i.e., how the prices of the assets in the portfolio are correlated) but the default correlation (i.e., how defaults of assets are likely to be correlated). Asset price correlation is a bad proxy for default correlation.

Valuation: Analytical Challenges in Modelling Cash CDOs

CDOs are typically modelled for rating and valuation purposes. However, there is no industry/academic standard for this process, unlike, for example, the Black-Scholes model used in options. Their adaptability to various asset classes, structural innovations and portfolio management strategies render them "challenging" to model in analytically tractable and computationally convenient means. I quote from Morgan Stanley's primer on CDOs:

"The complex waterfall structures and the potential for diversion of cash flows because of structural protections and coverage triggers imply that analytical models have to take into account the default probabilities as well as the determinants of the different coverage ratios in mutually consistent fashion. This, coupled with the optional redemption feature of most CDOs, calls for the modelling of interest rate risk in conjunction with the default risks of assets. Since the underlying collateral pools are managed, albeit according to predefined guidelines, the impact of future trading activities of collateral managers is difficult to model. Some analyses model the trading provisions assuming that the managers will trade at the extremes of all possible trading constraints, which has the effect of painting all managers with the same brush, constraining relative value judgment. Trading further complicates the already difficult problem of modelling and parameterization of correlation."

Typical models in vogue for cash CDO analysis still rely on deterministic scenario analysis using annual constant default rates incorporating prepayment and recovery assumptions. Recently, there has been a gradual shift towards Monte Carlo simulation based analysis.

There is not even a system for the industry to agree common values for inputs into the various models.

The enormous degree of discretion in pricing allow 'marking to model' to be closer to 'marking to my needs' (everyone can get a price that works for them) than 'marking to market' and, is in the worst cases, 'marking to myth' (as Warren Buffet called it).

Why CDOs Exist (in theory at least)

Investor demand for CDOs is strong for a variety of reasons.

i) The CDO structure divides and distributes the risk of the underlying collateral to investors with differing appetites for risk.

ii) A second reason investor demand for CDO issues is strong is that buyers of CDO equity receive nonrecourse term financing with leveraged exposure to CDO assets. CDO equity provides nonrecourse financing because CDO equityholders own stock in a remote entity – the CDO – and are not liable for the losses of that entity. Asset financing is in place for up to 15 years, during which time it cannot be withdrawn, the rate cannot change, and under the cash flow credit structure, a forced liquidation of collateral will not occur. CDO debtholders provide the financing for the equityholders, and the equityholders sustain the risk of collateral asset payment delays and credit losses. Equityholders own a leveraged position in the assets of the CDO and receive all cash flows in excess of the debt tranche requirements and thus collect all the upside on the CDO's assets.

iii) Debt investors like CDOs because they offer high rating-adjusted yields. The higher yield is primarily because of the liquidity premium and the inherent complexities of the CDO structure.

iv) Another reason investors are interested in CDOs is because of the exposure they provide to a diversified portfolio of collateral, often of hard-to-acquire assets, such as bank loans and ABS assets. For example, investors mandated to limit investments to investment grade securities have very limited opportunities to invest in emerging market securities, few of which are rated investment grade. However, CDOs make it possible for such investors to get such exposure through investment grade tranches of CDOs with a collateral pool of emerging market securities. The same analogy is extendible to several other asset classes, such as leveraged and middle market loans.

Virtues of CDO Equity

CDO equity has four positive attributes: Investors in the equity tranche (1) receive nonrecourse term financing, (2) may earn a significant return even when CDO debtholders have lower than expected returns, (3) hold two options that further increase the value of their investment and (4) hold a security with the potential to be part of a defensive investment strategy.

Effectively, equity investors seek to obtain a leveraged return as the positive difference between post-default yield on the CDO's assets and their cost of financing- the funding gap.

The spread over the risk free rate in an asset's yield of a non-callable fixed-rate instrument is a measure of the reward for the credit risk and liquidity risk. As such, CDO equity investors are betting that the difference between the expected credit losses and experienced credit losses in the portfolio will be favourable and thus seek to capture risk and liquidity premiums in the assets in the collateral portfolio.

In contrast to competing alternative asset classes, the cash flow return profile for CDO equity investors begins from deal inception. It is front-end loaded and not dependent upon the discretion of the collateral manager but on a predetermined set of rules...Therefore, for the first few years of the transaction, there may be residual cash flow available to equity tranche investors, which explains the front-loaded nature of CDO equity investments. For investors with exposure to first-loss, the likelihood of residual cash flows being available decreases over time as assets default.

Options Embedded in CDO Equity

CDO equityholders hold options on the *market value* of CDO collateral and on the *after-default cash flows* of those assets.

After-default cash flows

In situations where the market value of the CDO portfolio has deteriorated, equityholders continue to receive payments, provided coverage tests are not violated.

Through put-call parity (an options arbitrage identity), one can see that a CDO equity position has all the characteristics of a call option. In other words, a CDO equity investor has a portfolio of collateral on the one hand, and he or she has borrowed or sold a bond (or a series of bonds) on the other hand. In addition, the investor has purchased put protection because this is a nonrecourse investment, i.e., the equity cannot be worth less than zero.

The put premium that the equity investor is essentially paying to all the senior debt lenders, the expected return over LIBOR, is the cost of that put option. Viewed that way, a CDO equity investor potentially has very efficient financing for term leverage (if the embedded put option is not priced correctly).

Market value of CDO collateral

Finally, debt tranches are typically callable at the option of the equity shareholders after a stated non-call period, usually 2-5 years. The call option embedded in senior CDO notes is generally a Bermuda-style option, in that the call is exercisable on discrete exercise dates after the non-call period. Structurally, the embedded callability is intended to provide a means for equity investors to unwind the CDO transaction once it has de-levered to the point that on a forward-looking basis, returns are no longer deemed attractive.

As an option holder, the CDO equity class is long volatility. The greater the market risk and the after-default cash flow risk of the underlying assets of the CDO, the greater potential benefit to the equityholder.

In summary CDO equity is not quite as subordinated as one might think.

Correlation and CDO equity

Owners of CDO equity are said to be long correlation. Intuitively, this can seen because individual asset specific failures are the things that hurt the equity most. Think of 2005's failed correlation trades. When GM and Ford were being downgraded this was a negative event for equity holders of

CDOs since a specific default by one of them would have likely wiped out the equity in CDOs that held either company's debt. Many hedge funds had shorted mezzanine tranches to buy equity tranches as a bet that any defaults in the CDO would be correlated (a general economic event) and so what would be lost on the equity would be more than made up for by gains on the short mezzanine position. The auto downgrades caught these players out, and because there was so little liquidity in the mezzanine tranches they could not cover their shorts. Instead they shorted the auto stocks to hedge out the long equity tranche exposure. Unfortunately, Kerkorian's bid for 10% of the equity then squeezed this hedge, inflicting double whammy pain.

Other related instruments

CLO – collateralised loan obligations. The underlying assets are bank loans rather than bonds. In the corporate space, the cash CDO market has been dominated by structures backed by leveraged loans, i.e., CLOs. Shorter maturities, more debt seniority, and higher historical recoveries have made CLOs more accepted in the market than high yield bond backed CBOs that dominated the market pre 2002.

FTD – First to default baskets. The investor receives a premium in exchange for taking on first-loss risk on the basket of credits.

CDO squared – these are CDOs whose underlying assets are tranches (usually the rated tranches) of other CDOs. Intuitively, it is a way to get leveraged credit risk while minimising the idiosyncratic risk. The cynic might just think 'split caps'- I'll buy your tranche if you buy mine.

Leveraged Loan Default Swaps – CDS on leveraged loans.

Long-term performance

Ruffer performance versus FTSE All-Share Index July 1998 – June 2009 with income reinvested

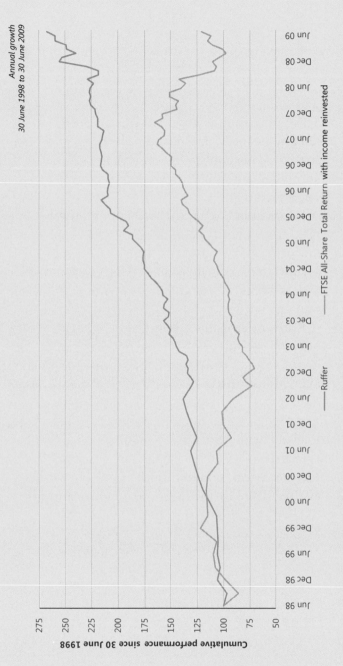

Annual growth
30 June 1998 to 30 June 2009

────── Ruffer   ────── FTSE All-Share Total Return with income reinvested

Cumulative performance since 30 June 1998

Source: Thomson Datastream, Ruffer. Full details of performance are included in the appendix. All figures include reinvested income. Ruffer performance is shown after deduction of all fees and management charges.

This publication is not a solicitation, or an offer, to buy or sell any financial instrument or to participate in any trading strategy. This publication reflects Jonathan Rufer's opinions at this date only and the opinions are subject to change without notice.

Information contained in this publication has been compiled from sources believed to be reliable but it has not been independently verified; no representation is made as to its accuracy or completeness, no reliance should be placed on it and no liability is accepted for any loss arising from reliance on it.

Rufer, its affiliates and any of its or their officers, directors or employees may have a position, or engage in transactions, in any of the financial instrument mentioned herein. Ruffer, may do business with companies mentioned in this publication.

Ruffer LLP is a limited liability partnership, registered in England with registration number OC305288. The firm's principal place of business and registered office is 80 Victoria Street, London SWIE 5JL. Ruffer LLP is authorised and regulated by the Financial Services Authority.